ODDITIES

LES
PROPHETIES
DE M. MICHEL·
NOSTRADAMVS.

*Reueuës & corrigées fur la coppie Imprimée
à Lyon par Benoiſt Rigaud. 1568.*

M. DCV.

TITLE-PAGE OF NOSTRADAMUS' "CENTURIES" (1605 EDITION)
British Museum

ODDITIES

A Book of Unexplained Facts

By RUPERT T. GOULD

Introduction by
LESLIE SHEPARD

BELL PUBLISHING COMPANY · NEW YORK

INTRODUCTION

THE LOVE OF MYSTERIES is deeply engrained in mankind and is responsible for a vast output of ghost stories, detective yarns, thrillers and other mystifications.

There is a special branch of literature dealing with *true* mysteries — the unsolved problems of everyday life and the enigmas of history. Various authors have specialised in the factual and historical mystery, notably Andrew Lang, Sabine Baring-Gould and the iconoclastic Charles Fort. It is a field in which the late Rupert Thomas Gould excelled.

Gould was a remarkably talented and versatile man: a nautical and mechanical expert, author and broadcaster. He was born at Portsmouth 16 November 1890. He was educated at Dartmouth College and entered the Royal Navy in 1906, serving in the Mediterranean, on the Yangtze and in the Home Fleet. In 1915 he was invalided, and from 1916 to 1927 worked as a naval assistant in the Hydrographic Department of the Admiralty. Several of his studies deal with naval mysteries.

In 1920 he undertook a major labor of love — the cleaning and restoration of the four historic marine chronometers made by John Harrison in the eighteenth century, the famous instruments which first definitely solved the problem of finding longtitude at sea. The work of cleaning and restoration occupied Gould over a period of *twelve* years. In 1923 Gould published his magnificent history *The Marine Chronometer*.

Gould was also the preeminent expert on the history of the typewriter, from the eighteenth to the twentieth century. In his house at Ashtead, Surrey, was a large room filled with ancient machines, and a notice on the door of the room read:

HOME OF REST FOR AGED AND DECAYED TYPEWRITERS
SUPPORTED ENTIRELY BY VOLUNTARY CONTRIBUTIONS
NO DESERVING CASE EVER REFUSED ADMISSION

The droll humor is an indication of the human touch that characterised so much of Gould's scientific work. His knowledge was formidable, but he could always write entertainingly with the warmth that brings a subject to life.

In 1934 he began a series of fascinating talks in the British radio program "The Children's House." He was billed as "The Stargazer" and the intention was that he should speak primarily on astronomical matters, but at his own request he was allowed a wide range of subjects. In those days he spoke extempore from a few rough notes, for fifteen minutes at a time, covering subjects like "The Indian Rope Trick," "The *Mary Celeste* Mystery," "Jules Verne," "The Canals of Mars" and "Sea Serpents." It is not surprising that these delightful talks were immensely popular with adults too, and they were issued in book form a few years later. Later he became a familiar and well loved member of the original "Brains Trust" radio program.

His wonderfully entertaining two volumes *Oddities* and *Enigmas* were first published in 1928 and 1929 respectively. These books are remarkable for their unprejudiced and penetrating enquiry and their incidental scholarship. They are also grand entertainment. Gould brings to these mysteries the charm of the born story-teller who cannot resist adding all those perceptive asides of odd or diverting information gathered in years of patient alert curiosity.

This wholesome spirit of curiosity runs through all Gould's work. No matter how bizarre the subject, Gould brought to it the same patient analysis that distinguished his practical work with the marine chronometer or the intricate mechanism of old typewriters. He wrote with the care of a scientist, the wit of a tolerant and humane man, the background knowledge of a scholar and the romantic interest of a schoolboy. He was a member of the bibliophile club, the *Sette of Odd Volumes,* founded by the antiquarian bookseller Bernard Quaritch.

Oddities and *Enigmas* went through a number of editions and are as fascinating today as when they were first written. Amongst Gould's other popular works are: *The Case for the Sea-Serpent* (1931) and *The Loch Ness Monster* (1934).

Gould specialised in the odd, eccentric, neglected, or mysterious, yet these are not idle mysteries. Gould had no interest merely in rehashing hackneyed material. He investigated only those matters which engaged his own unusual interest and called out his painstaking analysis, deduction and erudition, and on which he left, unobtrusively, his own originality.

He died 5 October 1948 at the age of 57. His splendid practical work and his entertaining books and radio talks have enriched our knowledge, but they also hint at a more fundamental impulse.

Behind the questing curiosity of the scientist to solve the mysteries of everyday environment are deeper, less practical urges. Much of the appeal of real-life mysteries is the doubt which they throw upon the immutable physical laws of a materialist world. Deep down, many of us more than half believe in the ghosts and fairies which modern science and technology has purged from the everyday scene. This feeling is an expression of that mystical sense of a deeper meaning in life than the day-to-day ephemera and technical triumphs with which we are surrounded.

But the essence of a good real-life mystery is that there should be no cheating, either to support a mystical theory or to eradicate belief in the supernatural. A sympathetic investigator solves mysteries where reliable practical solutions apply, or opens the mind to stranger possibilities when the answers are beyond present knowledge and belief.

It was in this sense that Gould spent his life in trying to solve mysteries, and achieved a rare balance between science and romance. In all his pursuits, practical and literary, he is judicious and fairminded, and always animated by good humor and human sympathy. It is difficult to read his account of the John Harrison timekeepers (published in 1935) without being deeply moved. Gould spent twelve years overhauling these neglected masterpieces which nowadays you may see beautifully cared for at the National Maritime Museum, Greenwich. At his 1935 lecture to the Society for Nautical Research Gould demonstrated these chronometers and reviewed the long years of restoration. He posed the question: Was it worth doing? Was it worth while to spend twelve years upon a few pieces of obsolete and over-complicated machinery? Gould's answer gives a clue to his own preoccupation with mysteries.

He thought it had been very well worth doing. John Harrison, a simple self-educated Yorkshire carpenter, had spent fifty years' thought and labor in the face of every obstacle and official discouragement to solve a problem — a problem that had baffled professional clockmakers and the finest scientific brains in Europe. Harrison, said Gould, was a truly great man...

Rupert Thomas Gould, who gave so many years to solving problems, was also a truly great man.

London, England   Leslie Shepard

BIBLIOGRAPHY OF RUPERT T. GOULD

The Marine Chronometer. 1923. (recently reprinted by Holland Press, London).

Oddities. A Book of Unexplained Facts. P. Allan & Co., London, 1928. Revised edition Geoffrey Bles, London, 1944.

Enigmas. Another Book of Unexplained Facts. P. Allan, London, 1929. Second edition Geoffrey Bles, London, 1946.

A Book of Marvels. Methuen & Co., London, 1937.
    ...this contains seven of the twenty essays in *Oddities* and *Enigmas* with some corrections and additions, but is superseded by the second edition of each book published by Geoffrey Bles, above.

The Case for the Sea-Serpent. Philip Allan, London, 1930.

John Harrison and His Timekeepers. A lecture... (reprinted from "The Mariner's Mirror"). 1935.

Captain Cook. Duckworth, London, 1935.

The Charting of the South Shetlands, 1819-28... (reprinted from "The Mariner's Mirror"). 1941.

The Stargazer Talks... (broadcast talks). Geoffrey Bles, London, 1943.

The Story of the Typewriter, from the Eighteenth to the Twentieth Centuries. (reprinted from "Office Control and Management"). London, 1949.

                                                        L. S.

PREFACE

BY WAY OF APOLOGY

The essays contained in this book, although apparently disconnected, were written at one time and with one object—to collect and digest the facts relating to a number of incidents which have not, at present, been satisfactorily explained.

In order to present those facts as clearly as possible, I have quoted rather extensively from the original sources. As most of these are not very accessible, I hope that I may be spared the reproach that the book has mainly been put together with scissors and paste.

I have ruled out such hackneyed and merely historical mysteries as the fate of Louis XVII, the identities of Junius and the Iron Mask, the disappearance of Mr. Bathurst, and other enigmas which have already been fully discussed in print.

I fear that the book might more appropriately have been called *Old Wives' Tales* or (following Scott) *Tales of My Grandmother*. Scientifically-minded persons can, with good reason, call it superficial; the general reader may, with no less justice, find it dull; and both will, I have no doubt, be tempted to echo the Irish bishop who remarked of *Gulliver's Travels* that it seemed to him to be full of improbable statements, and that for his part he scarcely believed half of it. Still, I have done my best to show, by giving chapter and verse, that my facts are facts; for such opinions as I have offered I am, of course, solely responsible.

RUPERT T. GOULD

Ashtead, 1928

PREFACE
TO SECOND EDITION

In revising *Oddities* for re-issue I have done my best to incorporate—either as text, footnote or postscript—the bulk of the information which, in consequence of much correspondence and a certain amount of research, has come my way since the book was first published sixteen years ago.

A few hasty views have been modified or withdrawn: but in general it is fair to say that while a good deal has now been added, hardly anything beyond the index—an unwilling sacrifice to the needs of war-time typography—has been omitted.

My grateful thanks are due to all those correspondents, known or unknown, whose collaboration has lightened the task of revision. To two friends, Mr. R. J. Cyriax and Mr. G. R. Hayes, I am under special obligation.

RUPERT T. GOULD

BARFORD ST. MARTIN, 1944

PUBLISHER'S NOTE
TO THE THIRD EDITION

The present edition includes a new Index, putting an end to the "unwilling sacrifice" the author had to make in 1945.

New Hyde Park, New York, 1964

CONTENTS

ILLUSTRATIONS

PLATES

FIGURES

ODDITIES

A Book of Unexplained Facts

I

THE DEVIL'S HOOF-MARKS

A Scottish minister once preached a sermon upon the text "The voice of the turtle is heard in our land".* He was literally-minded, and unaware of the fact that the "turtle" referred to is the turtle-dove, and not that member of the *Chelonia* which inhabits the ocean and furnishes the raw material of such "tortoise-shell" articles as are not made of celluloid. In consequence, the deductions which he drew from his text were long remembered by such of his hearers as were better-informed.

"We have here", he is reported to have said—"we have here, my brethren, two very remarkable signs and portents distinctly vouchsafed to us. The first shall be, that a creature which (like Leviathan himself) was created to dwell and abide in the sea shall make its way to the land, and be seen in the markets and dwelling-places of men; and the second shall be, that a creature hitherto denied the gift of speech shall lift up its voice in the praise of its Maker."

A visitation of a somewhat similar and hardly less startling kind occurred in Devonshire on February 8, 1855. The following account of it was published in *The Times* of February 16th.

"Extraordinary Occurrence

"Considerable sensation has been evoked in the towns of Topsham, Lympstone, Exmouth, Teignmouth, and Dawlish, in the south of Devon,† in consequence of the discovery of a vast number of foot-tracks of a most strange and mysterious description. The superstitious go so far as to believe that they are the marks of Satan himself; and that great excitement has been produced among all classes may be judged from the fact that the subject has been descanted on from the pulpit.

"It appears that on Thursday night last there was a very heavy fall of snow in the neighbourhood of Exeter and the south of Devon. On the following morning, the inhabitants of the above towns were surprised at

---

* *Canticles* ii. 12. † See Fig. 1.

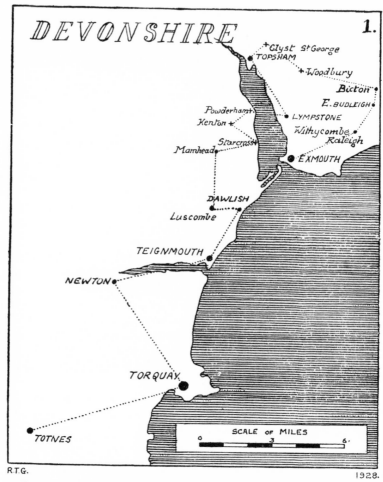

FIG. 1.—Sketch-map showing the localities in which the "Devil's Hoof-marks" were observed, February 8, 1855.

The marks are definitely recorded as having been seen at all the places whose names appear on the map. The dotted line, whose route is quite arbitrary, is merely inserted as an indication of the minimum distance which *must* have been traversed, had the marks been made by one creature only.

discovering the tracks of some strange and mysterious animal, endowed with the power of ubiquity, as the foot-prints were to be seen in all kinds of inaccessible places—on the tops of houses and narrow walls, in gardens and courtyards enclosed by high walls and palings, as well as in open fields. There was hardly a garden in Lympstone where the foot-prints were not observed.

"The track appeared more like that of a biped than a quadruped, and the steps were generally eight inches in advance of each other. The impressions of the feet closely resembled that of a donkey's shoe, and measured from an inch and a half to (in some instances) two and a half inches across. Here and there it appeared as if cloven, but in the generality of the steps the shoe was continuous, and, from the snow in the centre remaining entire, merely showing the outer crest of the foot, it must have been convex.*

"The creature seems to have approached the doors of several houses and then to have retreated, but no one has been able to discover the standing or resting point of this mysterious visitor. On Sunday last the Rev. Mr. Musgrave alluded to the subject in his sermon, and suggested the possibility of the foot-prints being those of a kangaroo; but this could scarcely have been the case, as they were found on both sides of the estuary of the Exe.

"At present it remains a mystery, and many superstitious people in the above towns are actually afraid to go outside their doors after night."

So far—and, unfortunately, no further—*The Times.* The *Illustrated London News*, however, took up the question, and opened its columns to what proved to be quite an extensive correspondence, which I have used as the source of most of the information here given. In the West Country the affair gradually blew over—although I believe that it is still well remembered. There was no repetition of the occurrence, but it took a long time for the "excitement" and "superstitious folly" to die down. One correspondent† speaks of

". . . labourers, their wives and children, and old crones, and trembling old men, 'dreading to stir out after sunset, or to go half a mile into lanes or byways on a call or message, under the conviction that this was the Devil's walk, and no other, and that it was wicked to trifle with such a manifest proof of the Great Enemy's immediate presence. . . ."

The correspondence presents, as might be expected, a curious medley of additional facts and half-baked theories. I will first summarize the facts, premising that *The Times* account, while giving a good outline of the events, necessarily omitted one or two very curious details.

An eye-witness, signing himself "South Devon",‡ sent in an able account, from which the following extract is taken.

". . . The marks which appeared on the snow (which lay very thinly on the ground at the time) and which were seen on the Friday morning,

---

* Read "concave". On the facts stated, the centre of the foot making the impression must have been farther from the ground than the outer parts of the foot.

† He signed himself "G. M. M." (*Illustrated London News*, 3.3.1855.)

‡ *Illustrated London News*, 24.2.1855.

to all appearance were the perfect impression of a donkey's hoof—the length 4 inches by 2¾ inches; but, instead of progressing as that animal would have done (or as any other animal would have done), feet right and left, it appeared that foot followed foot, in a *single line*; the distance from each tread being 8 inches, or rather more—the foot-marks in every parish being exactly the same size and the steps the same length.

"This mysterious visitor generally only passed *once* down or across each garden or courtyard, and did so in nearly all the houses in many parts of the several towns above mentioned, as also in the farms scattered about; this regular track passing in some instances over the roofs of houses, and hayricks, and very high walls (one 14 feet), without displacing the snow on either side or altering the distance between the feet, and passing on as if the wall had not been any impediment. The gardens with high fences or walls, and gates locked, were equally visited as those open and unprotected.

"Now when we consider the distance that must have been gone over to have left these marks—I may say in almost every garden, on door-steps, through extensive woods of Luscombe, upon commons, in enclosures and farms—the actual progress must have exceeded a hundred miles. It is very easy for people to laugh at these appearances and account for them in an idle way. At present no satisfactory solution has been given. No known animal could have traversed this extent of country in one night, besides having to cross an estuary of the sea two miles broad. Neither does any known animal walk in a *line* of single foot-steps, not even man.

"Birds could not have left these marks, as no bird's foot leaves the impression of a hoof, or, even were there a bird capable of doing so, could it proceed in the direct manner above stated—nor would birds, even had they donkey's feet, confine themselves to one direct line, but hop here and there; but the nature of the mark at once sets aside its being the track of a bird.

"The effect of the atmosphere upon these marks is given by many as a solution; but how could it be possible for the atmosphere to affect one impression and not another? On the morning that the above were observed the snow bore the fresh marks of cats, dogs, rabbits, birds, and men clearly defined. Why, then, should a continuous track, far more clearly defined— so clearly, even, that the raising in the centre of the frog of each foot could be plainly seen—why then should this particular mark be the only one which was affected by the atmosphere, and all the others left as they were?

"Besides, the most singular circumstance connected with it was that this particular mark removed the snow, wherever it appeared, clear, as if cut with a diamond, or branded with a hot iron; of course, I am not alluding to its appearance after having been trampled on, or meddled with by the curious in and about the thoroughfares of the towns. In one instance this track entered a covered shed, and passed through it out of a broken part of the wall at the other end, where the atmosphere could not affect it.

"The writer of the above has passed a five months' winter in the backwoods of Canada, and has had much experience in tracking wild animals and birds upon the snow, and can safely say he has never seen a more clearly-defined track,* or one that appeared to be less affected by the atmosphere. . . ."

Another correspondent, signing himself "G. M. M."†, also afforded a good deal of supplementary information, as the following extracts will show.

". . . As an amateur accustomed to make most accurate drawings from nature, I set to work soon after these marks appeared, and completed the accompanying exact facsimile‡ of those that were visible on the lawn of our clergyman's garden in this parish. He and I traced them through a low privet hedge, by a circular opening of 1 foot diameter. On applying a rule, the interval between each impression was found to be undeviatingly 8½ inches. This, in my opinion, is one of the most remarkable and confounding circumstances we have to deal with. . . .

"It was quite inexplicable that the animal, considering the scale of the foot, should leave, in single file, one print only, and as has already been observed, with intervals as exactly preserved as if the prints had been made by a drill or any other mechanical frame. No animal with cushion paw, such as the feline tribe—diminutive or large (cat or tiger)—exhibit, could have made these marks; for the feet of most quadrupeds tread in parallel lines, some widely divaricated, others approximating very closely. The ass, especially, among the animals daily seen, approaches the single line. The fox leaves round dots in a single line; the stoat two and one alternately. Moreover the feline tribe leave concave prints; whereas, in each of these mystic prints, the space enclosed by the bounding line was convex,§ as in the print of a patten.

"A scientific acquaintance informed me of his having traced the same prints across a field up to a hay-stack. The surface of the stack was wholly free from marks of any kind, but on the opposite side of the stack, in a direction exactly corresponding with the tracks thus traced, the prints began again! The same fact has been ascertained in respect of a wall intervening. . . . Two other gentlemen, resident in the same parish, pursued a line of prints during three hours and a half, marking their progress under gooseberry-bushes and espalier fruit-trees; and then

* See Fig. 2, which is taken from a drawing accompanying his letter.
† Rev. G. M. Musgrave.   ‡ See Fig. 3.
§ He was correct in calling the hoof-marks, themselves, convex—*The Times* was wrong in applying this term to the foot which made them.

missing them, regained sight of the impression on the roofs of some houses to which their march of investigation brought them. . . .

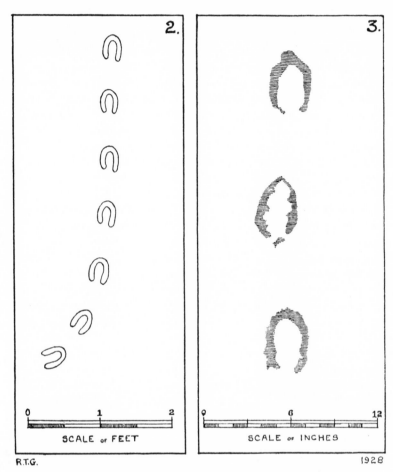

FIG. 2.—A drawing of the hoof-marks, accompanying a letter signed "SOUTH DEVON", published in the *Illustrated London News* of Feb--ruary 24, 1855.

FIG. 3.—Another drawing of the hoof-marks, accompanying a letter signed "G. M. M.", published in the *Illustrated London News* of March 3, 1855.

"I have addressed communications to the British Museum, to the Zoological Society, to the keepers of birds and beasts in the Regent's Park menagerie, and the universal reply is, they are utterly unable to form any conjecture on the subject, however correctly the impressions had been copied.

"I am emboldened to address you with more than the ordinary confidence of a correspondent 'well up in his facts', inasmuch as I am living in the centre of the district where the alarm, so to speak, was first given. Sir L. Newman's park, at Mamhead, is exactly opposite my own residence. Starcross Tower is an object of the picturesque, and beautiful to gaze upon from my study window: and Powderham Castle gleams in the sunshine half a mile further up. These are on the other side (west) of the River Exe, two miles in its breadth; and the marks were as abundant throughout the places just specified, and their neighbourhood—Kenton, Dawlish, Newton, etc.—as here at Exmouth, Withecombe Ralegh, Lympstone, Woodbury, Topsham, and the vicinity of Bicton and Budleigh. . . ."

In view of the very remarkable facts detailed in these letters, it will be admitted that the Devonshire rustics had every excuse for indulging in what their betters were pleased to term "superstitious folly". A natural explanation of the facts seemed impossible to find, and difficult even to suggest; while any explanation certainly postulated the visit of something very uncanny—something which walked upon small hooved feet with a very short, mincing stride, which sought darkness and solitude, which had never rested, which had crossed a river two miles wide, which had hung round human habitations without daring to enter them, and which had on some occasions walked up walls and along roofs, while at other times it had passed through such obstructions as if they did not exist. Assuredly the peasants were not to be blamed if their minds went back to such grim texts as Isaiah xxxiv. 14:

"The wild beasts of the desert shall also meet with the wild beasts of the island, and the satyr shall cry to his fellow."

Of course, many naturalistic explanations were offered, but none can be regarded as satisfactory. In the words of Maginn's *Aunciente Waggonere*,

> Somme swore itte was ane foreigne birde,
> Some sayd itte was ane brute. . . .

The various candidates who, by their "next friend", claimed the authorship of the marks comprised (among birds) cranes, swans, bustards, and waders; and (among beasts) otters, rats, hares, polecats, frogs, badgers, and —*mirabile dictu*—kangaroos.

The theory that a bird made the marks is obviously untenable, as "South Devon" pointed out. But an anonymous writer, one "W. W.",* made a pathetic attempt to evade the various fatal objections. By his account, five days after the appearance of the Devonshire hoof-marks a

---

* His letter to the *I.L.N.* on the subject was considered (3. III. 1855) but not printed. So he published a small pamphlet—*The Swan with the Silver Collar* (Wells, *Journal* Office, 1855, price 2d.)—of which I possess a copy.

swan turned up, alive but exhausted, at St. Denis in France, wearing a silver collar "with an inscription engraved on it, stating that the bird belonged to the domain of Prince Hohenlohe, in Germany". "W. W." maintained that this bird, whose feet had probably been "padded in the shape of a donkey's hoof or shoe" by its owner, to prevent damage to the garden in which it was normally kept, had no doubt made the mysterious marks!

Some of the other theories were ingenious. For example, one Thomas Fox sent in a very clever drawing (Fig. 4) to support his view that the marks had been made by the four feet of a leaping rat. There was a good deal, too, to be said for the otter theory. But the opinion most generally accepted was, of course, that put forward by the famous naturalist Richard Owen.

Here is his letter.*

"To the Editor of the *Illustrated London News*.

"An esteemed zoological friend has submitted to me a carefully-executed drawing of one of the more perfect impressions left in the snow at Luscombe, South Devon, on or about the 8th of last month. It was of the hind-foot of a badger. This is almost the only plantigrade† quadruped we have in this island, and leaves a foot-print larger than would be supposed from its size.

"The sketch, of which you have given a cut in p. 187‡ (February 24th), gives a correct general idea of the shape and proportion of these foot-prints, but without the indications of the pads on the sole, and the five small claws, which the drawing sent to me exhibited. Such perfect foot-prints were rare, because those of the fore- and hind-foot are commonly more or less blended together, producing the appearance of a line of single foot-steps; which appearance, if a bear had been abroad in the five winter months spent by your correspondent in Canada, would have shown him was not peculiar to the foot-steps of man, but characteristic of other plantigrade mammals, though they may be quadrupedal. The badger sleeps a good deal in his winter retreat, but does not hibernate so regularly and completely as the bear does in the severer climate of Canada. The badger is nocturnal, and comes abroad occasionally in the late winter, when hard-pressed by cold and hunger; it is a stealthy prowler, and most active and enduring in its quest of food.

"That one and the same animal should have gone over a hundred miles of a most devious and irregular route in one night is as improbable as that

* *Illustrated London News*, 3.3.1855.
† *I.e.* flatfooted—walking with the whole sole of the foot applied to the ground.
‡ Fig. 2.

one badger only should have been awake and hungry out of the number concealed in the hundred miles of rocky and bosky Devonshire which has been startled by the impressions revealed by the rarely spread carpet of snow in that beautiful county.

"The onus of the proof that one creature made them in one night rests with the assertor, who ought to have gone over the same ground, with a power of acute and unbiased observation, which seems not to have been exercised by him who failed to distinguish the truly single from the blended foot-prints in question.

"Nothing seems more difficult than to see a thing as it really is, unless it be the right interpretation of observed phenomena.

"RICHARD OWEN."

In the mid-Victorian era, that "period of digestion", the authority of an established name counted, in scientific as in other matters, for more than it does now. Probably all but a very few, such as the unfortunate observers who saw something different from what Owen so clearly tells them they ought to have seen, regarded this letter as absolutely decisive.

Nowadays, we know a little more about scientific dogmatism—and we also know a good deal more about Owen himself. He was, undoubtedly, a very able man; but on several important occasions he showed himself capable of making dogmatic assertions, in defiance of fact, which proved him to be possessed of a singular and not entirely "scientific" type of mind.

A good example of this tendency is his controversy with Huxley, in 1857, over the *hippocampus major*. Owen, coming forward "on the side of the angels" as the great scientific gun of the anti-Darwinians, committed himself to the dogmatic assertion that there were certain anatomical features—such as the above singularly-named structure—which were peculiar to the brain of man, and afforded ample ground for classifying him as a genus apart from all other mammals. Actually, as Huxley soon afterwards showed, such structures are common both to man and to all the higher apes, as well as many of the lower ones.

Proxime accesserunt may be placed Owen's exploded theory that the adult skull is a modified vertebral joint—a theory originally suggested by Oken—and his utterly childish "explanation" of the "sea-serpent" seen by H.M.S. *Dædalus* in 1848: an explanation flatly contradicting the observed facts, and postulating that the naval officers who observed them were, one and all, half-witted.

His explanation of the Devonshire hoof-prints is more plausible; but it does not fit the facts—nor is he fair to "your correspondent". "South Devon" nowhere stated, as Owen asserts, that man is the only creature which makes single foot-prints in snow—he said that no creature, not even man, makes a *single line* of prints: and this is generally true.* It is quite possible that the prints of a badger's hind-foot might be super-imposed on the last impression but one made by the fore-foot on the same side of the body, and so produce an apparently single foot-print. But such prints would undoubtedly be "staggered", for the badger has quite a wide "tread", and the result would then be a double line of imprints, not a single one. Badgers, also, are not commonly credited with the ability to scale walls and walk along roofs. As between the claims of the badger and the ótter, the latter certainly seem better founded.

In Figures 5 and 6 I have drawn foot-prints of a badger and an otter for comparison with the Devonshire hoof-marks. It will be admitted that the resemblance is not striking. It is only fair, however, to say that one or two of the writers to the *Illustrated London News* stated that faint traces of claws had, as Owen remarks, been seen, or imagined, at the edges of the hoof-marks.†

And Owen was entirely right in questioning the assertion that *one* creature had made *all* the marks. If, as alleged, they extended for some-thing like a hundred miles, it is in the last degree unlikely that this track, while it endured, could have been traced throughout its whole extent by a competent observer. And even if (as shown on Fig. 1) we reduce its length to a minimum of some forty miles only, the application of simple arithmetic is still fatal to the hypothesis of a single creature. Allowing this fourteen hours of darkness in which to make a 40-mile line of hoof-marks 8 inches apart, it must have kept up an average of more than *six steps per second* from start to finish!‡ And that is the absolute minimum—an addition of 30% for loopings and turnings, which seems reasonable enough, would necessitate the creature's taking ten steps per second for fourteen hours continuously. This, I submit, is simply unthinkable. The conclusion that more than one creature made the hoof-marks naturally follows—a conclusion, unfortunately, which neither explains the marks away nor identifies their authors. And it is worth noting that, on this supposition, "South Devon's" estimate of 100 miles for the total length of the track may easily have been *below* the truth.

Another naturalist, Frank Buckland, in spite of being one of Owen's disciples and admirers, rejected his "badger" theory—going further and faring worse. Writing long after the event he gravely asserted (in his *Log-Book of a Naturalist*) that the hoof-marks had been *proved* to be the

* Mr. Musgrave's letter, already quoted, indicates one or two exceptions. He might also have instanced the camel.

† E.g. "Ornither" and an anonymous correspondent, both of whose letters appeared on March 3, 1855. The correspondence terminated on March 17th.

‡ I am indebted to Mr. H. V. Garner for drawing my attention to this point.

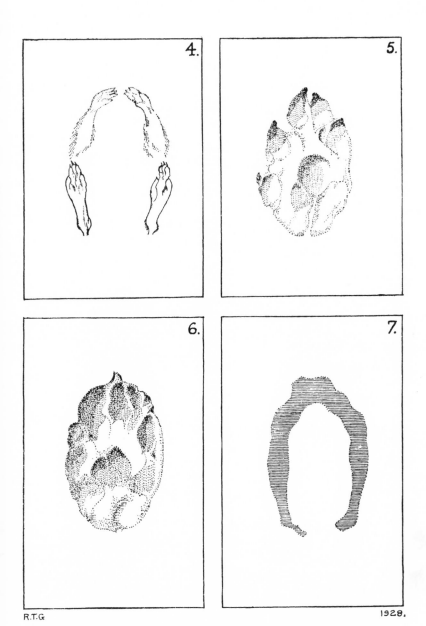

R.T.G.   1928.

Fig. 4.—From a letter, signed "Thomas Fox", in the *Illustrated London News* of March 10, 1855, suggesting that the hoof-marks were made by a leaping rat.

Fig. 5.—Impression of an otter's hind-foot.

Fig. 6.—Impression of a badger's hind-foot.

Fig. 7.—One of the hoof-marks, enlarged from Fig. 3.

    Note.—For purposes of comparison, Figs. 4, 5, and 6 have been drawn on the same scale as Fig. 7 (a mark about 4 in. long by $2\frac{3}{4}$ in. wide).

track of a racoon! He must have been grossly misinformed. Besides possessing all the physical handicaps which put Owen's badgers out of court, the racoon adds one of its own—it is not a native of this country. In effect, Buckland was informing his readers that a pack of escaped racoons, arriving and departing with utter secrecy, had wandered singly, for one night only, over a large area of Devonshire—acquiring, during their excursion, the difficult and previously-unsuspected accomplishment of walking up vertical walls and through haystacks.

But, putting aside the reported facts which are inexplicable on any naturalistic theory (such as the unobstructed passage of the tracks through walls, etc.), there is a crucial objection which appears to me to dispose of the claims not only of the badger and the otter, but of *all* the birds and animals supposed, by someone or other, to have made the mysterious marks. I except the kangaroo—that theory does not require serious discussion. It was only mooted, originally, because the private menagerie of a Mr. Fishe, at Sidmouth, contained a couple of these animals.

The objection is this. We can be quite certain, from the alarm the hoof-marks occasioned among the rustics, that they were most unusual—that nothing like them had ever been seen within living memory. It is therefore indisputable that they were not made by any *common, well-known,* creatures. If such had been the case—if, for example, they had been the foot-prints of badgers or otters—they would have been seen in Devonshire every winter. Instead of being a nine days' wonder, and scaring the feebler brethren into fits, they would have been looked upon as a perfectly familiar sight, not worth a second glance.* Yet, with one exception, there is no record of such marks having been seen on any other occasion before or since.

Unbeknown, apparently, to the correspondents of the *Illustrated London News,* a very similar case had occurred some fifteen years earlier, in a very different part of the world. The story had been published for eight years; but it is a curious fact that while the authority for it, Captain Sir James Clark Ross, R.N., was in England in 1855 and must, one would think, have heard of the Devonshire hoof-marks, he did not, apparently, direct attention to the very similar incident which was within his own knowledge.

The following is an extract from Ross's *Voyage of Discovery and Research in the Southern and Antarctic Regions,* vol. i. p. 87. His ships,

* But for this, and the fact that the hoof-marks were seen on walls and roofs, a candidate whose qualifications were not put forward at the time—the common rabbit —would seem to have as good a claim as any. In snow of a certain depth, a leaping rabbit *does* leave a track not unlike a series of hoof-marks. But it is clear, from "South Devon's" letter, that he saw, and examined, rabbit-tracks made at the same time as the hoof-marks, and did not associate the two.

the *Erebus* and *Terror*, were then at Kerguelen Island, a large sub-antarctic island in the Southern Indian Ocean. The date is May 1840.

"Of land animals we saw none; and the only traces we could discover of there being any on this island were the singular foot-steps of a pony or ass, found by the party detached for surveying purposes, under the command of Lieutenant Bird, and described by Dr. Robertson as 'being 3 inches in length and 2½ in breadth, having a small and deeper depression on each side, and shaped like a horseshoe.'

"It is by no means improbable that the animal has been cast on shore from some wrecked vessel. They traced its footsteps for some distance in the recently fallen snow, in hopes of getting a sight of it, but lost the tracks on reaching a large space of rocky ground which was free from snow."

One wonders, if they had "got a sight of it", what they would have seen.*

It is scarcely a far-fetched conjecture to suppose that the creature which made the "singular foot-steps" seen by Ross was akin to those whose tracks were observed in Devonshire. If we accept this, one or two conclusions seem to follow.

The Kerguelen creature was not a denizen of Kerguelen itself—at least, what we now know of the fauna of that island makes this exceedingly improbable. Presumably, then, it made its arrival from seaward. Either, as Ross suggests, it was a survivor from some wrecked vessel, or it was a sea-creature which, for some reason, had made an excursion on land. As to what manner of sea-creature it may have been, if it was one, I offer no opinion. The available selection is wider than might be at first supposed—it may be recalled that some years ago a seal was found half-way up a Scottish mountain, and miles from the sea. The locale of the Devonshire hoof-marks points to a similar conclusion. All the places mentioned by name lie, as will be seen from Fig. 1, close to the sea-coast or to the estuary of the Exe.

On the other hand, it is possible that in both cases the agents were land-animals—presumably tropical land-animals.† The appearance of their foot-prints in snow would normally be a matter of inference, rather than observation, while they would never, except by a rare accident, be ob-

---

* Dr. R. M'Cormick, R.N., who was supposed to be the official zoologist (and geologist) of Ross's expedition, does not refer to these marks in the account of the voyage given in his *Voyages of Discovery in the Arctic and Antarctic Seas, and Round the World* (London, 1884). It is probable, however, that he never saw them himself (his journal at Kerguelen is mostly devoted to a trivial and querulous account of his teal-shooting expeditions): and he was not the man to give prominence to the work of others. His book, also, was published forty years after the voyage.

† It was not, obviously, a common denizen either of the British Isles or of Kerguelen; localities whose climates are respectively temperate and sub-Polar.

served in either of the temperate zones. Land-animals swimming ashore from a ship would naturally seek for food—and, if timid, might easily cover a very considerable distance in a single night, and hang round buildings without daring to enter them.

On either supposition, it is possible that there is some quite simple solution of the Devonshire hoof-marks to be found, if one knew where to look for it. But there is a caveat to be entered. If land-animals made the marks, the available data are probably sufficient to enable a competent zoologist, with an unbiased mind, to make a reasonable suggestion as to their identity. But no authority on earth—not even the Ministry of Agriculture and Fisheries—can set limits to the number and variety of the creatures which, even though unknown to science, may yet live and move and have their being in the sea.

II

THE VAULT AT BARBADOS

In the churchyard of Christ Church,* Barbados, overlooking Oistin's
Bay, stands a small but massive vault, differing in no very obvious way
from its neighbours except that there is no stone or other barrier at its
entrance. The passer-by, looking in, sees nothing but bare walls and
casual rubbish. The vault has stood thus, open and untenanted, for over a
century—and until, if ever, the traditions relating to it have perished
there is little doubt that it will remain so.

For it is not, apparently, a quiet resting-place for the dead. Not once
nor twice, but five times in all, at intervals varying from a few months to
several years, have coffins entrusted to its keeping been found, when it
was next opened, to have been overturned, scattered in confusion, and
even set on end. All conceivable precautions have been taken—the walls,
roof, and floor sounded for concealed passages, the floor sanded to detect
foot-marks, the entrance closed with a block requiring four men to move
it, and that block sealed and marked by several independent persons. The
result has always been the same. At the next opening, while there has
never been a trace of any human being having made the smallest attempt
even to reach the interior, the coffins, on each occasion, have undergone
the same shameful treatment as before. It is not wonderful that after the
fifth occurrence of the kind (in 1820) the dead whom the vault could not
protect should, by common consent, have been removed to a more peace-
ful asylum elsewhere.

The story has often been told in print. Several versions exist, which
differ slightly in detail, but are in remarkable agreement as to the main
facts. Discrepancies and agreement alike, however, are capable of a simple
explanation. Practically all the versions, excluding such as are obviously
mere repetitions at fifth-hand or so, can be traced back to one account—
or, rather, several varying transcriptions of one account—written by the
Rev. Thomas H. Orderson, Rector of Christ Church during the whole
period of the disturbances in the vault (1812–20). Mr. Orderson seems
first to have drawn up a complete account for his own reference and then,
at different times, to have made several copies of this for curious corres-

---

* Destroyed by a hurricane in 1831. The foundation-stone of a new building
(designed, as its appointments clearly indicated, by Capt. Senhouse, R.N.) was laid on
Oct. 1, 1835; and that of a third exactly a century later—the 1835 church having been
burned to the ground in 1935.

pondents. As time went on, he may have grown weary of the whole subject; at any rate, the versions which he circulated do not agree in all respects—for example, one which has been declared* to be "absolutely authentic" (which it is, though no more so than several similar documents) omits an important interment in the vault altogether, and gives a wrong date for the first appearance of the disturbances.

While, however, Orderson's narrative provides the backbone of the evidence, we are not, as will be seen, entirely dependent on it. There is a considerable body of other testimony, which will be discussed in its place. In brief, it may be said that the evidence for the bulk of the happenings within and without the vault during the period of the disturbances is quite unassailable.

The first appearance of the story in print appears to have been in 1833, when Sir J. E. Alexander gave a short résumé of the facts in his *Transatlantic Sketches*. As his account, although short and incomplete, gives a useful introduction to the question, I reprint it here.

"It is not generally known that in Barbados there is a mysterious vault, in which no one now dares to deposit the dead. It is in a churchyard near the seaside. In 1807 the first coffin that was deposited in it was that of a Mrs. Goddard; in 1808 a Miss A. M. Chase was placed in it; and in 1812 Miss D. Chase. In the end of 1812 the vault was opened for the body of the Honourable T. Chase; but the three first coffins were found in a confused state, having been apparently tossed from their places. Again was the vault opened to receive the body of an infant, and the four coffins, all of lead, were much disturbed. In 1816 a Mr. Brewster's body was placed in the vault, and again great disorder was apparent in the coffins. In 1819 a Mr. Clarke was placed in the vault, and, as before, the coffins were in confusion.

"Each time that the vault was opened the coffins were replaced in their proper situations, that is, three on the ground side by side, and the others laid on them. The vault was then regularly closed; the door (a massive stone which required six or seven men to move) was cemented by masons; and though the floor was of sand, there were no marks of foot-steps or water.

"The last time the vault was opened was in 1819. Lord Combermere was then present, and the coffins were found confusedly thrown about the vault, some with their heads down and others up. What could have occasioned this phenomenon? In no other vault in the island has this ever occurred. Was it an earthquake which occasioned it, or the effects of an inundation in the vault?"

* By the late F. M. Alleyne. See Sir A. Aspinall's *Pocket Guide to the West Indies* (London, 1923, p. 97).

Schomburgk, in his *History of Barbados*, published in 1844, gives a similar version, adding that at the time of the opening in 1820 (the correct date of Alexander's "last time the vault was opened") a sketch was made of the disarray of the coffins. He also states that the sand on the floor was deliberately put down for the purpose of detecting foot-prints.

In 1860 a pamphlet with the alluring title of *Death's Deeds*, giving an account of the disturbances in the vault, was printed in England. It was anonymous, but appears to have been the work of a Mrs. D. H. Cussons. It formed the basis of another account printed in the *Memoirs and Correspondence of Field-Marshal Viscount Combermere*. I regard both accounts as entirely untrustworthy. The pamphlet I have not seen; nor do I know whether the inflated style of the Combermere account is native or transplanted. Judging by the clap-trap title of the Cussons pamphlet, there is no difficulty in believing it to be the fountain-head from which flowed the annexed "old abusing of God's patience and the King's English".

"When they endeavoured to remove the stone it resisted with unwonted weight. . . . For a moment all hands were paralysed, and a look of wondering dismay passed from each to each; but it was only for a moment. The next, excitement lent a powerful energy to their efforts, and the stone yielded half an inch, enough to afford a glimpse inside. Nothing was distinctly visible in the darkness of its buried night. Still, the light which entered through the narrow crevice seemed to cut across some black object close to the portal, so near that the thread-like ray lay brilliantly visible, prevented by this massive black substance from dispersing itself into the reigning darkness within.

"Terror a second time palsied the energies of those engaged in this operation. Suspense deepened the intensity of interest and awe which transfixed the anxious spectators. Every breath was hushed lest they should fail to catch the first whisper of those near the tomb that might afford a solution to the problem before them."

And much more, in the style of Mrs. Amanda McKittrick Ros.* Actually, this turgid narrative is an attempt to relate that when the vault was opened for the last time, in Lord Combermere's presence, one of the coffins was found to be jamming the door; an event which, as shown later, probably occurred only in the imagination of the authoress.

In the early years of this century the late Andrew Lang made a careful examination of the available evidence, with the aid of several MS. accounts

* Of Larne. Authoress of *Irene Iddesleigh* (1897), *Delina Delaney*, *Poems of Puncture*, and *Fumes of Formation* (1933). Easily the world's worst novelist, and second only to Mrs. Julia A. Moore, "The Sweet Singer of Michigan", as a manufacturer of unconsciously-funny doggerel.

Not to be confused with Mrs. Amanda Ross, whose novel *The Balance of Comfort*, or *the Old Maid and the Married Woman* appeared in 1818.

of the disturbances. He gave a very complete account of his results in the *Folk-Lore Journal* for December 1907, in an article entitled "Death's Deeds; a Bi-located Story", which I regard as the fairest and clearest account of the whole matter extant.

The story was also retold by Sir Algernon Aspinall, in an essay, entitled "A Barbados Mystery", forming part of his book *West Indian Tales of Old*. He also summarized it in his *Pocket Guide to the West Indies*. It is to be regretted that the particular Orderson version used by him was, as can easily be seen, erroneous in two important particulars.* Following him, Sir Arthur Conan Doyle gave a short and similarly inaccurate account in an article "The Law of the Ghost" which appeared in the *Strand Magazine*,† forming part of a series with the general title of "The Uncharted Coast".

I turn now to the MS. sources of information, most of which, as previously remarked, are slightly different versions of the facts from the standpoint of a principal witness—all written by Orderson, and communicated by him at various times to different persons. In fairness, I should add that I have not had the opportunity of seeing any of these MSS.; I take the details of them from Lang and from Sir A. Aspinall.

The burial register at Christ Church, which was examined by the late Hon. Forster M. Alleyne (Lang's brother-in-law), contains a complete record of the various interments in the vault, signed by Orderson, but no indication that anything out of the common had ever occurred there. The Parochial Treasurer's accounts, and the files of contemporary newspapers, were similarly found to be barren of interest.

He discovered, however, a description by an eye-witness, the Hon. Nathan Lucas, of the scene at the last opening of the vault in April 1820. This document, which also embodies one of the Orderson versions, is printed in full in Sir A. Aspinall's *Pocket Guide to the West Indies*. Mr. Alleyne also found allusions to the subject of the disturbances in the correspondence of a member of his family in 1820, and it is quite possible that more material of the kind may still be brought to light.

As to the Orderson versions, one (called "A" by Lang) was, in 1907, in the possession of the Hon. F. M. Alleyne already mentioned. His father, Mr. Charles Thomas Alleyne, had been in the island in April 1820, when the vault was opened for the last time. F. M. Alleyne told Lang that he had heard the story from the lips of an eye-witness of that event, Sir Robert Bowcher Clarke. "A" contained sketches of the coffins,

---

* It states that the coffins were first found disturbed on July 6, 1812 (interment of Dorcas Chase): and it omits the interment of Thomas Chase on August 9, 1812. It was on the latter occasion that the disturbance of the coffins was first noted.

† No. 348, vol. 58, December 1919.

both in order and when disarranged. On the back of one of the sketches was said to be written "J. Anderson, Rector"—probably a mistake for "T. Orderson".

Another version (called by Lang "O") was printed for private circulation by one Robert Reece, who afterwards contributed an article on the subject to *Once a Week*.* This version formed the basis of the account given in *Death's Deeds*, and hence also of that in the *Memoirs of Lord Combermere*.

A third version, which Lang does not name, but which it will be convenient to call "B", since it is "written on thin blue paper" (following the celebrated sergeant-major who filed the Wesleyan parade-states under letter H because they fell in at Half-past nine), was sent to Lang by F. M. Alleyne, who had copied it from a document once in the possession of a sister of Sir R. Bowcher Clarke. This version, signed by "Thomas H. Orderson, Rector", Lang prints in full, collating it with his "A" and "O".

The following chronological account, containing what I hope will be found a fairly faithful narrative of the events at the vault, has been compiled from all the foregoing materials. As is natural, most weight has been attached to the MS. documents—Lucas's statement and a synoptic combination of "A", "O", and "B". The printed versions have been used chiefly as comments upon these, but here and there a detail which they omit, and which is not in contradiction to them, has been adopted.

First, a few details of the vault itself. It was built early in the eighteenth century. It is partly above ground and partly below; the lower half being excavated, to a depth of about 2 feet, out of the solid limestone rock (which is common in most parts of Barbados). The upper portion is of exceedingly solid masonry, composed of large blocks of the local coral most firmly cemented together. The roof, seen from the inside, is arched; from the outside it appears flat. The sides have a slight inward slope as they rise. The floor-space is 12 feet long by 6½ feet broad. The back is composed of two separate masonry walls, an inner and an outer, not united. The interior is reached through a doorway, formerly kept closed by a large slab of blue Devon marble resting against the sloping sides. From this entrance a few steps lead down into the vault.

On the tombstone is, or was, an inscription recording that the vault was erected by the "truly sorrowful widow" (*née* Elizabeth Walrond) of the Hon. James Elliot, who was "snatched away from us the 14th of

* March 11, 1865. This article gave rise to a controversy between Reece and one John Arnold, who maintained, ably but erroneously, that the disturbances at Barbados had been caused by surface-water flooding the vault. See *Once a Week* for 22.4.1865, 13.5.1865, 27.5.1865 and 12.8.1865.

A letter from Reece to a Major Clarke, describing the disturbances, also appeared in *The Lamp* for June 1864.

May, Anno Domini 1724", and who (as the student of epitaphs, particularly eighteenth-century ones, will readily anticipate) was "lamented by
all who knew him".

Curiously enough, although the vault was undoubtedly erected for
Elliot's benefit, he does not seem to have been interred there; or else his
coffin was removed later. The first recorded interment in the vault is that
of Mrs. Thomasina Goddard, on the 31st of July 1807 . . . "and when it
was opened for her reception it was quite empty, without the smallest
appearance of any person having been buried there". Mrs. Goddard's
coffin appears, although the evidence is not conclusive, to have been of
wood—a point which, as will be seen, is of some importance.

It may be noted that Lucas, in his statement, draws attention to a
difference between the English and Barbadian practices of coffining the
dead. In Barbados, apparently, it was then the practice to enclose the
body first in a wooden coffin and then, at the grave, in an outer leaden
one; not, as we do, to have first a wooden shell, then the leaden coffin,
and then an outer one of wood. Mrs. Goodard's may have been a single
one of wood, without the usual leaden covering. With one exception
(noted), all the succeeding coffins placed in the vault had leaden outer
shells.

How Mrs. Goddard came to be buried in the Elliot vault does not
appear; but by 1808 the vault seems to have passed into the possession
of the Chase family, three members of which were buried there between
1808 and 1812.

The first was Mary Ann Maria Chase, the infant daughter of the
Hon. Thomas Chase, who was buried on February 22, 1808. Mrs.
Goddard's coffin was found undisturbed.

The second was Dorcas Chase, also a daughter of Thomas Chase, who
was buried in the vault on July 6, 1812. She appears to have been an
adult,* but there is no information as to her age. On this occasion, also,
the coffins (two) already in the vault were found undisturbed.

The case was otherwise when the coffin of Thomas Chase himself was
brought to the vault on August 9, 1812. The coffins of M. A. M. Chase
and Dorcas Chase were found to have been displaced, that of M. A. M.
Chase having been thrown from the north-east corner of the vault across
to the opposite angle, where it had lodged almost on end, head downwards.

The negroes employed in the work of bestowing the coffins appear,
with good reason, to have been much alarmed; but little notice seems, at
the time, to have been taken of their stories. As it was obviously not their

---

* Or, as a young French lady once phrased it in her anxiety to speak correct English,
"an adulteress".

business to demand an inquiry into reports which, *prima facie*, convicted them or their predecessors either of negligence, theft, or practical joking, the matter seems to have blown over for the time; although this may have been the first occasion on which special precautions were taken to ensure that the vault was securely closed.

A second infant, Samuel Brewster Ames, was buried in the vault on September 25, 1816—an interval of just over four years since the last interment. All the coffins (except, possibly, that of Mrs. Goddard) were found in confusion.

It is a little difficult, even with the aid of the various narratives (or possibly, it may be thought, with their hindrance), to determine whether, in fact, the coffin of Mrs. Goddard was disturbed as well as the remainder. The point is of some little importance, since it has been suggested by Sir Arthur Conan Doyle that the forces inside the vault, whatever they were, betrayed antipathy to the leaden coffins only, and left Mrs. Goddard's, which was of wood, alone. I reserve the question for discussion later.

Thomas Chase's coffin, be it noted (about whose disturbance at this date there is no question), was an exceedingly heavy affair, requiring eight men to lift it. It had an outer leaden shell, and its occupant is stated to have been of great bulk and weight.

On November 17th of the same year (1816) the vault was reopened to receive the coffin of Samuel Brewster (a different person from S. B. Ames above), who had been murdered in an abortive slave-rising in the preceding April and temporarily buried at St. Philip. On this occasion the same confusion was observed among the coffins (which, of course, were carefully and reverently replaced every time they were found disarranged).

It is a little difficult to understand how the vault, which until 1816 had been, except for its first occupant, reserved for members of the Chase family, came now to be used, apparently, as the burying-place of several other persons of differing names. They may all have been relations; but on this point the available information gives no light.

On July 17, 1819 (so "A" and "O": "B" and Lucas say the 7th), Thomazina Clarke was buried in the vault in a wooden coffin (all the records are in agreement on this point: "B" states that it was of cedar). The coffins were again found in disorder.

This was the last burial in the vault. By this time public attention was fully roused. Lord Combermere, Governor of Barbados, was present at the interment, attended by his aides-de-camp and a considerable crowd.

The interior of the vault was carefully examined and sounded, but no trace of any secret entrance could be found. The floor was next covered with sand, and after the coffins had been carefully replaced in rows the vault was closed, and the slab at the entrance cemented. Lord Combermere put his seal on it, and several witnesses added private marks of their own.

It may be noted that as the vault only measured 12 feet by 6½ feet in plan, six coffins (even though three were those of children) must have needed careful stowage. The accounts and sketches of their arrangement vary slightly; but it seems generally agreed that the three largest coffins were laid side by side on the floor of the vault, and the other three arranged one on top of each of these. The only divergent account is that given by Lucas, who states: "The Children's coffins were placed on bricks in the Vault; Mr. Chase's on the Rock, the bottom of the Vault". This is entirely at variance with the sketches accompanying his account.

The seventh coffin, that of Mrs. Goddard, had by this time decayed and fallen to pieces. The "shakings" were tied together in a bundle, and left inside the vault, stacked against the wall. What had become of the body does not appear.

Some eight months elapsed, and then, on April 18, 1820, the vault was reopened in the presence of Lord Combermere and of "two other persons of the first respectability" ("B").* The determining cause of this opening of the vault is uncertain—I imagine it to have been simply curiosity, stimulated by the accident of Lord Combermere's presence in the neighbourhood. This, at any rate, is the reason given by Lucas. The "B" Orderson version states that Combermere determined to have the vault reopened upon hearing that a noise had been heard in it by night— interesting, if true, but not confirmed by any of the other versions. At all events, the opening was undoubtedly deliberate, and made for the express purpose of seeing whether the coffins had been again disturbed—not of adding to their number.

The coffins were found in a bewildering state of confusion—bewildering because the seal and private marks on the slab and other parts of the vault were found perfect and undisturbed, while no trace of footmarks appeared on the sanded floor. The remains of Mrs. Goddard's coffin stood, as they had been left, against the wall.

It was enough. Combermere—who had fought all through the Peninsular War with Wellington and, but for a piece of official jobbery, would have commanded the cavalry at Waterloo—was not, it will be conceded, a man easily daunted; but he seems to have concluded that the matter was beyond his powers as Governor to unravel, and to have offered no opposi-

---

* Lucas's statement is more specific:

"... The Rector, the Rev. Dr. Thos. H. Orderson, ... very soon arrived. His Lordship, myself, Robert Bowcher Clarke, and Rowland Cotton, Esq., were present during the whole time."

tion when the Chase family gave instructions for the vault to be cleared and left empty, the coffins being buried elsewhere. One imagines that if Combermere had hadany suspicion that trickery could have been practised, he would have made it his business, in view of the great popular excitement caused by the proceedings at the vault, to have the problem investigated further.

Such, in outline, were the happenings at the Chase vault, Barbados, during the years 1808–20.

As previously mentioned, sketches were made, when the vault was opened for the last time, showing the state in which the coffins were found, and that in which they had previously been left. Unfortunately, there are at least two separate sets of these sketches extant; and they conflict in a very puzzling manner.

Drawings based on one set of these sketches are shown in Figs. 8 and 9. The sketches annexed to the Orderson version forming part of Lucas's statement have been published by Sir A. Aspinall in the two works already mentioned. The originals are in very exaggerated perspective, and appear to be drawn as if looking into the vault from the entrance. The second of these sketches, which shows one of the coffins (that of Thomas Chase) leaning against the back wall, is probably the foundation of the story, apparently related in *Death's Deeds* and repeated in the Combermere memoirs, that this coffin, when the vault was last opened, was found jamming the door. Neither Lucas nor Orderson, who were both present, makes any mention of this occurrence, which it is quite impossible that they could either have forgotten or failed to notice. I regard the statement as a pure fiction—a misguided attempt to add to the gruesome horrors of a plain tale which needs no such embellishment.

Figures 8 and 9 are based upon sketches published by Lang in *The Folk-Lore Journal*, and taken from "B".* Personally, I regard them as more authentic than Lucas's, because being in plan, and in simple outline without detail, they look much more like sketches made on the spot and at the time, which both sets of drawings profess to be. The Lucas sketches, with their complications of perspective and detail, have an air of afterthought. That, however, is a matter of personal preference. It does not seem possible to reconcile the discrepancies between the two sets of sketches.

For the sake of completeness, it may be as well to give now some

* A third pair of sketches, agreeing practically *in toto* with these, were published by Reece in his *Once a Week* article. He states that his father ". . . . some years since, had two models constructed, exhibiting the various displacements to which the coffins were subjected; one of these models he presented to the late Bishop Blomfield, who took a great interest in this mysterious matter of the vault; the other is, I believe, deposited in the British Museum".

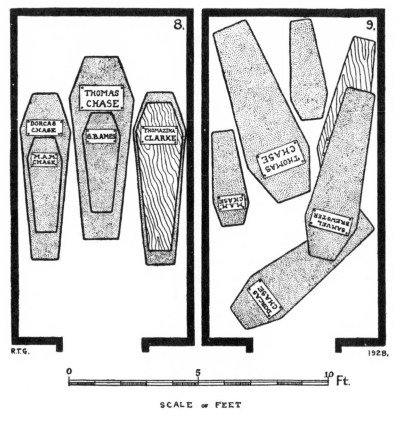

SCALE of FEET

FIG. 8.—Sketch showing the positions in which the coffins were left in the
Chase vault, Barbados, on July 17, 1819—the vault being closed and
sealed immediately afterwards.

FIG. 9.—Sketch showing the positions in which the coffins were found when
the vault was reopened on April 18, 1820.

NOTE.—The sketches are based upon contemporary drawings, corrected in details by means of a scale-plan of the vault and model coffins
(also to scale).

account of various similar events recorded as having happened elsewhere
—for the Barbados mystery, although the most completely documented
and the best-authenticated case on record, is not the only one. There are
at least three others—although one is more than a little suspect.

Of these three, two occurred in England. Of the first, which seems to
have happened about 1750, nothing more is known than can be gathered
from the following extract from the *Annual Register*, 1760 (p. 121).

ENTRANCE TO THE CHASE VAULT, BARBADOS

"To the Author of the *London Magazine*.

"Sir,—At Staunton, in Suffolk, is a vault belonging to the family of the French's. On opening it some years since, several leaden coffins, with wooden cases, that had been fixed on biers, were found displaced, to the great astonishment of many of the inhabitants of the village. The coffins were placed as before, and properly closed; when, some time ago, another of the family dying, they were a second time found displaced; and two years after they were not only found all off the biers, but one coffin, as heavy as to require eight men to raise it, was found on the fourth step that leads into the vault.—Whence arose this operation, in which, it is certain, no one had a hand—? N.B. It was occasioned by water, as is imagined, though no signs of it appeared at the different periods of time that the vault was opened."

So far as I know, the text of this passage (here given verbatim), has not previously been printed in full except by Sir A. Aspinall, who has followed a slightly inaccurate copy of it made long ago by Lucas and embodied in his account of the events at Barbados. Lang does not appear to have seen this text when he wrote his article originally; and although he mentions, in a postscript, the discovery of Lucas's account by Mr. Alleyne, and notes his reference to the *European Magazine*,* he assigns a wrong date to it (1814 for 1815), suggesting that he had not verified the reference personally.

I have not found any other mention of this case in the *London Magazine* or its contemporaries. Sir James Alexander instances it in his book (1833). The name should be Stanton—a mistake which has led astray several later inquirers, including Lang. There is no "Staunton" in Suffolk: but there is a "Stanton", about nine miles north-east of Bury St. Edmunds. Lewis's *Topographical Dictionary of England* (1831) gives it as then consisting of two united parishes, Stanton All Saints and Stanton St. John, which suggests a doubt as to which parish churchyard includes the vault in question. Lucas seems to have known of this, as he notes on his copy of the *European Magazine* extract: "(Qy. Which of the Stantons? N.L.)". The late Sir Arthur Conan Doyle stated that inquiries made "from the present vicar of the parish" had not yielded any further evidence or details.

I shall return later, so far as it concerns the happenings at Barbados, to the very natural theory that these disturbances of coffins have been occasioned by water flooding the vaults.

---

* The *European Magazine* for Sept. 1815, apparently hard-up for copy, "lifted" this paragraph from the *Annual Register* of fifty-five years earlier, practically verbatim and without acknowledgement. In consequence, the epoch of the Stanton case has generally been taken to be the beginning of the nineteenth century, instead of the middle of the eighteenth.

The evidence for the second case of the kind in England is contained in a communication made to *Notes and Queries* in 1867 by Mr. F. A. Paley, of Cambridge, a well-known scholar.

"DISTURBANCE OF COFFINS IN VAULTS.

"As attention has been directed to this rather curious and perhaps novel subject, I beg to add an instance which occurred within my own knowledge and recollection (some twenty years ago) in the parish of Gretford, near Stamford, a small village of which my father was the rector. Twice, if not thrice, the coffins in a vault were found on reopening it to have been disarranged. The matter excited some interest in the village at the time, and, of course, was a fertile theme for popular superstition: but I think it was hushed up out of respect to the family to whom the vault belonged.

"A leaden coffin is a very heavy thing indeed; some six men can with difficulty carry it. Whether it can float is a question not very difficult to determine. If it will, it seems a natural, indeed the only explanation of the phenomenon, to suppose that the vault has somehow become filled with water.

"I enclose an extract from the letter of a lady to whom I wrote, not trusting my own memory, as to the details of the case.

'PENN., *Oct.* 15, 1867.

'. . . I remember very well the Gretford vault being opened when we were there. It was *in the church* and belonged to the . . . family. The churchwarden came to tell the rector, who went into the vault, and saw the coffins all in confusion: one little one on the top of a large one, and some tilted on one side against the wall. They were all *lead*, but of course cased in wood. The same vault had been opened once before, and was found in the same state of confusion, and set right by the churchwarden, so that his dismay was great when he found them displaced again. We had no doubt from the situation and nature of the soil that it had been full of water during some flood which floated the coffins. I dare say . . . is still alive, and could give the date, and I almost think . . . saw what had happened. I felt no doubt myself that lead coffins could *float*. We know a large iron vessel will, without *any* wood casing, and I suppose the flood subsiding would move them. The vault had been walled up, so that no one could have been in it. . . .' "

The good lady's notions of hydrostatics are a little crude, but, as will be seen later, she was quite correct in supposing that a coffin could float. Mr. Paley's caution in suppressing every other name in connection with the case was perfectly proper and considerate, but is a trifle exasperating at this distance of time. It is reminiscent of Theodore Hook's parody of the style in which Moore wrote his emasculated and cryptic life of Byron:

".... He told me one night that —— told —— that if —— would only ⸻ him, —— she would —— without any compunction; for her ——, who though an excellent man was no ——, and that she never ——; and this she told ——, and ——, as well as Lady —— herself. Byron told me this in confidence, and I may be blamed for repeating it; but —— can corroborate it if he happens not to be gone to ——."

The third case is alleged to have occurred in 1844 at Arensburg, on the island of Oesel, in the Baltic. Unfortunately, although we have a most circumstantial narrative of all that happened, or is supposed to have happened, it is at third-hand; it is the work of a man who, while honest and sincere, seems to have possessed very little power of weighing evidence; and comparatively recent attempts to obtain corroborative evidence have only succeeded in throwing considerable doubt on the whole story.

With these reservations, I give the account, which is too interesting to omit. It was first published in Robert Dale Owen's *Footfalls on the Boundary of Another World* (1861). I have condensed it a good deal; the original (which, be it noted, forms the sole authority for the story) is rather verbose, and written in the "succulent bivalve" manner.

The story was told to Owen in Paris on May 8, 1859, by the son and daughter of one of the principal actors in it—the Baron de Guldenstubbé. The events were said to have occurred in the summer of 1844—fifteen years earlier.

The cemetery of Arensburg, the only town in Oesel, contains several private chapels, each owned by some "family of distinction", with its vault annexed. It was the custom for the coffins (of heavy oak) to be left for a time in the chapel and then transferred to the vault, where they were placed side by side on iron cross-bars.

A highway runs by the cemetery, and from this three of the chapels, facing the road, are very conspicuous. It was in one of these three chapels, belonging to the family of Buxhoewden, that the disturbances occurred; and it was, indirectly, the nearness of the road that first caused attention to be drawn to them.

On Monday, June 22, 1844, a peasant woman named Dalmann had driven to the cemetery to visit her mother's grave, which was close to the Buxhoewden chapel. She made her horse fast (presumably to some "hitching-post", or to the railings, if there were any) opposite that chapel. On coming away, she found the animal in a state of mortal terror, and went for a "vet". The latter sapiently, if cautiously, declared that the horse "must have been excessively terrified from some cause or other", and did what he could for it. The animal, one is glad to say, recovered—

the terror of dumb animals is a pitiable thing to see. A day or two later Mme Dalmann told the story to the Baron de Guldenstubbé, a member of "one of the oldest noble families of Livonia", at his château, near Arensburg. He, as was natural, treated it lightly.

The following Sunday several persons who, like Mme Dalmann, had fastened their horses up opposite the Buxhoewden chapel (presumably during service) found them trembling and sweating with terror when they returned. Suspicion focused itself on the chapel; and several people heard, or thought that they heard, rumbling noises or groans coming from it. One day in July the same thing happened again. Eleven horses had been tethered close to the chapel; some passers-by, hearing noises coming from the chapel, raised an alarm; and when the owners reached the spot, they found the horses in a dreadful state. "Several of them, in their violent efforts to escape, had thrown themselves on the ground, and lay struggling there; others were scarcely able to walk or stand; and all were violently affected, so that it became necessary immediately to resort to bleeding and other methods of relief". This, be it remembered, was in 1844, when bleeding was a very ordinary method of treatment; in fact, the sheet-anchor of most medical men. Three or four of the horses were too far gone to recover.

Their owners, quite rightly, felt that this nuisance ought to be abated. They addressed a complaint to the Consistory—an ecclesiastical court sitting periodically at Arensburg—which they apparently considered the most appropriate tribunal. But the Consistory, doubtful of its legal or material power to put things right, did, for the moment, "nothing in particular, and did it very well".

About this time there was a death in the Buxhoewden family, and during the funeral service in the chapel some of the congregation thought that they heard groans in the vault below. This, however, was probably the effect of imagination, excited by rumour. But after the service some of the bolder spirits went down to the vault—and although they heard nothing they found that almost all of the coffins in it "had been displaced, and lay in a confused pile". They could find nothing to account for this. The vault was usually kept locked, and the locks were intact. They replaced the coffins, and locked up the vault again.

The cemetery had by now acquired rather a bad name in the neighbourhood; and as its ill-fame continued to spread the Consistory found itself obliged to do something. They proposed to make an official inquiry. The Buxhoewden family at first opposed this, on the ground that some enemy of theirs, wishing to start a scandal, was probably at the bottom of the whole thing. They came round, however, after satisfying themselves that, on the face of it, no one could have got into the vault without their knowledge. As a first step the Baron de Guldenstubbé, who was President of the Consistory, visited the vault with two of the Buxhoewdens, and found the coffins again in the same disorder. This decided matters; and after replacing the coffins an official investigation was put in hand, and a committee appointed to make it.

The committee consisted of De Guldenstubbé, as President of the Consistory; the bishop of the province, as its Vice-President; two other members of the Consistory; a doctor named Luce; Schmidt (the burgomaster) and one of the syndics, as representing the authorities of the town; and a secretary—in all eight persons.

Very naturally, they began by examining the vault. They found that all the coffins, except three, had again been displaced—the third recorded disturbance within a very short period. It may be noted that the number of coffins in the vault is not stated by Owen; but as he uses the expression "many of the coffins", and gives one to understand that the three left undisturbed did not form a very striking exception, we may safely put the total number down at over a dozen.

The committee first looked for traces of robbery, without success. None of the ornaments of the coffins had been touched; and, on opening one or two, the trinkets forming part of the funeral attire were found *in situ*. Robbers had entered a near-by vault some time before and stolen the gold-fringed velvet coffin-palls; so that it was natural, though mistaken, to suppose that robbery was at the bottom of the disturbances in the Buxhoewden vault.

The committee then took up the hypothesis which the owners of the vault had already abandoned—that some lewd fellow of the baser sort, "not having the fear of God before his eyes but rather seduced by the craft and malice of the Devil", had gone so far as to dig a tunnel, from some distant coign of vantage, underneath the chapel and into the vault. To test this not very probable theory, they employed workmen to take up the floor of the vault and examine the foundations of the chapel. No traces of tunnelling were found. One wonders that they did not, as in the Crippen case, adopt the simple plan of putting down an inch or so of water on the floor of the vault; the water would have sunk quickest, in all probability, on the line of a tunnel; and if it had remained, or sunk very slowly, it would have indicated that the vault was likely, in heavy weather, to be flooded—a theory which the committee does not seem to have considered.

It declared itself baffled for the moment. The coffins were replaced, the inner and outer doors of the vault were closed and sealed, both with the Consistory and municipal seals, and fine wood-ashes were scattered over the stairs leading from the chapel to the vault, and over the floor of the chapel. A similar layer of ashes had already been laid down in the vault itself. "Finally, guards, selected from the garrison of the town, and relieved at short intervals, were set for three days and nights to watch the building and prevent anyone from approaching it."

At the end of the three days the committee returned to the charge, and had the vault reopened. In view of the very short interval, it would not have been surprising had they found everything just as before—whatever might have happened had the opening been postponed, say, for some months. But the vault, as if flattered by the attention paid it by such dignified bodies as the Consistory and the municipality, rose most punctually to the occasion.

"Both doors were found securely locked and the seals inviolate. They entered. The coating of ashes still presented a smooth, unbroken surface. Neither in the chapel nor on the stairway leading to the vault was there the trace of a foot-step, of man or animal. The vault was sufficiently lighted from the chapel to make every object distinctly visible. They descended. With beating hearts they gazed on the spectacle before them. Not only was every coffin, with the same three exceptions as before, displaced, and the whole scattered in confusion over the place, but many of them, weighty as they were, had been set on end, so that the head of the corpse was downward. Nor was even this all. The lid of one coffin had been partially forced open, and there projected the shrivelled right arm of the corpse it contained . . . (that of one of the Buxhoewdens who had committed suicide)."

The committee satisfied themselves, as on the former occasion, that no robbery had been committed, and that there was no secret entrance to the vault; and then, as at Barbados, the coffins were removed, and buried elsewhere.

Owen concludes his story with the following important passage:

"An official report . . . was made out by the Baron de Guldenstubbé, as president, and signed by himself, by the bishop, the burgomeister, the physician, and the other members of the commission, as witnesses. This document, placed on record with the other proceedings of the Consistory, is to be found among its archives, and may be examined by any traveller, respectably recommended, on application to its secretary."

In view of this very categorical statement, the sequel is unfortunate.

In 1899, in the course of some correspondence on the subject of "The Poltergeist" in the *Journal of the Society for Psychical Research*, the late Dr. Alfred Russel Wallace quoted Owen's account of the disturbances at Arensburg, and spoke of it as ". . . the best evidence as to occurrences which were, and are, wholly inexplicable".[*] He elicited a rather disquieting rejoinder from the late Frank Podmore.

[*] *Journal of the Society for Psychical Research*, (February) 1899, pp. 28, 29.

"(7) THE DISTURBANCES AT ARENSBURG.—As Dr. Wallace tells us, the facts were communicated* to Dale Owen by Mlle de Guldenstubbé and her brother. They had heard them from the late Baron. The account, as it reaches us, is therefore third-hand. Neither Dale Owen nor his informants profess to have seen the documents which constitute the strength of the evidence. Until we have a certified copy of those documents, the case, I submit, is not before the court."†

Podmore's scepticism was quite justifiable; particularly in view of what, I believe, is the rule of the S.P.R., that save in very exceptional circumstances it will not accept evidence at second and remoter hands.

The question thus raised in 1899 waited for its answer until 1907, when the *Journal of the S.P.R.* published the results of some inquiries made by Count Perovsky Petrovo-Solovovo.‡

The Consistory of Arensburg, in which the all-important documents were said by Owen to have been deposited, was closed in 1889 as the result of the ecclesiastical reforms initiated by the Czar Alexander III. Its archives were transferred to the "Livländisches Evangelisches-Lutherische Consistorium" at Riga. Solovovo applied to this body for information, and received the reply that the Oesel archives in their custody contained no documents bearing on the subject; they referred him to the archives of the Church of St. Laurentius at Arensburg. A letter addressed there brought a reply from the Rev. Lemm, "Ober-pastor" of the church in question, "which was wholly negative". Mr. Lemm also mentioned that, some years before, the present Baron Buxhoewden, who had seen an account of the 1844 disturbances in a Warsaw newspaper, had communicated with him on the subject, but had failed to find any further information either at Arensburg or at Riga.

It would seem, then, that the document paraded with such a flourish of trumpets has, if it ever existed, vanished into thin air; while both its existence and the facts of Owen's narrative are rendered, to say the least, doubtful. But the proof is not quite conclusive. In spite of the unsuccessful searches, it is quite possible that the document still exists.

Benjamin Franklin once delivered himself of the excellent aphorism, "If you want a thing done, go: if you don't, send". A search made by a third party, at a distance, for documents with whose special importance he is not personally impressed, is rarely satisfactory. An experience of my own is a case in point.

Some years ago, while compiling a book on the marine chronometer, I

---

* "Not, it is to be presumed, in writing: Dale Owen's words are, 'the facts above narrated were detailed to me', etc." [Note by Podmore.]

† *Journal of the S.P.R.*, (June) 1899, p. 93.

‡ *Journal of the S.P.R.*, 1907-8, pp. 30, 128, 144, 158-60.

came across a statement by Sir George Airy, Astronomer. Royal, in his Annual Report for 1841, that a set of elaborate drawings of John Harrison's first three marine timekeepers had been transmitted to the Observatory by Messrs. Arnold and Dent, and placed in safe custody there. I very much wanted to inspect those drawings; and, from what I knew of Airy's elaborate system of filing and indexing every scrap of paper that passed through his hands, I thought it would be no very hard job to find them. The Observatory authorities, with their customary kindness, made a search—which drew blank. Of the drawings, not a trace could be found —only a letter written by Airy to the Admiralty, stating that they had been received and that "every care will be taken of them". As a sarcastic, if unintentional, comment on the efficiency of his methods of filing papers, this would be hard to beat.

Luckily, however, I persisted. It would have been unreasonable to expect the Observatory authorities, who had already spent a good deal of valuable time over the matter, to make a further search. But I obtained their permission (a privilege which I appreciated) to make a personal search in their archives; and, after a long hunt in all likely and unlikely places, I unearthed (in one of the latter, needless to say) most of the missing drawings, securely hidden at the end of a volume of miscellaneous papers.

But if Solovovo's inquiries as to the documentary evidence mentioned by Owen resulted in casting some doubt (but scarcely absolute discredit) upon the latter's story, support was, at the same time, lent to it by a letter to the Count from "a leading member of the Buxhoewden family"— probably the "present Baron Buxhoewden" mentioned by Mr. Lemm. The letter, written from Arensburg, stated that the writer—aware that the archives of the Arensburg Consistory had been removed to Riga, and that there was nothing (officially) to be found there—had visited Oesel, and examined the archives of the former "Landgericht", but had not found, at present, anything bearing on the matter. It added, however (I translate from the original French):

". . . All of the old persons whom I have questioned upon the subject remember the incident in question perfectly, and the greater number of them affirm that they have heard it said that an official report (*procès-verbal*) was drawn up. With a few exceptions, the details mentioned in your English journal have been entirely confirmed, but, to my great regret, it has been impossible for me to discover a trace of the official report."

Although this is only hearsay evidence, it suggests at least that Owen was not the victim of an elaborate practical joke on the part of the two Guldenstubbés. It is possible, but not very probable, that the report in question may still be brought to light.

The letter also indicates that the Buxhoewden family considered the disturbances to have been caused by water making its way into the vault—a point which will shortly be discussed.

Such is a synopsis of the evidence for the cases, apart from that at Barbados, in which coffins have been found disturbed by some recondite cause. All four cases are curiously similar in outline, and I propose, while not asserting that any one explanation is equally applicable to all of them, to use the other three as a basis of comparison while discussing the explanations which have been put forward in connection with the disturbances at Barbados, which I consider the best-authenticated and, if the expression be permitted, most inexplicable case of the four.

Whatever may be thought of the evidence in the three other cases, particularly that at Oesel, I imagine that few will deny the actual fact of the coffins at Barbados having repeatedly been found disturbed, and the equally certain fact that the witnesses to the occurrence were completely puzzled to account for it.

Starting here, it may be premised that the agency producing the disturbances was either

1. Natural, or
2. Human, or
3. Neither human nor natural.

And, like the negro preacher who announced that he would divide his sermon into two parts, I propose to "wrastle with de easy part first". We have no right to postulate the existence of any agency of the third order unless and until discussion of the other two has failed to throw light on the matter.

Of natural causes, those which have been suggested are

(a) Earthquakes.
(b) Gases escaping from the coffins.
(c) Flooding of the vaults by casual water, which has afterwards subsided.

This classification appears to be exhaustive.*

The West Indies are undoubtedly subject to earthquakes; it may be remarked in passing that this cannot be said, in the same degree, of either England or the island of Oesel. But an earthquake so extraordinarily limited in scope as to produce violent motion in an area 12 feet by 6 feet, without the slightest tremor being felt elsewhere, is unknown to seismology; while to imagine that such an earthquake could occur repeatedly in exactly the same spot is an abuse of one's intelligence.

---

* I exclude, as clearly untenable, the suggestions that the coffins might have been displaced by animals entering the vault, or by the effects of lightning.

The gas theory I have mentioned only for the sake of completeness. There is no need to discuss it in detail. I will only say that no volume of gas that could conceivably be generated would be able, even if it escaped suddenly at a single small vent, to produce any motion of the coffin in which it had been confined; unless, indeed, the latter were balanced on knife-edges or floating in water, or otherwise relieved of the effects of weight and friction. As to its floating in water, it will be seen that this supposition is inconsistent with the assumption of gas escaping from the coffin.

The supposition that the disturbance of the coffins was due to intermittent flooding of the vault has far more to be said in its favour; in fact, it is one which, *on the evidence*, completely explains the occurrences at Stanton and at Gretford. I do not think, however, that it is applicable in the Oesel case (upon which, however, I do not much rely), and I am quite certain that it does not explain the events at Barbados.

Let us see what is to be said in its favour.

In the first place, Mr. Paley's correspondent was perfectly right when she asserted her belief that the coffins in a flooded vault, if freely laid therein, would float. They would undoubtedly do this *so long as they were watertight* (or, which is the same thing, gastight). This can be proved both by calculation and by direct evidence.

A coffin of ordinary size (actually, the size does not affect the question) and constructed in the English fashion, with a wooden shell, an inner lead casing and a heavy outer shell of wood, weighs in all about 8 cwt., and would displace, if wholly immersed in water, some 18 cubic feet. The weight of this displaced water, assuming it were fresh (if it were salt, the buoyancy of the coffin would be increased about $2\frac{1}{2}$ per cent.) would be about 10 cwt. Allowing $1\frac{1}{2}$ cwt. for the body, the coffin would still just float with a 50-lb. weight attached to it.

The following extract from the *London Evening Post* for May 16, 1751, provides excellent direct evidence on the point:

"We have an account from Hambourg that on the 16th April last, about six leagues off the North Foreland, Captain Wyrck Pietersen, commander of the ship called the *Johannes*, took up a coffin made in the English manner, and with the following inscription upon a silver plate, 'Mr. Francis Humphrey Merrydith, died 25 March, 1751, aged 51', which coffin the said captain carried to Hambourg, and then opened it, in which was enclosed a leaden one, and the body of an elderly man embalmed and dressed in fine linen. This is the corpse that was buried in the Goodwin Sands a few weeks ago, according to the Will of the deceased."

No doubt the coffin was buried at low water, when the sands were uncovered, and was freed by the scour of the tide. But its buoyancy must have been more than a little to extricate it entirely, for the Goodwins are proverbially tenacious of anything that comes into their keeping.

The Times of August 3, 1907, reports a sitting of the Consistory court of London, at which a petition for a faculty was presented by the vicar and churchwardens of Edgware parish church. It was desired to remove various remains buried in the church itself, in a series of brick graves under the aisle and the transepts, covered with large flagstones. It had been found that these graves were full of water to a depth of from 4 to 6 feet, in which some of the coffins, and also decayed bones, were floating.

The Edgware case is, if anything, more significant than that of the coffin found floating at sea, for two reasons. The floating took place in fresh water, not salt; and the coffins, although much older, had obviously remained watertight. It may be pointed out that a non-watertight coffin of ordinary pattern would certainly not float in water.

It is also an excellent proof, if any were needed, that vaults do sometimes become flooded. And it will be conceded that if this occurred in any of the cases I am considering, the result would necessarily be some disturbance of the coffins. Even if the rise and fall of the water were very gradual, there would probably be some slight currents and eddies, and it is too much to expect that the coffins should all come down again exactly in the positions from which they rose. If some floated and some remained submerged, it would be about an even chance that, when the water sank, one or more of the floating coffins would subside across the lower ones in an unstable position, and so be found tilted, or even bottom upwards. Even if all floated, they might not necessarily be all found side by side on the floor.

The theory put forward by the Buxhoewden family, in the letter previously mentioned, takes this factor into account. Shortly, it was stated that Oesel is subject to periodical accumulations of surface water (*Grundwasser*), which are common in the autumn and spring, and rise, at those periods, almost to ground-level in some parts of the island, only to disappear very rapidly in the summer and the winter. Underground tombs, in such circumstances, become tanks. The letter adds that other tombs have since been found, occasionally, to be full of water, in which the coffins were floating—some of them, singularly enough, head downwards.

This is not impossible. If the coffin were only just buoyant, it would have a negligible "metacentric height", and would tend to turn into its most stable position, whatever that might be. As compared with a coffin of considerable buoyancy, which would undoubtedly float in a horizontal position, the stability of such a coffin would be analogous to that of a submarine, awash, contrasted with that of a surface craft; and it is well known that submarines have no great stability. When one reflects that the head is, bulk for bulk, by far the heaviest part of the body, it is not at all wonderful that some coffins might, if the depth of water allowed, float head downwards, and retain that position when the water in the vault subsided.

Again, it is by no means certain that water entering a vault would leave any very obvious traces, provided that the inundation did not last very long. Most vaults are more or less damp, so that traces of extra damp would not be very obvious. Readers of that classic of Bacchanalian literature, Professor Saintsbury's *Notes on a Cellar-book*, will remember his account of the cellar which, "at certain times of the year, used to be filled about a foot deep with the most pellucid water, apparently rising from the earth. This remained some time, and disappeared as it came". It does not seem to have done any great harm, and it certainly did not prevent the use of the adjoining cellar as a repository for nobler liquids.

It does not even seem likely that traces of the flooding would be found upon the sand or ashes covering the floor; the effect of the water on this, if gradual, would probably be to make it smoother than before.

The flooding theory, then, has much to be said in its favour. It provides a natural explanation of the whole mystery; it produces an agency of quite sufficient power to displace the coffins, overturn them, and even stand them head downwards; and it does not involve any disarrangement either of seals or private marks on the outside of the vault or of the material strewn on the floor for the purpose of detecting foot-marks. In the Stanton and Gretford cases there seems to be no valid reason for declining to accept it; although there might be such reason if we knew more of these two rather obscure and vaguely documented cases.

But I cannot think that it entirely explains the disturbances at Oesel; and it is quite inapplicable in the case of the Barbados vault.

At Oesel we have to assume that the flood-water rose from well below the floor-level of the vault to a height of at least 6 feet above it (as shown by the inverted coffins) and again sank, so as to disappear completely, within the period of a few days. Not only must it have done this, but it must have done it again and again, at quite short intervals, at least four times. In the case of the official investigation, the whole operation must have been performed in three days only; and I cannot conceive any hypothesis which would make this rapid flux and reflux even plausible. In addition, the coffins would certainly not have had time to dry; and, in common with anything of perishable material, such as a pall, etc., left in the vault, they would have exhibited most obvious traces of damp.

The same reasoning applies, although not with so much force, to the Barbados case. The intervals were longer; though one was of a month only, and in the early autumn. But there are other and much more cogent objections.

In the first place, the churchyard stands on a headland overlooking Oistin's Bay, a situation not very favourable to any accumulation of surface water. On the other hand, the vault is partly dug out of the limestone rock, in which the presence of springs is not impossible.

But the possibility of the disturbances having been due to the action of water was not overlooked at the time, as at Oesel. Lucas, in his account, is specific as to the point:

"There was no vestige of water to be discovered in the vault; no marks where it had been; and the vault is in a level churchyard, by no means in a fall, much less in a run of water."

Just previously he has remarked:

"Why were the coffins of wood *in situ*? and why was the bundle of Mrs. Goddard's decayed coffin found where it had been left? Wood certainly would first float."

His second question is the crux of the matter. We have the written testimony of two eye-witnesses, Lucas and Orderson, that the remains of Mrs. Goddard's wooden coffin, tied together in a bundle, were found undisturbed when the vault was last opened. Unless we disregard this testimony altogether—in which case we might as well disbelieve the whole story and be done with it—this seems quite conclusive evidence that whatever agency may have caused the disturbances, it was not water. If the flood were deep enough to float the coffins, it must, *a fortiori*, have floated the bundle—and, short of a miracle, this could not afterwards have been found undisturbed. It may also be pointed out that all but two feet of the vault was above the ground-level, so that it is difficult to imagine it being flooded to a greater depth—while two coffins of ordinary height lying one on top of the other would not be floated by two feet of water.

There arises, in consequence, the question whether the disturbances were the work of some human agency. Three other questions at once suggest themselves, assuming this to be the fact:

1. Who did it?
2. Why was it done?
3. How was it done?

To the first two questions there are several possible answers, but they can only be the merest guesses. The disturbances began when a member of the Chase family was buried in the vault; and Thomas Chase, the head of the family, who shortly followed there, seems to have been a man of strong and possibly cruel character—one who might easily make bitter and vengeful enemies, particularly among his negro dependents. As against this, one imagines that nothing but the most powerful inducements could have prevailed upon a superstitious negro to break into a vault, probably by night; although there is a case on record of an occurrence almost as unlikely, when a negro broke *into* Dartmoor prison, having an account to settle (by means of a razor, or other convenient implement) with the Chief Warder—an errand happily bootless in more senses than one.*

Admittedly, the Barbados story has a hint of Voodooism, which would at once have been suspected had the scene been laid in Hayti; but if we concede, for the moment, that some negroes or other enemies of the Chases had made their way into the vault, it is difficult to imagine why they (there must have been more than one) should have contented themselves with merely throwing the coffins about, and not have attempted to open them for the purpose of mutilating or defiling their occupants. They must, on this supposition, have had several opportunities of doing so.

It is true that, as far as we know, the coffins, once deposited, were never opened for examination, and it is therefore a matter of inference that their contents went unmolested: but they were undoubtedly scrutinized, and we can at least conclude that they showed no external signs of having been opened, and that their weight was not appreciably altered.

But to the third question—how it was done—there can scarcely be any answer. In view of the repeated examinations of the walls, sides, and floor of the vault, and the precautions taken, it seems impossible during the period when Combermere's seal was on the slab, and most extremely unlikely at earlier dates, that anyone, even if they had the will, could have had the power to enter and leave the vault undetected.

If, then, natural causes and human agency must both be rejected as an explanation of the disturbances at Barbados, what is left? We must conclude, I submit, that the agency producing the disturbances at Barbados was neither human nor natural. As to its nature, apart from this combination of negatives, I do not feel called upon to offer any opinion—which, after all, would be of little value.

Others, however, such as Dale Owen and the late Sir Arthur Conan

---

* The story is told by Sir Basil Thomson, in his book *The Criminal* (London, 1925, pp. 129, 130). The negro (a discharged convict) had walked to Dartmoor from London with the intention of killing the Chief Warder and setting fire to the prison. He made his attempt on the night of August 17, 1890.

The unknown intruder who, under cover of night and "to gain some private ends," broke into Geelong Prison (Victoria) in Jan. 1936 was more fortunate. He sawed through a $\frac{1}{2}''$ lock-plate, lowered himself 30 ft. to the prison-yard at the end of a rope, did his errand (suspected to be the transfer of gaol-breaking tools to some of the inmates), and got safely away before dawn.

Doyle, have been less Pyrrhonic. The latter, in particular, who had no doubt as to the psychic nature of the phenomena, reached three principal conclusions which I will summarize briefly but, I hope, fairly.

1. That the disturbances were the work of forces desiring the more speedy decomposition of the bodies. It is claimed that this explained the particular animus directed against those with leaden casings, while the wooden ones were left undisturbed; and that the desired result was achieved, in that the coffins were ultimately buried elsewhere.

2. That the physical force necessary to move the coffins was derived in some manner from the "effluvia" of the overheated negroes employed in carrying the coffins; which "effluvia" were necessarily retained in the confined space of the hermetically-sealed vault.

3. That the disturbances were facilitated, or even occasioned, by the presence in the vault of the corpses of two persons who had committed suicide. "There is some evidence . . . that when a life has been cut short before it has reached its God-appointed term, whether the cause be murder or suicide . . . there remains a store of unused vitality which may, where the circumstances are favourable, work itself off in capricious and irregular ways. This is, I admit, a provisional theory, but it has been forced upon my mind by many considerations. . . ."

Dale Owen, reaching the same conclusion as to the "spiritualistic" character of the disturbances at Oesel (he does not seem to have known of any of the other cases), goes no farther than to suggest that their *raison d'être* may have been the (alleged) conversion of an infidel member of the committee at Arensburg, one Dr. Luce—a pennyworth of sack to an intolerable deal of bread. But Sir Arthur Conan Doyle's views, however far-fetched they may appear to ordinarily-minded people (and as, I admit, they seem to myself), certainly deserve careful examination.

As to the actual fact of wooden coffins in the vault at Barbados having been left undisturbed while the leaden ones were scattered, the evidence is somewhat conflicting. There are but two stated to have been of wood only; those of Mrs. Goddard (the first occupant of the vault) and of Thomazina Clarke (the last person buried there); the Alpha and Omega of the inmates.

Turning to the four MS. authorities, "A", "O","B", and the Lucas-Orderson version, I find that "A" and "O" agree in two statements.

"(July 6, 1812) Dorcas Chase buried. The two other coffins were in their proper places. They were leaden coffins.

"(August 9, 1812) Hon. Thomas Chase buried. The two leaden coffins were found out of place."

The Christ Church burial register supports these statements. "B" omits any mention of Mrs. Goddard's interment, and accordingly makes no specific reference of any kind to her coffin. The Lucas-Orderson version agrees with "A" and "O" in saying that when Dorcas Chase was buried "the two *leaden* coffins" were displaced.

Now when Dorcas Chase was buried, there were only two other coffins in the vault, those of Mrs. Goddard and M. A. M. Chase. On the evidence of the entries relating to Dorcas Chase's burial, it most certainly appears that Mrs. Goddard's coffin was a leaden one.

On the other hand, the entries relating to the burial of Thomas Chase suggest equally strongly that the third coffin then in the vault—Mrs. Goddard's—was undisturbed, and was of wood. This is also confirmed, at first sight, by the statement in the Lucas-Orderson version about the remains of Mrs. Goddard's coffin having been tied up in a bundle. If her coffin had been of English pattern one could reconcile the discrepancies by supposing that the outer wooden casket had decayed and come away, converting the coffin to a leaden one of the Barbados type, which would have taken its place with the others and so accounted for the silence on the subject of what happened to her body—one of the most remarkable features of the whole story. But there is a strong objection to this theory, for none of the sketches depicting the state of the vault at the last two openings show seven coffins.

I must leave the question of Mrs. Goddard's coffin, noting that while it *may* have been of wood only, the evidence for this is not very satisfactory.

There seems to be no doubt that Thomazina Clarke's coffin was of wood; whether this had a lead lining does not appear. But there is still a difficulty, for we cannot be certain that this coffin was left undisturbed. It was the last buried, so that we must look to the narratives of the final opening of the vault for information.

The authorities are equally divided on the subject. "A" is not specific on the point, but allows it to be inferred that the Clarke coffin was displaced along with the others. "B" does the same. The sketches accompanying "A" (for which I have already indicated my own preference) support this view.

Not having been able to consult "O", I am unable to say whether it remarks specifically on the point. Lang says, "The sketches given by O vary much from A". I infer that the sketches accompanying "O" probably agree with those in Lucas's statement.

The latter does not say in what state any of the coffins were found; it merely refers to "the annexed drawing". In this, the Clarke coffin is shown as undisturbed, and that of Samuel Brewster also. This fact casts some doubt on the authenticity of the drawing. Such a striking exception as two coffins left untouched out of six would surely, one thinks, have been commented on in the other narratives.

The balance of evidence, I suggest, is in favour of the view that the Clarke coffin was disturbed. Summarizing, the case for supposing that wooden coffins were immune from the forces disturbing those of lead does not appear to be at all clearly made out.

I turn to Sir Arthur Conan Doyle's second conclusion.

I am far from denying that the "effluvium" emitted by an overheated Negro is very strong indeed*; but I find it difficult to believe that the concentrated aroma of even half a dozen buck-niggers could, unaided, shift a coffin whose weight was a good load for their united arm-muscles—or, for that matter, disturb even a much lighter object. Sir Arthur suggested that these "effluvia", under the more dignified style of "emanations of the living", were concentrated in the vault as in the cabinet of "a genuine medium", and used (apparently by its inmates, or some of them) in the same manner as that practised by the medium, whatever that may be.

On this I am not competent to pronounce. I have never met a genuine medium—on the other hand, I have made no great efforts to do so, although from my casual encounters with mediums of the other kind I should imagine that the earnest searcher would do well to equip himself, after the manner of Diogenes, with a powerful lantern and a stout pair of shoes.

On the question of the power, if any, permitted to suicides everyone must judge for himself. There is this to be said *in limine*, that Reece (writing in 1864) states that both Thomas and Dorcas Chase died by their own hand, the daughter having starved herself to death owing to her father's cruelty, "wherefore the other corpses were desirous to expel her". And, whatever we may think of the truth of the almost innumerable recorded cases of supernatural phenomena, it is undeniable that a connecting thread links the bulk of them together; they are almost all associated with persons who have undergone strong emotions, often terminated by a violent and/or premature death. Those who die peacefully in their beds at the close of the three-score years and ten are not often alleged to return as ghosts—that appears to be the privilege of the victim of accident or murder, the suicide, the revengeful and the remorseful. In the common phrase, then, "there is something to be said" for the idea that the presence of two suicides in the vault at Barbados "might have something to do with" the disturbances there.

I do not accept this view. But if I reject it, it is not on the ground that I am an absolute disbeliever in all forms of "supernatural" phenomena—on that subject I neither affirm nor deny anything. My reason for reject-

---

* The negro says the same thing of the white man. "... *cuiusque stercus sibi bene olet.*"

ing it may irritate the "unco' guid", but I should think myself wanting in common honesty if I avoided the subject.

We have gone a long way from the days when, as Hood puts it,

> . . . They buried Ben in four cross-roads,
> With a *stake* in his inside,

but even in those days there was a queer refinement of kindliness and charity in that apparently barbarous treatment. The stake, it is true, was intended to ensure that the suicide did not haunt the neighbourhood— did not, as they still say in Rumania, become Un-Dead. But the burial at the cross-roads served a more noble purpose. As the rubric said, and still says, ". . . *the Office ensuing is not to be used for any that . . . have laid violent hands upon themselves*". But the suicide, if huddled by night into the ground at the cross-roads, might still, even though he were denied Christian burial, have the cross over his grave.

Nowadays we are more charitable. In default, and sometimes in defiance, of the clearest evidence coroners' juries find, in their verdicts,. that "unbalanced mind" which averts the angers of the Church. And if the latter still formally records its readiness to cast the first stone, its practice is uniformly more kindly and, I suggest, more Christian.

Putting aside those well-known cases in which every man of common sense will agree that suicide was not only justifiable but even a duty— such as the case of that "very gallant gentleman" Captain Oates—there is much to be said for the view put forward by Winslow in his *Anatomy of Suicide,** that *all* suicides are, in effect, insane when they take their lives. And when we reflect on the anguish of mind which they must have undergone, and the agonies of physical pain which they often undergo in struggling to cut the Gordian knot of life and troubles simultaneously, it is difficult—and not only is it difficult, but it is harsh and callous—to shut out of one's mind the belief, or at least the hope, that they have already been punished enough, and may now take their rest.

> The Gods may release
> That they held fast.
> Thy soul shall have ease
> In thy limbs at the last.
> But what shall they give thee for life, sweet life that is overpast?

If we come to be judged, assuredly it will not be upon the circumstances of our deaths alone, but upon the fabric and pattern of our whole lives. And if we ourselves are charitable to the suicide, and if we look for a larger charity elsewhere, what right have we to assume that the dead —sinners like ourselves—would, if they could, be less charitable?

* *The Anatomy of Suicide.* Forbes Winslow, M.R.C.S. (London, 1840, pp. 221–45.)

POSTSCRIPT

The diary of William Bulkeley, published in the Transactions of the Anglesey Antiquarian Society, 1931, refers to a similar case which occurred in the Meyrick family vault at Llangadwaladr.

The vault, excavated from the solid rock and roofed with brick, was built about 1734; and, when opened in 1742, already contained three coffins, originally laid on a wide bench (of rock) running all round the vault. One of the three was found set obliquely on end, its head resting near the middle of the floor and its foot just supported by the edge of the shelving. The other two coffins were entirely undisturbed—thus negativing the supposition that water had flooded the vault.

I have notes, but no details, of similar occurrences in the crypt of Borley Church, Essex (about 1882); in the Terry-Hughes vault at Camden, N.S.W.; and (recently) in another vault at Barbados.

III

THE SHIPS SEEN ON THE ICE

Of all bygone Polar explorers one name, I think, springs most readily to the mind—that of Sir John Franklin. It will always be remembered, not so much for his actual explorations (considerable though they were), as for the tragic disaster which overtook his last expedition, the long-drawn uncertainty as to his situation, and the halo of mystery which still, in great measure, surrounds his fate.

He sailed with the *Erebus* and *Terror*, two excellent ships manned by the pick of the Navy, on May 19, 1845, the object of his voyage being to complete the North-West Passage. The ships were last seen in Melville Bay, Greenland, about July 30th of the same year, by the whaler *Enterprise*. All was then well, and they were impatient to begin their progress westward, delayed hitherto by the ice. The *Enterprise* turned southward, not knowing that she had seen history made; yet on that day Franklin and his companions·vanished for ever from the sight of civilized men.

The years went by without any tidings of the missing explorers. During 1848–53 a perfect spate of rescue-expeditions poured out to search for Franklin in all quarters, except the line of his intended route—a region which, through some species of judicial infatuation, was left practically neglected. Our Government dispatched several expeditions, and others were equipped by private enterprise.* But all was to no purpose. The British Government abandoned the fruitless search soon after receiving information in 1854 from Dr. Rae (of the Hudson Bay Company) which, although only at second-hand, left no doubt that complete disaster had overtaken Franklin and his men. It was reserved for the *Fox*, under Captain F. L. McClintock, R.N., sent out by Lady Franklin in 1857, to bring back the only written record of the disaster which has ever come to light.

It was found in a cairn at Victory Point, King William Island, where it had been deposited by Franklin's expedition.

It is tantalizingly brief, and curtly formal in manner. It could scarcely

---

* Most of these were instigated and supported by Franklin's devoted wife and her friends. Two, it should always be remembered, were financed from motives of pure humanity by Henry Grinnell, a New York merchant. Franklin's gallant but muddle-headed friend, Sir John Ross, also went back to the Arctic at the age of seventy-three in search of him, sacrificing his pension to raise funds for that purpose.

PLATE II

THE SHIPS SEEN ON THE ICE

From Parliamentary Paper No. 501 of 1852. By permission of the Controller H.M. Stationery Office.

[*Facing page 52*

have been otherwise. It was written, in circumstances of great difficulty, on the margin of what used to be called a "bottle-paper"—a printed form designed to be buried or jettisoned for the information of succeeding explorers, and bearing a request, in six languages, that the finder would return it to the Admiralty. The final message on it—the paper had been deposited earlier, and subsequently brought up to date—is well known, and has often been reprinted.* I do not propose to give it in full, but the following extracts form a useful starting-point.†

"[April 25], 1848.—H.M. ships *Terror* and *Erebus* were deserted on the 22nd April, 5 leagues NNW. of this, [ha]ving been beset since 12th Septr. 1846. The Officers & Crews consisting of 105 souls—under the Command of [Cap]tain F. R. M. Crozier, landed here—in lat. 69° 37′ 42″, long. 98° 41′. . . .

"Sir John Franklin died on the 11th June, 1847, and the total loss by deaths in the expedition has been to this date 9 officers & 15 men . . . start on to-morrow 26th for Back's Fish River."

For the time being let us leave these men, doomed but uncomplaining, starting on what their leader must have known in his heart was a perfectly hopeless attempt. I turn to a problem for which a very singular solution offers itself. What became of the *Erebus* and *Terror* after they were abandoned?

If we accept as gospel the stories told later by the Eskimo, one ship drifted into a position off Adelaide Peninsula, and was there crushed by the ice and sunk. The other drifted round King William Island to meet a similar fate off Matty Island.

These stories (like many of the Eskimo statements relating to the fate of Franklin's expedition) lack confirmation. None of the searchers who have been over the ground, from McClintock in 1858 to Major Burwash, a Canadian who visited the reported locality of the wreck in 1926 and flew over it in 1930, has ever seen a vestige of either ship. Nor, if they were actually wrecked anywhere along the North-West Passage, has any other white man.

* Every now and then one of these reprints, believed to be the original, is sent to the Admiralty by someone who considers it to be of great importance. I believe that the Scottish police once telegraphed that they had arrested, on general principles, the bearer of one of these documents, and were "holding him pending the receipt of Admiralty instructions".

† The portions in brackets are conjectural, the paper of the record having been eaten away by the rust of the cylinder enclosing it. The record is now in the Naval Museum at Greenwich. The latitude and longitude mentioned are, of course, N. and W. respectively. It will be noted that the former is given to seconds of arc: a most unusual proceeding, particularly when one remembers that the document was only a brief note scrawled with half-frozen fingers in a temperature below zero.

But there is some ground for thinking that even if McClintock's search had been made under perfect conditions of weather, and unrestricted as to time, he would still have completely failed to find the wreck of either ship; that they had never been wrecked at all; that they had long ago left the vicinity and, still locked in the ice, been carried out into Lancaster Sound and then down Davis Strait towards the North Atlantic.

In April 1851 the English brig *Renovation*, in the course of a passage from Limerick to Quebec, fell in with a very large ice-floe off the Newfoundland Banks. She passed this in clear weather, running about seven knots, at a distance of some three miles. On the floe were seen two three-masted ships, not far apart, one heeled over and the other upright.* They were painted black and corresponded both in size and appearance with the *Erebus* and *Terror*. They remained in sight for about an hour, and were seen, and examined through the telescope, by most of the *Renovation's* crew. Unfortunately, no attempt was made to close or board them; and not the least singular feature of the story is that although so much public interest had been excited about Franklin's fate, no one on board the *Renovation* knew that a large reward was on offer for authentic news of it, although several were impressed with the idea that what they had seen was undoubtedly the missing ships. The matter attracted no general interest whatever for several months.

It would be "another injustice to Ireland" to say that it went entirely unrecorded by the Press. It is to the enterprise of an Irish paper (unfortunately of limited circulation) that we owe its first appearance in print.

From "The Limerick Chronicle", May 28, 1851.

"Extract from a Letter of a Passenger† who sailed from this Port for Quebec, in the *Renovation*, on the 6th April last, to a Friend‡ in Limerick.

"Quebec,
"*May* 9, 1851.

"We arrived here on yesterday, after a passage which for the first 13 days promised to be one of the speediest almost on record, having been two miles to the west of the Bird Island, in the Gulf, at the time we met the ice, and having been for 16 days coasting along it, with a fair wind ever since. It has been very heavy, and a number of ships have suffered severely. Indeed, to attempt to give any description of the ice itself would be useless; we have sailed for sixty miles of a stretch seeking an opening without being able to effect, which was most vexatious, as had we not met with it we should have made the passage in 15½ days. The icebergs we met with were frightful in size, as the basis of some of them would cover three

* See Plate II.   † John S. Lynch.   ‡ Mr. Creilly, the writer's uncle.

times over the area of Limerick; and I do not at all exaggerate when I say that the steeple of the cathedral would have appeared but a small pinnacle, and a dark one, compared to the lofty and gorgeously-tinted spires that were on some of them; *and more to be regretted is that we met, or rather saw at a distance, one with two ships on it, which I am almost sure belonged to Franklin's exploring squadron, as from the latitude and longitude we met them in they were drifting from the direction of Davis's Straits. Was there but a single one, it might have been a deserted whaler, but two so near each other, they must have been consorts; they were to windward of us, and a heavy sea running at the time, with thick weather coming on, we could not board them."**

If this extract was reprinted at the time by any other paper, I have not been fortunate enough to come across it. I confess that when I first made its acquaintance I had never heard of the *Limerick Chronicle*.

Whatever we may think of the story itself, this extract is excellent evidence of its contemporary circulation. Here is another piece of evidence, part of a letter written at the time by a member of the *Renovation's* crew, but not published until later.† The letter is dated June 18, 1851, and is post-marked "Limerick", where it was received by John Silk, brother of its author, James Silk. I have not attempted to amend the delightful spelling, punctuation, and occasional redundances of the original.

". . . On the 14th day in the morning wee saw a very large hice Burgh to whindward of ous, and 12 o'clock 14th, wee saw as many as 6 hice Burg, and one of them we went very close to ous in which it appeared to be the High of 250 feeat, in wich there is but one third of third of them in the worter, in which makes the hice burgh 750 feat, that so, my dear friends, you might have read of the hice Burgh in the frosen reagenths, so, my dear friends, I am not Asay what I have read of, for this is what I have sean witnissed myself, and likewise, my dear friends, Apon one of the very large burghs in which wee see there was 2 large ships on them, 1 laying Apon her broad broad side, and the other where A laying as comfortable as if she was in the dock fast to her moreings. The wether was very fine and the wather very smouth, but the captain being laid up at the same time it was not reported to him untell 8 o'clock, and we out of sight of them,‡ so, my dear friends, I canot tell you whether there was

* As the learned "Beachcomber" remarks, "the italics, while not my personal property, have been inserted at my suggestion".

† In *The Times* of May 8, 1852.

‡ In view of this piece of natural poetry, how unjust it was to criticize as an "affected Hibernicism" Wolfe's

". . . the foe and the stranger would tread o'er his head
And we far away on the billow."

any living sould there are not. So, my dear friends, I canot tell you any more About them now. . . ."

But although the men of the *Renovation*, headed by Edward Coward (her captain), seem to have been no more reticent, at Quebec and elsewhere, about her strange adventure than seamen are accustomed to be, the story slumbered. The ship, having lost most of her foc'sle hand by desertion at Quebec, came home; her mate, Robert Simpson, who had been the first to sight the ships on the ice, left her to become master of his own ship, the *British Queen*; and the *Renovation*, still under Captain Coward, sailed again in the spring of 1852 for the Mediterranean.

Then, quite accidentally, the story attracted official attention; and officialdom exploded into a fury of activity.

The disclosure seems to have come about in what the old mast-and-yard seamen used to call "circumbendibus fashion". While at Quebec in May 1851 Coward said something about seeing two ships on an iceberg to two brother merchant-skippers, one of whom, named Storey, was a native of Tynemouth. In March 1852 (ten months later) Storey mentioned the matter, in conversation, to one James M. Shore, Second Master, R.N., who, "after mature deliberation", sat him down and wrote a chatty little letter on the subject, with two postscripts, to no less exalted a person than the Secretary of the Admiralty—a liberty, apparently, not justified by any personal acquaintance.

The Admiralty took immediate action. With a very proper regard for their own dignity, they began by giving the unfortunate Shore a rap over the knuckles in the course of a frigidly official letter to the Commander-in-Chief, Portsmouth.

"ADMIRALTY,
"*March* 22, 1852.
"SIR,

"I am commanded by my Lords Commissioners of the Admiralty to transmit to you the enclosed letter from Mr. James M. Shore, second master of Her Majesty's ship *Sampson*, respecting two three-masted ships having been seen drifting with an iceberg, and to signify their direction to you to forward the same to Captain Jones of the *Sampson*, desiring that officer, first, to inform Mr. Shore that my Lords would have expected that he knew enough of the rules of the service not to address a letter to the Admiralty excepting through his commanding officer. . . ."

I cannot say whether Captain Jones told the unfortunate Shore that he wouldn't have such a —— on board his ship; but no doubt that worthy (whose offence, really, was no more than "Zeal, all zeal, Mr. Easy") had a *mauvais quart d'heure*. He passes out of the story—having performed, like an alarm-clock, a useful but irritating function.

The tale of the Admiralty's subsequent enquiries fills a moderate-sized Blue-book—one of a number devoted to the Franklin Search Expeditions. They are a most singular collection. A complete set would rival in bulk the four Shakespeare Folios, and contain even more words, of all kinds, than the minutes of the *Royal Oak* court-martials (happily left unprinted). Nothing like selection appears to have been attempted—every scrap of paper that found its way into official channels, from the most valuable hydrographic and other information down to begging letters and mediumistic ravings, was sure to be cast up in one of these Blue-books, in an order partly chronological, largely fortuitous, and, as a whole, defying analysis. In some cases the Blue-books must now be regarded as the best procurable authorities, the original documents from which they were compiled being no longer extant—but they are by no means easy reading, and probably were never, even in their heyday, widely read.

The Blue-book which, under the prosaic title of "Vessels in the North Atlantic",* successfully disguises the extraordinary character of the story which it contains, differs little, in the above respects, from its more ordinary comrades. The information afforded is copious—those unacquainted with the official mind might perhaps be pardoned for considering a little of it to be redundant. Yet, for all this wealth of detail, necessary or otherwise, there are one or two loose ends left over and allowed to dangle; for the enquiries seem to have started more than one hare which, unlike those of the electric variety, was never caught. The arrangement of the matter is chronological (of which usually valuable method one can only say, in this case, that it is better than alphabetical would have been) and there is no comment or other attempt to connect the links of the chain. As a whole, the book is quite as repulsive and difficult to read as any ordinary Blue-book dealing with some far less interesting subject: like the *Hortulus Animæ*, "er lasst sich nicht lesen"—it does not permit itself to be read.

The Admiralty began, quite sensibly, at the beginning. Shore's statement was obviously of no value, being third-hand; but he had given some information about Storey, his informant, and Their Lordships, although not quite satisfied that Storey really existed, directed Commander H. C. Hawkins, R.N., of the Coastguard, stationed at Sunderland, to get into touch with him, cautiously adding "if there be such a person".

Hawkins acted with energy. He saw Storey at Tynemouth, who

* VESSELS IN THE NORTH ATLANTIC.—Copies of Communications between the Admiralty and any (*sic*) Public Authorities at Home and Abroad, in reference to certain Vessels observed on an Iceberg in the *North Atlantic* in 1851, and supposed to have been Abandoned (*Sir R. H. Inglis*).
Ordered, by the House of Commons, *to be Printed*, 22 June, 1852.
501. [*Price* 1s. 2d.]

repeated and confirmed the account previously given to Shore. He also visited at Shields Mrs. Coward, wife of the *Renovation's* captain, and learned that during the last two or three months her husband had mentioned to her the sighting of the ships on the ice. Later inquiries made at Shields by Commander Hawkins elicited that the owner of the *Renovation*, Mr. Emmanuel Young, had never heard Coward mention the incident, and that the ship's log for 1851 was still on board her.

Following up a minor clue obtained by Hawkins, enquiries made at Weymouth brought to light one George Cleugh, the other merchant-skipper who had been present when Coward told the original yarn to Storey at Quebec in May 1851. He confirmed this, and added that "it was generally spoken of at Quebec".

Attention was now focused on two witnesses capable of affording valuable evidence: Simpson, on his way to Limerick in the *British Queen*, and Coward, now nearing Venice in the *Renovation*. There was also a third who, although a nebulous figure at the moment, soon took definite shape as John Supple Lynch (spoken of by Their Lordships as "a most intelligent and willing witness"), who had been the *Renovation's* only passenger during her eventful voyage, and who was ultimately located and interrogated at Prescott, Canada.

The Admiralty took prompt steps to obtain the evidence of all these witnesses. The Coastguard authorities at Limerick were ordered to visit the *British Queen* on her arrival and "make the most minute enquiries"; the Canadian Customs authorities were requested to take similar action with regard to Lynch; and the Foreign Office were rather curiously informed that Their Lordships *"require* that instructions may be sent to Her Majesty's Consul-General at Venice to go on board the *Renovation*, and to make the most strict and searching inquiry". The use of "require" for "request" was probably a slip of the pen; as, no doubt, was the employment, in a letter written (I believe) during the War, of the unfortunate phrase: *"Even* my Lords Commissioners of the Treasury will appreciate the necessity for this expenditure. . . ."

It might be thought that in taking and giving all this trouble the Admiralty were attaching altogether too much importance to an item of stale and not very plausible news. But it must be remembered that in the spring of 1852 the Franklin problem was rapidly assuming the proportions of a pronounced Admiralty bugbear. Seven years had gone by without news of him; several expensive search-expeditions had resulted in total failure, complicated, in one case, by bickerings and recriminations calling for an official enquiry. Another expedition, still more expensive, was fitting out; a reward of £20,000 for succouring Franklin was on offer; and the Press was exclaiming freely and not at all politely against Admiralty apathy and ineptitude—and, after the manner of its kind, declaiming in the same breath against the expenditure of any more money upon a search-expedition. Last but not least among this catalogue of official worries, the dependents of the expedition were still drawing the ample allotments made to them, out of their double pay, by their missing husbands seven years earlier; Franklin's officers were still on the Navy List and complicating the promotion of others about whose existence there was, unfortunately, much less doubt; and Franklin himself was drawing near to the head of the Captain's List, and would shortly fall due for his Rear-Admiral's flag,* adding one more (on paper) to an already plethoric list of unemployed flag-officers. In these circumstances it would be very natural for the Admiralty to consider that a strict investigation into the *Renovation's* story was a paramount duty for several reasons besides the "common dictates of humanity"—of which they had possibly heard enough.

If it could have been definitely established that the ships seen by the *Renovation* were the *Erebus* and *Terror*, the last naval search-expedition —Belcher's fiasco—would probably not have been undertaken, and the Admiralty might have felt themselves free to act as they did some years later: to remove the names of Franklin and his men from the Navy List, to pay part of the reward to the most acceptable candidate who claimed to have brought news of Franklin's fate, and to wash their hands of the whole business. They saw, I think, this chance, and they can scarcely be blamed for snatching at it.

Besides, Franklin's name was not yet forgotten by his countrymen. Events like the "Coup d'État" and the *Birkenhead* tragedy might divert public attention for a while, but the mystery surrounding the lost explorers had not yet lost its "news-value". That was to come later, with the Crimean War. The protracted bungle which has been called, more truly than judiciously, "Stratford Canning's revenge", gave the public its fill of fresh interests. What were the lives of a hundred miserable seamen, dead no doubt long ago, compared with the magnificent idiocy of Balaclava, the "four miles of beds eighteen inches apart" down which the Lady of the Lamp walked every night, and the slow eliciting (by the Roebuck Committee) of the stories of the cargoes of boots "all for the left foot",† and the innumerable other cases of that ineptitude, crass stupidity, and peculation which invariably make their appearance whenever this country draws the sword?

As was to be expected, the results of the enquiries initiated by the

* He was, in fact, promoted to Rear-Admiral on Oct. 26, 1852, when his fate was still uncertain. Actually, he had then been dead for more than five years.

† It has been claimed that, actually, these were the old-fashioned "straights", fitting either foot "indifferently"—an excellent example of *le mot juste*.

Admiralty came to hand in an order corresponding to the relative distances of Limerick, Venice, and Prescott (Canada) from London. Simpson, in the *British Queen*, arrived at Limerick on April 4, 1852, and at once furnished the Coastguard authorities with a statement for transmission to the Admiralty. Its contents left little doubt that the *Renovation's* story rested on a very solid foundation.

The Admiralty therefore took the additional precaution of having Simpson questioned by an expert. Captain Erasmus Ommaney, R.N., who had been second-in-command of Captain Austin's search-expedition in 1850-1, was now serving at the Admiralty as Inspector of Coastguard, and, as it happened, was about to make an official tour in Ireland. Their Lordships accordingly requested him to make first for Limerick, and to "put such questions to Mr. Simpson, in order to elicit further facts relating to this story, as your own judgment and acquaintance with such matters would suggest".

To naval officers the requests of the Admiralty are, of course, like those of Royalty; and to Limerick Ommaney accordingly "proceeded with moderate dispatch"—as a mere landsman would say, he went there as soon as he conveniently could. He was an excellent officer, who afterwards rose to very high rank. He had come out of the Austin fiasco with much more credit than his chief, and had been the first man to find any traces of the Franklin expedition (at Beechey Island, where they had wintered in 1845-6). He was as good a man as could have been selected for such an enquiry, and his subsequent report shows him to have been thorough and painstaking.

Unfortunately that report, as it appears in the Blue-book, is simply a verbatim report of question and answer. Simpson, in addition to his replies, made a sworn statement, but by some mistake (I imagine) the Blue-book has omitted it. The omission, however, may have been deliberate. The statement is available, for it was printed in the *Nautical Magazine* for May 1852. But with it there appeared what I regard as an even better piece of evidence.

Like "the man they called Ho" in *The Hunting of the Snark*, Simpson had an uncle, one Ebenezer Landells—an engraver who was something of a social success and had been one of the original founders of *Punch*. As soon as his nephew's name appeared in the Press in connection with the *Renovation's* story, Landells exercised the inalienable right of every Englishman,* and wrote to *The Times* (19.4.1852).

* I do not think that it is laid down in Magna Carta (which, by the way, was repealed in 1863), but it certainly should have been. Nowadays, alas, the palmy days of such topics as "Do we Believe?" are gone by, and "Paterfamilias" and "Fiat Justitia" are politely turned down, or fobbed-off into the "Points from Letters" column.

"Mr. Robert Simpson . . . is a nephew of mine, and I can answer for his strict probity and integrity. I have written to him at Limerick, and if he has not sailed I am sure he will furnish me with full particulars, and also a sketch. . . ."

His confidence in his nephew was justified. The letter duly arrived, and was published in *The Times* of April 22, 1852.

On the whole, I regard the letter as the fullest and best statement of Simpson's evidence. It has the advantage of having been written three days after his examination by Ommaney, and of correcting, by subsequent reflection, one or two slight details. I have compared it carefully with his two other statements and the cross-examination printed in the Blue-book, and I give it below in full.

"BRITISH QUEEN", LIMERICK,
April 19th.

MY DEAR UNCLE,*

I received your letter this morning, dated the sixteenth, and feel great pleasure in writing the particulars relative to the two ships which were seen by me and others when on our outward-bound passage to Qubec in April, last spring, in the brig *Renovation*.

It is now twelve months ago, and so many occurrences have happened in the interval that the real circumstances have nearly escaped my memory; but I shall feel great pleasure in relating them to the very best of my recollection.

On the 6th of April, 1851, we sailed from Limerick for Quebec in ballast, and one cabin passenger, a very respectable young man named Mr. Joseph (*sic*) Lynch. We experienced a most beautiful run at the rate of nine, ten, and eleven knots per hour† as far as the Gulf of St. Lawrence, nothing remarkable occurring until about the 18th or 19th, when we were surrounded by numerous gigantic icebergs; and I think it was on or about the 20th, at 6 a.m., my watch on deck, I discovered on the starboard bow a large iceberg, with two ships on it, as did also the men that were in my watch.

I immediately went below and informed Captain Coward, who being very ill at the time, did not notice at first what I said. I again repeated the circumstance, and asked him what he intended to do, but he only groaned out, "Never mind", or something to that effect.

I was anxious to get up on deck again, but before I went up called

* "Oh, skip your dear uncle," the Bellman exclaimed,
    As he angrily jingled his bell.
† This is a very common mistake, even among seamen. It should, of course, be "knots", *tout court*. A knot is a measure of speed, not a distance. "Knots per hour" is equivalent to "nautical miles per hour per hour".

Mr. Lynch, who immediately jumped up and looked at the vessels a few minutes, when he went below again and dressed himself, the weather being at the time excessively cold, the wind from the northward and eastward, blowing a fresh breeze, and I think, but am not certain, under double-reefed topsails, whole courses, jib and reefed trysail. This can easily be ascertained by a reference to the log-book, which is now on board the *Renovation*, and on her passage to Venice (*sic*).

However, in continuation of my story, Mr. Lynch, after putting on his clothes, came on deck, where he and I, in our turns,* stood watching the two ships for about three-quarters of an hour, when we lost sight of them, but not the berg, which was then on the starboard quarter. We pursued our course with the greatest regret that we did not board the ships, which, to all appearance, had been a considerable time on the ice.

The largest one was lying on her beam-ends, with her head to the eastward, and nothing standing but her three lower masts and bowsprit; the smaller one, which was sitting nearly upright, with her head to the southward, with her three masts, top-masts on end, and top-sail and lower yards across, and to all appearance having been properly stripped and abandoned.

These are the total circumstances which I can recollect; but as the Admiralty have ordered an investigation into the circumstances, letters from Mr. Lynch, at Quebec, together with the log-book, will help to throw some light and verification of the truth. Mr. Coward told me at Quebec he had reported the ships, when I, of course, supposed that the news would certainly reach England. All this has come out lately, from a letter which was written by Mr. Lynch, after his arrival, to an uncle of his, a Mr. Creilly, whom I know very well, and now residing in Limerick.

This letter, it appears, was published in the *Limerick Chronicle*, but, strange to say, the circumstances never got circulated, I believe, out of Limerick until Captain Coward, a few weeks ago, told a friend of his, a master of a ship residing at Tynemouth, who, it appears, had been conversing about icebergs to another gentleman, and thus the circumstance got spread about until it reached the Admiralty, who will (and no wonder) think it a very strange affair altogether. I never heard anything more about it from anyone but Mr. Lynch, and I used often to regret the ships not having been boarded. He stopped aboard of our ship a considerable time after we got to Quebec.

The first thing that I heard about it since was on my arrival at Tarbert, in the River Shannon, when an officer of the Coast Guard came on board, and I furnished him with all the particulars; likewise, on my arrival at Limerick, Captain Ommaney was sent from London, to whom I also related

---

* Taking turns with the *Renovation's* only telescope. Simpson says, "It was old, and a very indifferent one". Lynch calls it a "fair common ship's-glass".

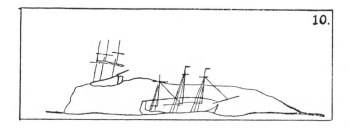

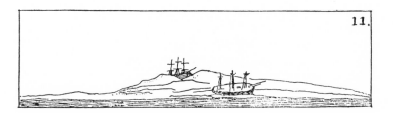

R.T.G. 1928

FIG. 10.—The ships seen on the ice, from a sketch by Robert Simpson, mate of the *Renovation*, published in the *Illustrated London News* of April 17, 1852.

FIG. 11.—The same, from a later sketch (also by Simpson), published in the *Nautical Magazine* for May 1852.

FIG. 12.—An Eskimo sketch, believed to represent the *Erebus* and *Terror* in 1848, when beset off King William I, and showing one vessel on her beam-ends.

From *Parliamentary Paper* No. 107 of 1850.

NOTE.—It is not absolutely certain that this sketch was intended to represent the *Erebus* and *Terror*: it may possibly refer to the *Enterprise* and *Investigator*, under Ross, beset off Port Leopold, 1848.

the circumstance, and the only thing I was mistaken in was the wind, which I informed him was from the southward and eastward; and I also gave him a sketch, which I am sorry is wrong, for now that I overhaul my memory, I am almost certain it was from the northward and eastward. However, this is of little import, merely that my story might coincide with Mr. Lynch's, who will also write, by order of the Admiralty, to the best of his recollection.

My time will not permit me to enter into anything more at present. You desired me to tell you what I entered into the log-book, which is out of my memory. I enclose a sketch,* which is only a very rough one, but it will give you an idea, and a better one than in writing.

I hope soon to hear from you, and I shall be much obliged to you by sending me a paper now and then, as there are very few to be had here. Give my kindest love to aunt and all my cousins, and accept the same yourself.

From your affectionate nephew,
ROBERT SIMPSON.

Ommaney's questioning of Simpson (and of Thomas Davis, A.B., late of the *Renovation*) brought out, as was to be expected, various special points omitted from this letter. The conclusion he reached is quite explicit, if indecisive:

". . . That two vessels were seen in the position described there seems to be no shadow of doubt, though it is to be regretted that, owing to the distance which the *Renovation* passed from the piece of ice with the ships laying on it, no fact can be elicited by which the vessels can be identified, though I have put every question which my experience dictates."

Putting aside for the moment the question of identifying the ships, we come next to the evidence given by Captain Coward and two of his apprentices before H.M. Consul-General at Venice, April 29, 1852.

I regard Coward's evidence as suspect—for there is an objection *in limine* to be raised against it. Simpson has testified that Coward was sick in his bunk when the ships were sighted, and would not even alter course to close them. Lynch, an independent witness and a friend of Coward, tells the same story in answer to a specific question on the point (which he had evaded in his first report). The following is an extract from the questions put to him at Prescott, Canada, by Lieut. F. C. Herbert, R.N., on May 14, 1852.

Q. Did the master of the *Renovation* come up to look at them?
A. My impression is he did not.

* See Fig. 10.

Yet here are the opening paragraphs of Coward's evidence.

Q. In the spring of 1851, was not an iceberg, with two ships on it, seen from your vessel, the *Renovation*?

A. Yes.

Q. On what day was the iceberg seen, and at what hour, and by whom was it first observed?

A. To the best of my recollection, the iceberg was seen on the 17th April, 1851—I cannot remember the hour—by the mate, Mr. Simpson, and Mr. Lynch, a passenger. I was sick in bed at the time, and I immediately got up on being called by the mate, and saw two vessels embedded in an iceberg.

Q. Did you see it yourself, and if so, how long after it was reported to you?

A. I saw the iceberg about five minutes after it was reported to me.

It must be remembered that Coward would have been half-witted if he had not realized that the Consul-General's inquiry might have serious consequences for himself. He had already had ample time to think over his proceedings in connection with the ships seen on the ice; and he must have realized that he had committed a very grave blunder. On the high seas, to meet with a wreck of any description is a comparatively rare event; two abandoned vessels high and dry on an icefloe are a portentous spectacle eloquent of catastrophe. If only on the off-chance that there might be some life to be saved, it was his bounden duty to have closed and, if possible, boarded them. Yet he had done nothing. Unless he now bestirred himself, he might easily find his master's certificate suspended—which meant a long spell of unemployment, as well as public obloquy. What was to be done—and, more urgent, what was to be said?

He might have told the exact truth*—which always pays best in the long run. But I do not think he did.

He might have pleaded that his illness had entirely incapacitated him, and that Simpson was, actually, in temporary command of the *Renovation* when the ships were seen. This, however, was a risky statement to make and fairly certain to be refuted sooner or later.

The excuse which he actually made was that he considered them to be mere wrecks; and that being pressed for time, and with bad weather imminent, he did not consider himself justified in examining them. This excuse, of course, postulated that he had formed a considered opinion as to the circumstances of the case—i.e. that he had seen for himself the ships on the ice. "As well be hanged for a sheep . . ."

---

* After the manner of the Scottish tradesman, counselling his son: "Honesty, laddie, is aye the better policy—Ah've tried baith".

It is only fair to point out that Coward, while he made no official report at the time of having sighted the ships, seems to have spoken of them quite freely in conversation when he reached Quebec—so that he must, at that time, have seen nothing blameworthy in his decision not to investigate them. And there is no suggestion of ill-feeling between Simpson and himself. Simpson, when questioned by Ommaney as to their relations, replied:

"We had perfect confidence in each other; we had been together four years in the *Renovation*. His orders were very strict, never to alter the ship's course without his permission."

And Lynch says of him:

". . . The master was timid in the ice, and a little irritable from sickness; else he was a man to risk his life to save a dog."

Still, although I may be doing his memory an injustice, it is my opinion that he did not come on deck to see the ships, and that his statement is worthless as evidence.

If he lied, he did so with circumstance. He supplied numerous particulars, from his own observation (or imagination) of the vessels' size, rig, appearance, etc., in general agreement with the accounts of Simpson and Lynch, but differing considerably in detail. He repeatedly stated that his answers were only "to the best of his recollection". Two of his apprentices, William Lambden and James Figgis, testified to having seen the ships, but their statements are short and present no features of interest.

The log-book of the *Renovation* was examined, but proved to contain no entry whatever relating to the subject. In conjunction with Simpson's statements to Ommaney, it enables the date of the occurrence to be fixed as April 17th, but it does not afford sufficient data for determining the exact position in which the ships were seen.*

There remains Lynch's evidence. He seems to have taken much more interest in the subject, both at the time and later, than anyone else on board the *Renovation*. As we have seen, he was the writer of the original account in the *Limerick Chronicle*. He had taken up a post in the Canadian Customs, at Prescott, and from it he transmitted to the Admiralty, through official channels, a fuller statement of what he had observed. He also answered numerous questions put to him personally by Lieut. F. C. Herbert, R.N., and Captain E. Boxer, R.N. He appears, as a witness, to have shown himself all that could be desired.

The following extracts contain the essential features of his statement.

". . . I do not recollect anything particular occurring until we fell in with the icebergs on or in the vicinity of the banks of Newfoundland.

"We came in view of one iceberg, on which I distinctly saw two vessels,

---

* From the evidence given to Ommaney by Simpson, the former determined it to be approximately 47° 23′ N., 50° 28′ W., which is probably not far from the truth.

one certainly high and dry, the other might·have her keel and bottom in the water, but the ice was a long way outside of her; this was as near as I can recollect on the 18th or 20th of April, 1851.

"I thought at the time we might have been about three miles from them. . . . I examined them particularly with the spy-glass; one, the larger, lay on her beam-ends, the other upright. I said to the mate on seeing them that they were part of Sir J. Franklin's squadron; he said very likely, and that it would be a good prize for whoever would fall in with them; the captain did not think it prudent to give orders to attempt to board them.

". . . On examining, which I did closely with the glass, the berg, I could see nothing that I could say were boats or tents, but there were a number of hillocks of different shapes, which might have been boats or stores covered by any of the snow-storms which we had at that time; of course I do not take on myself to say such was the case, as similar appearances were to be seen on many other bergs.

"My reason for supposing them to belong to Sir John Franklin's squadron was, there being two ships on one iceberg, they appearing to be consorts, and having no appearance of being driven on the berg in distress, as the rigging and the spars of the upright one was all as shipshape as if she had been laid up in harbour; also the one on her beam-ends had no more appearance of a wreck than a vessel with her top-masts struck and left by the tide on a beach; no loose ropes hanging from any part of her. My opinion is that she had been moored to the berg like the other, until coming in contact with field-ice, the collision threw her over in the position in which we saw her. . . .

"It is but justice for me to say, as far as regards Captain Coward, that nobody could regret more than he did his inability to board the vessel, and to my knowledge it preyed very much on his spirits after. Neither he nor his mate had ever been on the North American coast before; and though I was most urgent at the time to attempt to board them, I was convinced after that it would have been attended with imminent danger, and perhaps loss of vessel, as there was a heavy sea running at the time, and the vessel so short-handed.

"It would appear uncalled-for my making those remarks were it my first time at sea; but I had been at sea before for four years, and among the ice on the coast once before. On my arrival at Quebec I gave every publicity I could to the transaction.* . . ."

The questions put to Lynch were mostly upon details of the ships' appearance. One or two, however, are general and important.

* He and Simpson, while at Quebec, seem to have formed, but abandoned, the project of going back to find, and board, the two ice-borne ships.

(By Herbert);

Q. How long were you in looking at the vessels?

A. They were in view, fairly, quite half an hour, and I had a spy-glass two-thirds of the time.

NOTE.—Mr. Lynch says the berg and vessels were in sight for a much longer period; but by "fairly in view" he means to say the time they were under actual observation.

Q. When did you first observe that you thought they were Sir John Franklin's ships?

A. On first seeing them; that is, as soon as I had carefully observed their condition.

Q. Are you positive it was before they were astern?

A. Oh yes, positive.

(By Boxer)

Q. How was the weather while passing the ships on the ice?

A. The weather was clear.

Q. Do you think it possible you could have been deceived by any optical delusion as to the undoubted fact of the objects seen being really ships?

A. Having seen them in different positions and minutely, I can have no doubt upon the subject at all.

Two minor questions put to Lynch, and one or two other hints given elsewhere in the Blue-book, suggest that John Todd, the cook of the *Renovation,* had been posing as a hero who had nobly volunteered to board the ships, but had been ordered back to his pots and pans by a craven captain. The Admiralty seem to have sent a copy of his statement to Boxer, but this does not appear in the Blue-book. Todd was subsequently found to have been, at the time, confined to his bunk by dysentery.

While the Admiralty enquiries had certainly succeeded in collecting a considerable body of evidence, the most important item of all came to hand from an unexpected quarter.

Captain Robert Kerr, R.N., writing from Sligo on May 1, 1852, informed the Admiralty that he had recently been conversing with William Hill, master of the brig *Henderson,* lying in that port. Hill stated that he had sailed from Galway for New York on April 3, 1851, in company with a German brig, the *Doktor Kneip* of Wismar, which soon left him astern. He reached New York exactly a month later, having seen no ice during his passage, although he met with indications that it was not far off. To his surprise, the *Doktor Kneip* had not arrived—she entered next day. Her master and owner, Edward Lorentz, told Hill in conversation that he had fallen in with a great deal of ice on the Newfoundland banks, and had also seen "two vessels abandoned and water-logged". The date of the occurrence was not stated.

The Admiralty wrote to the Foreign Office on May 6th to inquire the present whereabouts of the *Doktor Kneip*, and received on the following day an answer—from Lloyd's. At least, that is what the Blue-book would have us understand: I imagine that actually the Admiralty wrote to both of them. The *Doktor Kneip* had sailed from Antwerp on April 6th "for Berdionski".* There is no indication of any further attempt having been made to follow up this clue—a regrettable omission.

Such is an outline of the evidence as to the fact of two ships having been seen on an iceberg off the Newfoundland Banks by the brig *Renovation* in April 1851. The truth of this seems indisputable; yet several attempts were made to throw doubt on the whole story.

One was purely laughable. It took the form of a short note contributed to *The Times* by its naval correspondent (15.4.1852).

". . . It is more than probable the vision seen by those on board the *Renovation* may have been the reflection of that vessel from two different surfaces of the iceberg to which it is said they were attached, as, if the objects seen had been real ships, some other vessels would have seen them on a coast so much frequented as Newfoundland is by trading and fishing vessels."

O sancta simplicitas! If the surface of the berg had been worked into an optically-perfect mirror, and the *Renovation* had happened to be on a line exactly perpendicular to it, even then reflection would only have given the impression of a ship at double the distance of the berg, not of one resting on top of it. And a telescope brought to bear on this reflection would at once have disclosed moving figures, etc.—let alone that the *Renovation* had all her top-hamper in place and a good deal of sail set, while the ships on the ice were partly dismasted and their yards stripped.

As for the second objection, the fatalities attending some early East-to-West Atlantic flights have shown very clearly how "frequented" the Newfoundland coast and Newfoundland waters are, even now.

An experienced whaling-captain, William Penny, smarting under the rather unfair censure of a naval court of enquiry which had investigated the lamentable differences between himself and Captain Horatio Austin, R.N., put forward some *a priori* reasons for supposing that no iceberg, or icefloe, of the size reported by the *Renovation* could ever have survived long enough to have reached the position where she claimed to have sighted it. Rather inconsistently, he also gave it as his opinion that what she

* Berdiansk, in the Sea of Azov.

had seen were "country ships", as the whalers called them—ship-like formations upon the summit of an iceberg.

The Newfoundland authorities went even further than Penny. The Governor, in a letter to the Colonial Office (6.5.1852), gave it as the general opinion that

". . . it is well-nigh impossible that two vessels on a field of ice, attached to an iceberg of the magnitude and description spoken of by the men of the *Renovation*, could have passed along this coast from the north, and have reached the latitude of Cape Race, without having been seen either by some of the numerous sealing-vessels . . . or by some of the many vessels . . . on their way to or from the Gulf of Saint Lawrence. . . ."

In the presence of facts supported by several independent witnesses, such arguments are, of course, utterly worthless; yet they have a perennial fascination for a certain type of mind. For example, when M. J. Brooks, of Oxford, jumped 6 feet 2½ inches at Lillie Bridge in 1876, Donald Dinnie, the celebrated all-round Scottish athlete, at once wrote to the papers proving, on *a priori* grounds, that such a feat was absolutely impossible. One wonders what he would have said about Howard Baker's British record of 6 feet 5 inches, or Walker's American jump of 6 feet 10 inches (1937).

We may, I think, take it that the ships seen on the ice by the *Renovation* were no illusion. The real question is—what ships were they?

It is hardly necessary to point out that before coming into the position in which they were seen they must have been in the Arctic for a considerable time. As everyone knows who has read of the *Titanic*, vessels in the North Atlantic often find themselves among icebergs—it is one of the risks of their trade—but although such an encounter is disagreeable, and often dangerous, such ships do not run the risk of being beset. A vessel so firmly enclosed in an ice-field as to have been lifted bodily out of water by its pressure, or by the sudden displacement of a berg, must have been in the Arctic regions—presumably on some definite errand.

The ships seen by the *Renovation* must, therefore, have either been exploring vessels or whalers. If they were the former, they must undoubtedly have been the *Erebus* and *Terror*. If they were whalers, their identification is much more difficult. On the other hand, most maritime nations—our own in particular—have a habit of keeping themselves informed as to the doings and fate of even their smallest craft—and the ships on the ice were not small coasters, but of a good size, and undoubtedly requiring a considerable crew.

The Admiralty made thorough enquiries as to the possibility of their having been whalers. Letters were sent to the port authorities of all the whaling ports, enquiring as to any losses reported in 1850 or 1851. None could be traced. Going back a year, it was found that three whalers—the *Prince of Wales* (one of the last ships to speak to Franklin), the *Lady Jane* of Newcastle-on-Tyne, and the *Superior* of Peterhead—had been lost in the ice in 1849: but the official "protests" recording their loss, and the statements of the survivors, left no doubt that all three had been abandoned in a crushed, dismasted, and sinking condition.

It is curious that while the Admiralty thought it worth while to make some inquiries from the emigration authorities at the out-ports as to whether any other vessels had sighted the ships seen by the *Renovation*—these enquiries were fruitless—they did not, apparently, extend to the other side of the Atlantic their researches on the subject of missing or abandoned whalers. The Newfoundland authorities had not received any reports of such losses in 1851; but no enquiry seems to have been addressed to the American shipping interests.

It is therefore possible, on this ground, that the ships might have been abandoned American whalers—but there are many objections to this theory.

In the first place whalers, when plying their trade, do not seek each other's company—it halves the chance of a good catch. On the other hand, nothing would be more natural than for two exploring vessels to be beset side by side—as we know, in fact, occurred to the *Erebus* and *Terror*.

Secondly, the appearance of the ships by no means suggested that they were abandoned whalers. Lee, master of the *Prince of Wales* (lost in 1849) told the Hull authorities that no whaler would be abandoned as long as her masts stood; and if such a vessel were to be abandoned, it certainly seems most unlikely that her crew would have left her in the carefully-dismantled state observed by the *Renovation*—a state which suggests the conscientious thoroughness of a naval crew doing their best, after the decision to abandon their ships had been taken, to ensure that these were left in as good and seaworthy a condition as possible.

Thirdly, there is the difference in appearance. The *Erebus* and *Terror* were flush-decked—i.e. without poop or forecastle—and so was, certainly, the vessel lying on her beam-ends (the other was not well-placed for determining this point). A whaler, on the other hand, would almost certainly have had a "t'gallant foc'sle", and probably a poop as well. On this point alone the appearance of the *Erebus* and *Terror* would single them out as different not only from any whaler, but from almost any other craft of their size afloat; and it is worth noting that the ship on her beam-ends in Simpson's sketch (the larger of the two, as the *Erebus* was) is as good a representation of the *Erebus* as could possibly be drawn in a few lines.

It remains, then, to be tested in detail whether the ships seen on the ice corresponded, in appearance, with what is known of the *Erebus* and *Terror*.

It is as well to recall, first of all, the rather unsatisfactory nature of the evidence. We are dealing with the testimony, not given on oath, and related long after the event, of men who had suddenly come into contact with officialdom, and who may have thought that not only their veracity but their humanity was open to question. What they had seen was not only remote in time, but had been remote in distance—a berg and its strange cargo, some miles off, seen from a rapidly-moving ship in the early morning light by the aid of a single and imperfect telescope. They had evinced no particular interest in the subject then, and yet they were being asked to give most precise details of it a year later. In the circumstances, it is somewhat remarkable that their separate accounts, in which there can be no suspicion of collusion, should agree so closely as they do.

On the other hand, at least two of the deponents, Simpson and Lynch, were, if not "expert witnesses", something better. They were, obviously, competent observers. Both had had considerable experience at sea, Simpson for thirteen years and Lynch for four. Simpson had some artistic ability, and was able to make a sketch which, as he truly said, ". . . will give you an idea, and a better one than in writing". Lynch had had previous experience of ice conditions, and was clearly a man of considerable intelligence. On the other hand, he was obviously imbued with the idea that the ships were Franklin's.

As I have already said, I regard Coward's testimony as being, at best, hearsay evidence. I rely chiefly on the statements made by Simpson and Lynch.

The facts about the *Erebus* and *Terror* are, shortly, as follows. They were bomb-ketches, built for special naval purposes.* The *Erebus* was slightly the larger, being 370 tons to the *Terror's* 326. They were of wood; and, being designed to stand the shock of mortars firing from their decks at high elevation, were exceedingly strongly built. For Polar work, of which they had their full share, they were still further fortified, their planking "doubled", their frames multiplied, and their bows and sterns built up internally until they became almost solid masses of wood. As already stated, they were flush-decked. They were three-masted and, for their last voyage, barque-rigged.

It may be noted that the difference in appearance between a barque-rigged and a full-rigged three-master is not great. The former has yards on her fore and main masts, and fore-and-aft rig on her mizen-mast; the

* The *Erebus* was built at Pembroke Dockyard in 1824–6, and the *Terror* in a private yard at Topsham in 1812–13.

latter has yards on all three masts. To a seaman the difference, except at a great distance, is obvious; but it is scarcely striking.

They were of great beam in proportion to their length, and exceedingly bluff in the bow, which made them "dull" (slow and unhandy) in sailing. Under Ross in the Antarctic, they had relied on sail alone, and with him they had performed feats of exploration hard to rival even in these days of steam and petrol;* but for Franklin's expedition they were also fitted with a single screw, rotated by a steam-engine of no less than twenty horse-power. In a flat calm their auxiliary power could send them along at four knots†; we have no record of whether it was much used—probably not.

Their hulls were painted black, the "weather-works" (the portions of the hull above deck-level) yellow, and the masts white. They had no stern-walks or figure-heads, but a practically straight bow and a long and prominent bowsprit. Their bottoms were not coppered—a protection usually fitted to H.M. ships, but not altogether suitable for work in the ice.‡

If the ships seen on the ice were the *Erebus* and *Terror*, they should have conformed, in all essentials, with these particulars so far as could be observed.

Combining the statements of Simpson and Lynch with the few trust-worthy details given by other witnesses, and noting all material dis-crepancies, the following is an account of what was seen by the *Renovation* at her point of nearest approach.

On the starboard beam, to windward of the ship and at a distance stated at from three to five miles, was an extensive ice-floe—or, possibly, an iceberg forming the nucleus of an extensive attached mass of pack-ice. On this were seen two ships close together (Lynch says about three-quarters of a mile apart, but this is clearly an over-estimate) and of slightly different size. The larger was considered to be 400–500 tons, the other somewhat smaller. Simpson considered her some 100 tons smaller, but Lynch states definitely that the difference was "nothing like 100 tons".

The larger was lying on her beam-ends, with her head eastward. Her decks were observed to be flush, and only her three lower masts and bowsprit were standing.

* ". . . Above all, Ross has shown the world what may be achieved in these inhos-pitable regions by a competent, energetic leader, and has proved it with ships that had no power of self-propulsion, spite of all their excellence and fitness. If any man deserves to be regarded as the hero of Antarctic exploration, surely it is James Clark Ross."—Karl Fricker, *The Antarctic Regions* (London, 1904, p. 117).

† The *Terror* reached this speed in a steam-trial off Woolwich, April 1845.

‡ They were originally coppered, and remained so until their return from the Antarctic. Their copper was stripped at Woolwich while fitting-out for the Franklin expedition.

The smaller ship was on a higher part of the ice, almost upright, with her head pointing southward (Lynch considered her to be heading northward, but this seems to have been an excusable mistake—she being nearly end-on). Her yards and top-masts were in place. According to Lynch, she crossed a mizzen-yard, and was therefore full-rigged, but this may be an error occasioned by mistaking the bow for the stern. Her decks could not be seen, but she did not appear to have a poop or a forecastle. Her bottom was not coppered.

Both ships were painted black, and their masts white. There was no opportunity of seeing whether either ship had a propeller. No sail was bent on either ship and no boats were visible. There were no signs of any life on board.

It will be admitted that there is no fatal discrepancy between these details and those of the *Erebus* and *Terror* already given. The two chief differences are in the size and (possibly) in the rig. But neither of these bears close examination. The size of the ships was, obviously, a matter largely of guess-work; and it should be remembered that the tonnage of a naval vessel is, in general, given as smaller than that of a merchant-craft of equal size, owing to the different methods of measurement. It may also be noted that (according to a statement in the *Dumfries Courier*) the *Erebus*, although only some 44 tons larger than the *Terror*, had the appearance of being at least 100 tons larger.

As for the rig, Simpson could not say whether they were full-rigged or barque-rigged—a very natural hesitation in view of the fact that one was partially dismantled aloft and the other end-on. Lynch considered that the smaller, at least, was full-rigged; but, as already pointed out, this may have been the result of a misconception.

On the other hand, the points of similarity are striking—so is the fact of two vessels, agreeing in size and appearance with Franklin's ships, being found in company abandoned but cared-for. On the evidence as it stands, one would be inclined to say that there was a strong case for supposing that the ships seen by the *Renovation* were the *Erebus* and *Terror*.

There are, however, two further points to be considered. Does this supposition agree with all that can be traced as to the movements of Franklin's ships after they were abandoned? And, granting this, how came they to be seen off Newfoundland when they were abandoned some 2,000 miles away, and separated from the Atlantic by a very considerable mass of land, divided only by comparatively narrow and tortuous channels, generally ice-blocked?

With regard to the first point, it has already been stated that the Eskimo told McClintock that both ships had been wrecked in the vicinity of King William Island—one actually on the shores of that island. But he never succeeded in seeing a vestige of either wreck for himself—later searchers, such as Hall (1869), Schwatka (1879) and Burwash (1926), were all equally unsuccessful—and, which is more remarkable, he hardly came across a single piece of wood in Eskimo possession that could have formed part of either ship. To those who know what value the nomadic Eskimo attach to wood, and how eager they are to acquire it, it will be obvious that their story of the wrecked ships requires a good deal of salt to make it palatable.

It should be noted, however, that a remarkable piece of evidence came to light not very long ago. In 1855 James Anderson, a chief factor in the service of the Hudson Bay Company, made, at their order, a singularly ineffective search down the Great Fish River (the line of Crozier's retreat) for traces of Franklin's expedition. As showing how thoroughly he was equipped, it need only be said that he had a very short allowance of provisions, no proper map, and not a single person with him who could speak Eskimo. He reached the mouth of the river and then returned, after finding nothing more than a few scraps of wood and clothing which had probably been dropped by some of the few survivors who reached the river itself.

But in 1909 there appeared in the *Transactions of the Canadian Institute* a statement to the effect that one of Anderson's Indian guides had confessed, many years later, that having been sent on ahead by Anderson, he had journeyed northward over the ice towards King William Island and had seen, a long way off, the masts of a wreck which must have been one of Franklin's vessels. Fearing that Anderson, if he heard of this, would insist on making for the wreck and thus imperil their lives (food was running short, and the ice, also, might soon break up), he suppressed this information and reported, on his return, that he had seen nothing.*

If this statement be accepted, there is an end of the supposition that the ships on the ice off Newfoundland were the *Erebus* and *Terror*. But I confess that I am far from satisfied with it. It is a discreditable story, told by a self-confessed liar; it is very vague, and told long after the event; and it may easily be a product of imagination, narrated for effect—or a distorted recollection of some quite different event. If we must choose between this story and the *Renovation's*, I for one unhesitatingly select the latter.

Until, then (if ever), it can be definitely established that there is a basis

* See the article, "A story of a Franklin Search Expedition", by J. B. Tyrrell, M.A., in *Transactions of the Canadian Institute* (Toronto, April 1909). The guide's name was Paulet Papanakies. He told the story to a Mr. J. B. Johnston in 1893.

of truth for the reports of the *Erebus* and *Terror* having been wrecked off King William Island, such reports can scarcely be regarded as proving that the ships seen off Newfoundland were not Franklin's.

With regard to the second point—how they came there, if they did so —we are not altogether without data. There have been at least four cases of ships having been beset in the same regions and drifted for great distances along a route which would ultimately bring them to the Atlantic.

Captain George Back, R.N., in the *Terror* herself, was lying beset off Cape Comfort, in Hudson's Strait, in March 1837, when the *Terror* was lifted bodily out of water, and remained so for 118 days, meanwhile drifting some two hundred miles down the strait. When released she leaked like a sieve, but Back frapped her together with her chain-cables and finally beached her, more fortunate than the *Audacious*, in Lough Swilly.

This case is interesting, as showing both the *Terror's* great structural strength (a steel ship in like case would have broken her back in five minutes), and the fact that a ship of her size and build could be lifted bodily on to a floe by ice-pressure.

Sir James Ross, leader of the first and least successful of all the Franklin search-expeditions, was beset in Barrow Strait the day after he had cut his way out of Port Leopold (his winter quarters) and was drifted some three hundred miles into Davis Strait, extricating himself only to make his way homeward. It was an inglorious end to the career of the greatest of all Polar explorers.

The *Advance* of the Grinnell (American) search-expedition, under Lieutenant De Haven, U.S.N., was beset in Wellington Channel in 1850, and carried out into Baffin Bay. Before getting clear of the ice she had drifted nearly a thousand miles.

But the most remarkable case of all is that of H.M.S. *Resolute*. She was one of the five ships forming the squadron commanded by Captain Sir Edward Belcher, R.N., leader of the last Government expedition sent in search of Franklin, and the last man in the world who ought to have been put in charge of it. It was said of him, with truth, that he made a "hell afloat" of every ship he commanded; and, indeed, reading his account of this expedition, one is sometimes driven to suspect that the pain of an old and severe wound had unbalanced his mind, while one is lost in amazement at the preternatural patience shown towards him by most of his subordinates.

In the autumn of 1853 four of Belcher's ships were lying beset in or near Barrow Strait. As they were not released in the following spring, and means of returning to England were at hand, he decided to abandon what he referred to as "these purchased masses of timber". One almost expects to find him using the word "contemptible". For this act he was subsequently court-martialled, but unfortunately his original instructions had given him such wide discretion that he was, technically, acquitted.* Incidentally these Instructions, issued on April 16, 1852—soon after the *Renovation's* story had attracted official attention—directed Belcher to test this "by search and enquiry on the shores of Davis Strait": presumably, on the assumption that the Eskimo maintained a coastguard service in that region.

The *Resolute*, of Belcher's squadron, was abandoned, while still completely seaworthy, in May 1854. She was then firmly beset in lat. 73° 40′ N., long. 101° 20′ W.

In September 1855 she was picked up, floating freely off Cape Mercy, Davis Strait, by an American whaling-skipper named Buddington. She was not far from the Atlantic, and had covered nearly a thousand miles from the spot at which she was abandoned. It is pleasant to read that she was purchased by the U.S. Government, reconditioned, and given back to us "as a token of good will on the part of the American people". It is not quite so pleasant to record that she was then allowed to decay, neglected, in a corner of Portsmouth Dockyard. She could have served a most useful purpose if she had been lent to Lady Franklin for McClintock's expedition; but the Admiralty would not do this.†

There is, therefore, no great improbability in supposing either that the *Erebus* and *Terror* were lifted on to the surrounding ice by pressure, or that they drifted from where they were abandoned out into the Atlantic. The principal difficulty is to understand how they could have got from King William Island into Barrow Strait. The general trend of the ice where they were abandoned is south-eastward, whereas to reach Barrow Strait they would have had to make their way northwardly. It seems not altogether unlikely, however, that the south-eastward set of the ice down McClintock Strait—the original cause of their besetment—may occasionally set up a counter-drift up Franklin Strait and Peel Sound, which would bring them to Barrow Strait. From here they would be set down Lancaster Sound, and so, ultimately, reach the Atlantic (see Fig. 13).

Whether the ships seen on the ice by the *Renovation* were actually the lost *Erebus* and *Terror* is a matter of opinion. My own, for what it may be worth, is that they were—but it may be due simply to a subconscious prejudice in favour of the marvellous.‡ At all events the story, whatever

* One is, however, glad to learn that his sword was handed back in a silence more cutting than any words. He reported most unfavourably on two of his subordinates, who were immediately promoted. He was never employed again.

† She was, however, borrowed by Jules Verne to take Dr. Fergusson and his party to Zanzibar in 1862. See *Five Weeks in a Balloon*.

‡ In fairness, I must record that my friend Mr. R. J. Cyriax, the leading authority on the subject of Franklin's ill-fated expedition, does not share this opinion.

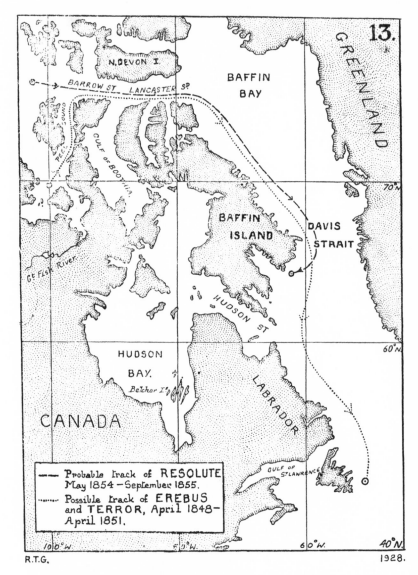

FIG. 13.—Routes followed by the *Resolute*, and (possibly) by the *Erebus* and *Terror*, when abandoned and drifting.

NOTE.—This sketch-map also shows the position of the Belcher Is., Hudson Bay, referred to in "The Auroras, and other Doubtful Islands".

its ingredients of fact, fiction, and error, has added one more to the mysteries which surround, and probably will always surround, the doings of Franklin's ill-fated expedition.

Of these, there are many. Why, for example, did Franklin leave no cairn at any point in the whole length of the Wellington Channel (which he was the first to explore) nor any record narrating his visit, proceedings, and intentions? Why did he leave his winter quarters at Beechey Island in such haste that even there he left no record?

Why did Crozier, second-in-command of the expedition and a most loyal subordinate, hint so darkly in his last letters home at having "my full share of troubles" before the voyage ended? What possessed him to make for the Fish River when he could more easily have crossed to Fury Beach, where, to his own knowledge, were many tons of stores of all kinds, and where he would have had much more chance of getting help from the whalers of Lancaster Sound? Why did he start long before he could hope to meet with any game?

Why was Franklin buried in the ice? Or, if on land (which was in sight from the ships), why has his grave never been found? Did Crozier die with his men, or is there any truth in the traditions collected by Hall that, knowing Eskimo ways and the Eskimo language, he survived the disaster and lived the life of a savage for some twenty years? Is Rae's story true, that some of Franklin's men ate each other?

Who were the two men whose headless skeletons McClintock found in the boat? Why had each fired a single shot? Did the Eskimo, as they claimed, assist the stragglers—or did they murder them? And why did they so carefully pull down every cairn they could find and remove the records left by Franklin's men along their line of retreat?

To these questions, and many others, there is no conclusive answer. All that we know with certainty is written on the record found by McClintock. No sadder story was ever told in a few lines. For the rest—

> The bodies and the bones of those
> Who strove in other days to pass,
> Lie withered in the thorny close,
> Or blanched and blown about the grass.

Some of the survivors possibly reached Montreal Island, at the mouth of the Fish River; one or two may even have started up the river; but none came back to civilization; and probably none could ever have done so. A small, healthy party of trained hunters might, as was shown later by Rae and Schwatka, have come and gone between King William Island and the nearest outpost of the Hudson Bay Company with perfect safety; but for a large party of men, most of them scurvy-ridden, short of food—and, most amazing of all, encumbered with heavy boat-sledges and quantities of useless lumber*—to attempt such a journey was utter madness. Had they stuck to the ships, and sent a few of their fittest men to the shores of Lancaster Sound on the chance of sighting a whaler, there might have been some hope still; but they abandoned their ships, and now the western coast of King William Island is dotted with the graves that show where they fell down and died as they walked.

What became of the ships on the ice? If they were whalers, they sank a few days later; for, if the report accredited to the *Doktor Kneip* be accepted (and there seems no reason to doubt it), the floe broke up shortly after the *Renovation* had left it astern and such vessels, badly strained, must soon have followed suit and sunk. But if they were the *Erebus* and *Terror*, the case is altered. The latter ship, as has been told, spent over three months on a floe in 1837, and yet reached England. Probably no wooden ships were ever more massively built or more strongly fortified. They would have been light, too, for most of their stores must have been expended before they were abandoned; and even if all their store-casks had been "shaken" to save room, the staves would still have been "floating ballast".

Looking at the immense amount of solid wood built into them, and their comparatively small amount of "dead-weight", I am by no means certain that, even if full of water, they would have sunk; it seems far more likely that they would float, awash or little more, until they fell to pieces or were driven ashore.

Where did they go? Did they drift round and round the North Atlantic, as many other derelicts have done, for years? Did they go northward again—or southward, back to the Antarctic? Did they find a last resting-place somewhere in the Pacific, as the ships of La Pérouse, the French Franklin, did at Vanikoro? Or are they still afloat?

POSTSCRIPT

Lord Cochrane, in his *Autobiography of a Seaman* (vol. I, pp. 63, 64, 1861 edn.) records that the *Renovation's* strange story "was scarcely credited at the time", and proceeds to relate an experience of his own in

* "... A great quantity and variety of articles lay strewed about the cairn, such as even in their three days' march from the ships the retreating crews found it impossible to carry farther. Amongst these were four heavy sets of boat's cooking stoves, pick-axes, shovels, iron hoops, old canvas, a large single block, about four feet of a copper lightning conductor, long pieces of hollow brass curtain rods ... and even a small sextant. ... The clothing left by the retreating crews ... formed a huge heap four feet high."—*A Narrative of the Discovery of the Fate of Sir John Franklin*, Capt. F. L. McClintock, R.N. (London, 1860, pp. 304–5).

support of it. While serving aboard H.M.S. *Thetis* in 1794, his squadron encountered a number of icebergs in mid-Atlantic. ". . . on passing one field of great extent we were astonished at discovering on its sides three vessels, the one nearest to us being a polacca-rigged ship, elevated at least a hundred feet; the berg having rolled round or been lightened by melting, so that the vessel had the appearance of being on a hill forming the southern portion of the floe."

I have a note (but no details) of a full-rigged ship, lying on a berg or floe, having been seen off the Falklands early in 1907 by a French steamer.

IV

THE BERBALANGS OF CAGAYAN SULU

It is not generally known (and I do not state it as a fact) that certain American citizens* possess the ability to quit their bodies for a short period, and to travel about in the form of fire-flies for the purpose of assaulting their neighbours.

If I asserted my personal belief in this somewhat surprising statement I should not expect to meet with much credence. I have no intention of doing so. I only wish to give a short account of the evidence which will enable someone bolder than myself, if he so desires, to show that it is not quite so devoid of foundation as it may appear.

The sole evidence is to be found in an article by Mr. Ethelbert Forbes Skertchley, of Hong-Kong, published under the ægis of the Asiatic Society of Bengal. It appeared in their *Journal* for 1896.†

The contents of the Society's *Journal* exhibit, like the *Philosophical Transactions* of an even more famous and dignified body, the Royal Society of London, a very wide range of subjects and interests. All is fish that comes to its net. The majority of the papers deal with ethnological subjects, but as a whole they embrace almost every branch of human knowledge: mathematics, astronomy, numismatics, biology, philology, anthropology, medicine, *et hoc genus omne*. They give the impression of composing a formidable body of hard and perfectly sincere spade-work done in the cause of scientific truth. *A priori*, one would not dream of accusing the author of any article which the Society has judged worthy of inclusion in its *Journal* of relating a mere "traveller's tale", or of stooping to perpetrate a hoax—such an occurrence would seem, on the face of it, as improbable as a police raid, in support of our chaotic Licensing Laws, upon the Athenæum Club. Never before, surely, did so strange a tale as Mr Skertchley's find so unimpeachable a sponsor.

* When this book was first published one or two of these, disregarding my preliminary caution, took this statement a little too seriously, and sent me learned disquisitions upon the exact legal status of the Filipinos under American rule.

† "Cagayan Sulu, its Customs, Legends, and Superstitions", by Ethelbert Forbes Skertchley. Communicated by the Anthropological Secretary (received July 6th; read 4th November, 1896).—*Journal of the Asiatic Society of Bengal*, vol. lxv, Part III, Anthropology and Cognate Subjects. No. 1, 1896. Printed in Calcutta, at the Baptist Mission Press, and published by the Asiatic Society, 57 Park Street.

His article begins reasonably enough with a description, rather in the manner of the Admiralty Sailing Directions, of the little island of Cagayan Sulu. It lies at the southern end of the Philippine group, and its inhabitants have in consequence, been quasi-citizens of the United States of America since 1898. They will remain so until the Filipinos both demonstrate their fitness for independence and receive it at the hands of their present overlords*—two separate contingencies, over the first of which there appears to hang, at the time of writing, some shadow of doubt, while the second . . . well, perhaps the less I commit myself about the second, the better.

At the date of Mr. Skertchley's visit the island was under Spanish rule —with whose blessings, apparently, he was not greatly impressed. The natives, mustering about fifteen hundred fighting men, held even stronger views, which they were at little pains to conceal from the local Spanish garrison, consisting of a captain and four men (chiefly employed guarding a tin flag nailed to a pole).

The middle portion of the article reads much like any other of its kind, and enters into a good deal of rather ordinary ethnological detail. Then, after one or two folk-stories have beeen related, come three pages in which Mr. Skertchley tells, both from his own experience and from local information, the remarkable story of the Berbalangs:

"In the centre of the island is a small village, the inhabitants of which owe allegiance to neither of the two chiefs. These people are called 'Berbalangs', and the Cagayans live in great fear of them.

"These Berbalangs are ghouls, and must eat human flesh occasionally or they would die. You can always tell them, because the pupils of their eyes are not round, but just narrow slits like those of a cat.

"They dig open the graves and eat the entrails of the corpses; but in Cagayan the supply is limited, so when they feel the craving for a feed of human flesh they go away into the grass, and, having carefully hidden their bodies, hold their breath and fall into a trance. Their astral bodies are then liberated. . . . They fly away, and entering a house make their way into the body of one of the occupants and feed on his entrails. . . .

"The Berbalangs may be heard coming, as they make a moaning noise which is loud at a distance and dies away to a feeble moan as they approach. When they are near you the sound of their wings may be heard and the flashing lights of their eyes can be seen like dancing fire-flies in the dark.

"Should you be the happy possessor of a cocoa-nut pearl you are safe, but otherwise the only way to beat them off is to cut at them with a kris, the blade of which has been rubbed with the juice of a lime. If you see the

* With whom, at the present time (1944) we may safely leave General MacArthur to deal.

lights and hear the moaning in front of you, wheel suddenly round and make a cut in the opposite direction. Berbalangs always go by contraries and are never where they appear to be.

"The cocoa-nut pearl, a stone like an opal* sometimes found in the cocoa-nut, is the only really efficacious charm against their attacks; and it is only of value to the finder, as its magic powers cease when it is given away. When the finder dies the pearl loses its lustre and becomes dead.

"The juice of limes sprinkled on a grave will prevent the Berbalangs from entering it, so all the dead are buried either under or near the houses, and the graves are sprinkled daily with fresh lime-juice."

So far, so good. The reader of the article naturally imagines that Mr. Skertchley is merely relating, more or less in the words of the Cagayans, one of their pet beliefs, which bears a close family resemblance to other stories of ghouls in other parts of the world. The "strigoi" of Rumania, for example, is supposed to prey on the dead, and also, when his food is scarce, on the living. Like the berbalangs, he is credited with the power to discard his body and assume other strange shapes at will. Against him, too, various symbolical precautions must be taken.

"The branch of wild rose on his coffin keep him that he move not from it; a sacred bullet fired into the coffin kill him so that he be true dead; and as for the stake through him, we know already of its peace; or the cut-off head that giveth rest. . . ."

Such are the words of the erudite Doctor van Helsing, a prominent figure in that classic of vampire literature, *Dracula*.† As among the Cagayans, too, the coffins menaced by vampires are also protected by similar methods; devices such as the "mort-houses" and "patent coffins" used in this country during the period of the Resurrection-Men are, apparently, of no avail against any competent vampire.

But the startling finale of Mr. Skertchley's article, in which he relates his own experience of the Berbalangs, entirely upsets this theory, and leaves it doubtful how far, in the portion already quoted, he is drawing on the native stock of folk-lore and how far he is detailing his own conclusions.

"Having heard so much about the Berbalangs, I was naturally anxious to see them, but could get no one to go as a guide, till after two or three days Hadji Mahomet's eldest son, Matali, volunteered to accompany me. . . . We set out at once.

---

* It is very similar to the silicious concretion, known by the Hindu name of "tabasheer", sometimes found in the joints of bamboos.

† The best-known novel of the late Bram Stoker. It is a mine of quite accurate information relating to the Rumanian customs and superstitions with regard to their "Un-Dead"—human beings whom they believe to have become vampires.

"We arrived in sight of the village about five o'clock, but Matali would not approach within half a mile, and tried to persuade me not to go nearer. Finding I was determined to go, however, he begged me to take his kris and a few limes and told me to accept no food unless I first sprinkled it with lime-juice, as the Berbalangs were in the habit of setting food before strangers which had the appearance of curried fish but was in reality human flesh, and should I once eat this my soul would be destroyed and I should become a Berbalang. If, however, before eating I sprinkled the food with lime-juice, it would resume its natural shape. . . .

"Taking the kris and limes, and leaving Matali praying for my safety, I soon arrived at the village. It consisted of about a dozen houses of the ordinary native type; but with the exception of a few fowls and a solitary goat there was no living thing to be seen. I was surprised at this and entered several of the houses, but all were alike deserted. Everything was in perfect order, and in one house some rice was standing in basins, still quite hot, as though the occupants had been suddenly called away when about to begin their evening meal. . . .

"I returned to Matali, and on telling him of the deserted state of the village he turned pale, and implored me to come back at once, as the Berbalangs were out and it would be dangerous to return in the dark.

"The sun was setting as we started on our homeward way, and before we had covered half the distance it was quite dark. There was not a breath of air stirring, and we were in the middle of an open valley with no trees about when we heard a loud moaning noise like someone in pain. Matali immediately crouched down in the long grass and pulled me down beside him: he said the Berbalangs were coming down the valley, and our only chance was that they might pass us by without seeing us. We lay there while the moaning sound grew fainter, and Matali whispered that they were coming nearer.

"Presently the sound died away to a faint wail and the sound of wings became audible, while a lot of little dancing lights, like fire-flies, only reddish, passed over us. I could feel Matali's grip tighten on my arm, and I felt a nasty creepy sensation about the roots of my hair, but after the lights had passed, the noise of wings ceased, the moaning grew louder, and Matali told me they had gone by, and for the time being we were safe.

"We continued on our way down the valley, and on passing an isolated house at some distance from the path the moaning grew faint again, and Matali said the Berbalangs had certainly gone into the house, and he trusted that Hassan, the owner, had a cocoa-nut pearl to protect him. . . .

"Now I knew Hassan, to whose house the Berbalangs had gone, and decided to call on him the next day and see what account he had to give of the night's occurrences.

"Accordingly, soon after daybreak, I started off alone, as I could get no one to accompany me, and in due course came to Hassan's house. There was no sign of anyone about, so I tried the door, but found it fastened. I shouted several times, but no one answered, so, putting my shoulder to the door, I gave a good push and it fell in. I entered the house and looked round, but could see no one; going farther in, I suddenly started back, for huddled up on the bed, with hands clenched, face distorted, and eyes staring as in horror, lay my friend Hassan—dead.

"I have stated above the facts just as they occurred, and am quite unable to give any explanation of them."

If Mr. Skertchley had read his paper to the Asiatic Society, instead of communicating it, I imagine that such of the members as might have been present would, unless they desired a breach of the peace, have concurred with his concluding remark. The first explanation which at once suggests itself is that the whole story is either pure or adulterated fiction.

Those who wish may think so; they have been provided with sufficient material to form their opinion. It is a hypothesis which I do not propose to adopt. I know nothing of Mr. Skertchley, and I should be sorry to accuse any man of deliberate lying merely on the ground that something he had narrated seemed to me to be intrinsically improbable. The utmost that I think myself justified in saying is that the story looks to me to be, in places, a little coloured—to be related in a manner which, here and there, tends a little too obviously towards literary effect. It almost reads like one of those haunting *Ghost Stories of an Antiquary* which it was the late Provost of Eton's* custom to relate for the delight of his friends, and sometimes (but too infrequently) to publish.

I confess that I cannot dismiss the story as a fable; and yet it seems to defy all explanation. Part of it—the account of the customs of the Berbalangs—may be dismissed as mere folk-lore. The death of the villager Hassan, again, might have been due merely to suggestion. Many such cases are on record. The Voodoo-fearing negro in Hayti who has been cursed by one of the "Papaloi", or the West African native upon whom a Porroh-man has put a ju-ju, very often pines away and dies at the bidding of his own imagination.

Civilized men have done the same. There is a case on record of an Oxford scout who got into the bad books of some of the undergraduates. They held a mock trial, conducted with the utmost solemnity, and sen-

---

* Dr. M. R. James. I can hear his voice now, reading Mr. Skertchley's account to my brother and myself, after dinner, in the Provost's Lodge at King's thirty years and more ago.

tenced him to be beheaded. He was made to kneel, blindfolded, at a block, and then the "executioner" flipped him lightly on the back of the neck with a wet towel. He was picked up stone-dead.

This occurrence, and many others that might be instanced—such as the old story of the healthy convict who, as an experiment, was told, with appropriately surgical *mise-en-scène*, that he was being bled to death and succumbed, like the walls of Jericho, to the noise of a tap kept running under the operating-table—may be explained as a simple case of heart-failure following shock; but I do not think it has been proved that such is invariably the true explanation. I suggest that it is quite likely that, if the unfortunate Hassan had been brought, in some way, to believe that he was beset by the Berbalangs, he might have died as the direct result of this suggestion.

The questions remain, how was that suggestion effected, and was it in any way connected with the appearances described by Mr. Skertchley? I leave it to entomologists to say whether the "dancing lights, like fire-flies, only reddish" could, actually, have been any known form of luminous insect capable of existing in the Philippines; and whether it is possible to train such insects to make, like bees or pigeons, for some designated spot. The Chinese, it is well known, can do much in the way of insect training, but I do not know whether such feats are within their capacity—or anyone else's.

If such things are possible they provide, I suggest, the groundwork of an explanation. The stage noises could have been provided by the Berbalangs accompanying, under cover of night, their swarm of trained fire-flies. As for their motives in carrying on this strange deception, it is surely permissible to regard them as a savage Mafia terrorizing a smaller Sicily.

I am not certain whether there is any close parallel to the details of the Berbalang story to be found in other parts of the world. The late Andrew Lang adapted Mr. Skertchley's account to the purposes of a novel, *The Disentanglers*, and quoted his authority, adding, in a footnote,*

"See also Monsieur Henri Junod, in *Les Ba-Ronga* (Attinger, Neuchâtel, 1898). Unlike Mr. Skertchley, M. Junod has not himself seen the creature."

I have read M. Junod's book, an ethnological study of an African tribe, with some care, but I have not been fortunate enough to find anything bearing even the remotest analogy to the doings of the Berbalangs.

It is a common saying, "out East", that if you live there long enough you will come to believe anything. Now that American civilization has reached the Philippines, however, we may hope that this reproach will be submerged in a great wave of "uplift". I trust that the Berbalangs—who

* *The Disentanglers*, Andrew Lang (London, 1902, p. 242, f.n.).

by all accounts are at least "most unpleasant people"—may be led to see the error of their ways; and that at the same time some thing may be done towards a scientific investigation of the powers which they are reputed to possess, and of their physical structure. An anatomical examination of the pupils of their eyes, for example, could not fail to provide confirmation or disproof of one of the many interesting pieces of folk-lore collected by Mr. Skertchley.

V

ORFFYREUS' WHEEL

The history of human folly, on any scale commensurate with the vast and ever-increasing amount of material available, remains to be written. A casual effort in this direction was made by Sebastian Brant, who published his *Ship of Fools** in 1494. But while this book may have inspired Erasmus to take up the cudgels "for self and fellows", and produce his *Praise of Folly*,† its satire fell, for the most part, on deaf ears. Centuries later an atrabilious Scotsman, peering at the world from an anacoustic study in Chelsea, recorded his conviction that it was peopled by "too many millions, mostly fools"—a sweeping statement, but embodying an essential truth. Most of those, for example, who have had experience (internal or otherwise) of Government Departments can testify to having, like Oxenstiern, been amazed at discovering how little wisdom it takes to govern the world; and if there be any truth in the often-quoted assertion that "a nation gets the government it deserves", Carlyle's apothegm must be regarded as resting upon a very solid—one might even say dense—basis of fact.

Of the many millions of fools who cumber the earth, I suppose that the fanatics, taking them all round, are the greatest nuisance—and, tested by old-fashioned notions of personal independence and "the liberty of the subject", the one most actively mischievous. Possessing, far too often, that misleading form of energy which it is fatally easy to mistake for capacity; restrained by no false modesty from minding everybody else's business; and simultaneously unbalanced and supported by a chronic inability to conceive that there can be two sides to any question, they are the bacteria of the civilized world—a fertile source of past, present, and future disorders.

But if the fanatic, generally speaking, is an unpleasant figure, the harmless "crank" can be very amusing—provided that you merely chuckle over his lucubrations, and sternly refuse to be drawn into correspondence with him. The latter caution is a *sine qua non*. He can never be converted from his mistaken notions, for the serene ignorance which gave them birth forms, also, a mental armour proof against the clearest demonstration. In addition, he is generally of irritable temperament; he has much spare time; he is blind to the decencies of ordinary controversy; and he wields a vitriolic, if halting, pen.

Such is the flat-earther, the circle-squarer, the Ten Tribes man, the

---

* *Das Narrenshiff.*

† *Encomium Moriæ*. The title is a joke at the expense of his friend Sir Thomas More.

Jacobite, and the man who, measuring the Pyramids with a foot-rule (or, more commonly, relying on similarly-accurate measurements made by other people) establishes to his own satisfaction that the early Egyptians were only a little lower than the angels, and, possessed of an amazing and unsuspected amount of scientific and other knowledge, took the eminently reasonable step of declining to commit any of it to writing, leaving it to be deduced from the dimensions and orientation of various Royal tombs (used, in the monarch's lifetime, as observatories).

Among this happy band (one can hardly add "of brothers", for in general one crank hates another most whole-heartedly) an honoured place will, I think, always be found for the man who is convinced that he has discovered the secret of "perpetual motion" (which, I ought perhaps to explain, happens to form the subject of this essay). That place is his of right, because, like the King, he never dies. He is always with us—and there are always a good many of him.

The reason is not far to seek. The necessary qualifications for a perpetual-motion seeker are few and simple. He must have a little mechanical skill—enough, say, for simple jobs about the house. He must have a little spare time and a certain amount of perseverance and self-confidence. And he must be ignorant, or all but ignorant, of two subjects in particular: the fundamental principles of mechanics and the work of his predecessors.

Of men of this type (the subject does not seem to have ever had much attraction for the other sex) there is always an ample supply—one might almost say a superfluity. And it is a curious feature of their unhappy obsession that it takes a variety of forms, and directs their attention to several different objects.

Some, for example, consider that what is required is a clock that will never need to be wound; that such a clock will, in particular, be of the utmost value for finding longitude at sea; and that there is an enormous Government reward on offer to its successful inventor. All three of these notions are baseless.

In the first place, many clocks have been made which do not require winding; their construction presents no great mechanical difficulty, and they can be fitted with any of several well-known systems of self winding. They are mechanical freaks, and generally poor timekeepers. Secondly, to find longitude we merely need a timepiece which keeps accurate time— it does not in the least matter how often it has or has not to be wound, except that in general the more often it is wound the better time it keeps.*

* No eight-day chronometer has ever gained first place in the annual trials at Greenwich, although many have competed. Frodsham 3593 (8-day) was second in 1883. Such eight-day chronometers as are used afloat generally go better if wound every day.

Thirdly, there is no Government reward on offer for such a timepiece—or for any other form of "perpetual motion" machine.

Others of the fraternity propose to obtain "perpetual motion" by means of mills worked by tidal water, or by fans placed in tall chimneys and exposed to a continual upward draught, or by various other applications of natural sources of power. Like the first class, such "perpetual motions" are, if not common, at least far from unknown.

But the inventor who is, at the same time, nearest of all his tribe to the real idea of "perpetual motion", and furthest of all from realizing it in practice, is the man who attempts to make a machine which will give out more work than is put into it; one which actually creates energy, and does not depend on external supplies of that useful commodity. Apart from occasional dabblings in hydrostatics and pneumatics, he generally looks to some application of gravity or magnetism for the mainspring of his machine; and he goes his way serenely unconscious of the fact that he is really doing his best to produce a working model of a contradiction in terms. He might, no less usefully, devote his time to drawing four-sided triangles.

I have said that he is usually ignorant of the work of his predecessors. Broadly speaking, this is a good thing. If he were to read up what he could find in print on the subject of perpetual motion, he could not go very far without coming across some mention of Councillor Orffyreus, and the wheel which he exhibited at Hesse-Cassel in 1717. And the more he looked into the story of that wheel, the more he would become convinced that while the secret of "perpetual motion" (in the true sense) might have died with Orffyreus, it had certainly been known to him.

Orffyreus' wheel, in fact, is the only instance on record of a machine, capable of doing external work and yet apparently independent of any external or known source of power, having been exhibited in public and subjected to official tests. These tests, while not stringent, certainly seem to have precluded the very natural supposition that the whole thing was a clever trick. The machine underwent them successfully, but its construction was never disclosed.

The making of the wheel, and its apparently successful performance, are historical facts for which there is ample evidence. But none of this evidence brings us much nearer to a plausible explanation of those facts. For example, there is in existence a contemporary pamphlet written by Orffyreus himself, in which he gives an outline of the mechanism and principles of his machine—but that explanation is at variance with all modern ideas of mechanics. If, as he claimed, he had discovered a new source of power, he was either unable or unwilling to give a correct description of it; yet, if he was a charlatan, he must have been an illusionist far superior to Buatier da Kolta or J. N. Maskelyne, for he certainly produced what was, judged by the standards of his day, a most consummate deception.

Here are the facts of the story, so far as they are upon record.

Johann Ernest Elias Bessler, called Orffyreus, was born at Zittau, Saxony, in 1680. "Orffyreus" seems to be an assumed name* which he adopted as a means of self-advertisement, precisely as a more famous countryman of his, afflicted from birth with the remarkable style of Philip Theophrastus Bombastus von Hohenheim, had done long before. P. T. B. von Hohenheim, even in its abbreviated form, is a name chiefly remarkable for its length—but there will always, I think, be some who have read of "Paracelsus".

Orffyreus seems to have had a restless and inquiring mind—he studied theology, medicine, and painting before turning his attention to mechanics. About 1712 he began to be known as the constructor of various self-moving wheels. He exhibited these freely, but always with their mechanism concealed by casings forming part of the wheel and revolving with it.†

He brought out the first of these at Gera, in the province of Reuss, in 1712. It was a wheel of about 3 feet diameter and 4 inches thick, capable not only of keeping itself in motion when started but of gradually working up its speed to a certain limit, and of raising a weight of several pounds. It should be noted, however, that the accounts of the work done by the first three of Orffyreus' wheels show that the tests applied to them were only "brake tests" of very short duration, during which the wheel lifted a weight by means of a rope coiled round its axle. The lifting effect was not exerted, apparently, for more than a minute or so, and was probably due, in great part, to the mere momentum of the wheel. As an apparent demonstration that the machines were self-moving, this was far less conclusive than their progressive acceleration when once set going.

Orffyreus seems to have derived no benefit, either in money or reputation, from the wheel which he exhibited at Gera. One suspects that the chief reason for this was to be found in his personal character. He seems to have been, intentionally or otherwise, one of the Old Masters of that "gentle art of making enemies" of which Whistler was so polished and caustic an exponent. At all events his admirers were few, and his detractors many. Some asserted that the machine was a bare-faced imposture;

* He arrived at it by writing the alphabet in a circle, and picking out the letters diametrically opposite to those of "Bessler"—thus obtaining "Orffyre" which he Latinised.

† The account here given of the various wheels is compiled from several sources, including the Leipzig Acts (*Acta Eruditorum*) for 1717, a German technical dictionary published in 1719–20, Orffyreus' own pamphlet, and Dirck's *Perpetuum Mobile*, second series (London, 1870).

others that it was, at all events, a mere model, and that a larger machine of the same type could not answer.*

Orffyreus—who, like Paracelsus, seems to have spent most of his life in a nomadic state, the remainder being passed in brief sojourns punctuated and terminated by controversies and recriminations—left Gera in dudgeon and went to Draschwitz, near Leipzig. Here, in 1713, he completed and exhibited a larger machine on the same lines. It was about 5 feet in diameter and 6 inches thick. It could reach a speed of fifty revolutions per minute and raise a weight of 40 lb.

Removing to Merseburg, he constructed a third and still larger machine. This was about 6 feet in diameter and 1 foot thick. He obtained certificates from several "learned men"—who, presumably, were at least competent to determine so simple a point—that it was not moved by any "outward agent": i.e. that it was not connected with any external source of power. It may be noted that only one man, the Landgrave of Hesse-Cassel, was ever permitted to view the internal mechanism of any of Orffyreus' wheels.

As at Gera, Orffyreus found that the exhibition of his wheel made him merely a target for detraction and abuse—not only oral but printed. Apparently in the hope of silencing his enemies, he again submitted the machine, on October 31, 1715, to the examination of a committee of eminent men, who signed, on December 4th, a certificate stating that they considered it a true "perpetual motion . . . having the property to move right and left, easily moved, but requiring great effort to stay its movement; with the power of raising . . . a box of stones weighing 70 lb., 8 ells high perpendicularly. . . ." But this carried no weight with his opponents—nor did the fact that the machine, unaffected by the controversy, continued to revolve during the remainder of Orffyreus' stay in Merseburg.

His adversaries attacked him in various ways. For example, one C. Steinbruck, in 1716, published a satirical pamphlet in which he made Orffyreus an offer of one thousand thalers to demonstrate that his machine could really, as he had claimed, go for a month continuously, or raise a weight of 70 lb. C. Wagner, a Leipzig mathematician, also issued a pamphlet proving to his own satisfaction that Orffyreus' experiments were offences against the laws of nature and punishable as such. He also professed to be able to exhibit a machine, constructed of copper, which could perform all that was reported of the Merseburg wheel—

* It is a well-known fact that in many cases an accurate model of a proposed machine is successful in its working, and the machine itself a failure. The reason for this, broadly speaking, is that the weight of a machine increases as the cube of its size, and its structural strength as the square. For the same reason a tall man, *cæteris paribus*, is proportionately weaker than one of normal size.

while at the same time confessedly a trick, operated by concealed machinery. Another of the pack, Andreas Gartner, a Dresden model-maker, more modestly professed only that he, too, could construct a "perpetual-motion" machine. Yet another, J. G. Borlach, published a treatise (Leipzig, 1716) showing that perpetual motion was contrary to nature, and containing a plate indicating how, in his opinion, Orffyreus kept his wheel turning. The plate (which Orffyreus contemptuously reproduced in his own later pamphlet) shows the wheel revolving close to a wall, on the other side of which a tired-looking servant is hauling on the end of a rope made fast to a rocking-beam overhead. The other end of the beam is connected by a crank with the axle of the wheel. It is scarcely necessary to say that such a contrivance would not have deceived a child—much less the intelligentsia who had testified that Orffyreus' wheel, whatever its mechanism, was at least unconnected with any external source of power.

There is, however, one curious point to be noted in connection with Borlach's suggestion, absurd though that was. The arrangement of wheel, rocking-beam, and crank is identical with that employed in the "beam-engine"—the earliest form of steam rotary power-plant—invented by James Watt. Watt's first engines were designed for pumping water, the pump being coupled direct to the beam—but in 1780 he designed a new engine in which he proposed to use a crank to transform the reciprocating motion of the beam into continuous rotary motion. At that date, the crank was in common use for such purposes as the treadle of a lathe—and, in consequence, Watt did not cover it by his patent. Much to his surprise, he found that gossip as to the details of the new engine had led to one James Pickard, a Birmingham button-maker, securing a patent for the use of the crank in steam-machinery. Pickard obtained this patent on August 23, 1780, about a month before Watt's engine was completed. The latter was, for some time, compelled to evade this patent by using a "sun-and-planet" motion instead of a crank—and it seems a pity that in the course of his wide reading he had not come across the pamphlets of either Borlach or Orffyreus, since he could have proved that a similar arrangement to that patented by Pickard had been designed and published sixty-five years earlier.

Either at the end of 1716 or early in the following year Orffyreus quitted Merseburg and settled at Hesse-Cassel, one of the small quasi-independent states endemic in eighteenth-century Germany. Here he attracted the notice of Karl, the reigning Landgrave (Count); or, to give him his full title as it appears in the Latin version of Orffyreus' pamphlet—

"... CAROLUS, Hassiæ Landgravius, Princeps Hersfeldiæ, Comes Cattimeliboci, Deciæ, Ziegenhaynæ, Nidæ, Schaumburgi, &c."

The Landgrave took the harassed and vagrant Orffyreus under his protection. A post was found for him as Town Councillor—an office apparently more important then than now—and rooms were set apart for his use in the Ducal castle of Weissenstein, near Cassel.

But although Orffyreus had put a considerable distance between himself and the scenes of his past exploits, and although he was, in a measure, protected from affront by the Landgrave's patronage, he could not, if he had wished to, shake off the reputation and the mystery attaching to his name. He may have pulled his weight as a Town Councillor, but there can be little doubt that he was chiefly regarded by the people of Cassel, and their ruler, as the possessor of a long-sought and valuable secret—that of perpetual motion. One imagines that he was looked upon by his patron somewhat as the Court alchemists of an earlier century were regarded by their hosts—and it is difficult to doubt that, before long, he was politely invited to give a specimen of his powers.

At all events, before 1717 was out he had constructed at the castle of Weissenstein his fourth, last, and largest wheel. Of this there exists an excellent description given by Professor 's Gravesande, of Leyden, in a letter to Sir Isaac Newton (whom he knew intimately).

". . . The inventor has a turn for mechanics, but is far from being a profound mathematician, and yet his machine hath something in it prodigiously astonishing, even though it should be an imposition. The following is a description of the external parts of the machine, the inside of which the inventor will not permit to be seen, lest anyone should rob him of his secret.

"It is an hollow wheel, or kind of drum, about 14 inches thick and 12 feet diameter; being very light, as it consists of several cross pieces of wood framed together; the whole of which is covered over with canvas, to prevent the inside from being seen. Through the centre of this wheel or drum runs an axis of about 6 inches diameter, terminated at both ends by iron axes of about three-quarters of an inch diameter upon which the machine turns. *I have examined these axes, and am firmly persuaded that nothing from without the wheel in the least contributes to its motion.** When I turned it but gently, it always stood still as soon as I took away my hand; but when I gave it any tolerable degree of velocity, I was always obliged to stop it again by force; for when I let it go, it acquired in two or three turns its greatest velocity, after which it revolved twenty-five or twenty-six times in a minute."

A similar account of the machine is to be found in a letter written by Baron Fischer (architect to the Emperor of Austria) to Dr. J. T. Desaguliers, F.R.S.

* The original is not italicized.

"I do myself the honour of writing the present letter to mark my esteem for you, and also to give you news of the Perpetual Motion at Cassel, which has been so much recommended to me since I have been in London. Although I am very incredulous about things which I do not understand, yet I must assure you that I am quite persuaded that there exists no reason why this machine should not have the name of Perpetual Motion given to it; and I have good reasons to believe that it is one, according to the experiments which I have been allowed to make by permission of His Serene Highness, who is the most amiable and gracious of princes that I have known in my life; and who had the patience to be present at the trials which I made during two hours.

"It is a wheel which is 12 feet in diameter, covered with oil-cloth.* At every turn of the wheel can be heard about eight weights, which fall gently on the side towards which the wheel turns. This wheel turns with astonishing rapidity, making twenty-six turns in a minute when moving freely. Having tied a cord to the axle, to turn an Archimedean screw for raising water, the wheel then made twenty turns in a minute. This I noted several times by my watch, and I always found the same regularity.

"I then stopped the wheel with much difficulty, holding on to the circumference with both hands. An attempt to stop it suddenly would raise a man from the ground.

"Having stopped it in this manner, it remained stationary; and (here, Sir, is the greatest proof of it being a Perpetual Motion) I restarted it very gently, to see if it would of itself regain its former rapidity—which I doubted, believing, as they had said in London, that it only preserved for a long time the impetus of the impulse first communicated. But, to my great astonishment, I observed that the rapidity of the wheel augmented little by little until it had made two turns, and then it regained its former speed, until I observed by my watch that it made the same twenty-six turns a minute as before, when acting freely; and twenty turns when it was attached to the screw to raise water.

"This experiment, Sir, showing the speed of the wheel to augment, from the very slow movement that I gave it, to an extraordinary rapid one, convinces me more than if I had only seen the wheel moving a whole year, which would not have persuaded me that it was perpetual motion, because it might have diminished little by little until it ceased altogether; but to gain speed instead of losing it, and to increase that speed to a certain degree in spite of the resistance of the air and the friction of the axles, makes me unable to see how anyone can deny the truth of so describing it.

"I also turned it in a contrary way, when the wheel performed as

* Not the modern "linoleum", but thin cloth oiled or waxed to give it a smooth surface, like glazed calico.

PLATE III

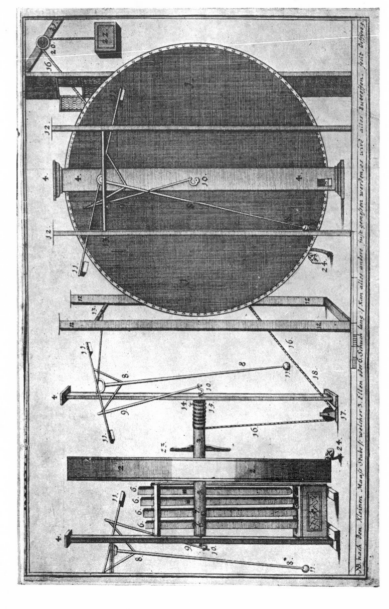

ORFFYREUS' WHEEL

NOTE.—This illustration is taken from a pamphlet published by Orffyreus in 1715, before the Weissenstein wheel was constructed. The plate of the latter given in his pamphlet of 1719 is very similar, but much more coarsely engraved.

before. I carefully examined the axles of the wheel, to see if there was any hidden artifice; but I was unable to see anything more than the two small axles on which the wheel was suspended at its centre."

The wheel seems to have remained on exhibition at Weissenstein for several months, and to have been examined by many persons of standing, including (in addition to 's Gravesande, Fischer, and the Landgrave) Julius Bernhard of Rohr, Wolff Dietrich of Bohsen, Friedrich Hoffmann (a celebrated physician), Christian Wolff, F.R.S. (Chancellor of the University of Halle), and John Rowley, a well-known English maker of mathematical instruments.* All were satisfied that the wheel was no fraud; Rowley, in particular, seems to have made himself quite notorious, later, by the pertinacity with which he asserted, after his return to England, that he had seen a genuine "perpetual motion" at Cassel.

The official test of the machine was performed in 1717–18. On October 31, 1717, Orffyreus was requested to transport the wheel from the room where it was installed to another (also in the castle of Weissenstein) "where there were no walls contiguous to it, and where one might go freely round it on every side". This he accordingly did.

On November 12th following, the Landgrave, with some of his officials, visited the wheel in its new situation and, after seeing it in free and rapid movement, caused the doors, windows, and all other conceivable means of access to the room to be closed, secured, and officially sealed.

On November 26th the seals were broken and the room opened. The wheel was found to be revolving as before. The room was reclosed and resealed with the same precaution.

On January 4, 1718, it was again opened. The seals were found intact. The wheel was revolving with its accustomed regularity.

The Landgrave gave an official certificate of these facts to Orffyreus (dated May 27, 1718), which the latter published in his pamphlet of the following year. The certificate expressly states that the precautions taken were such as to exclude the faintest "hint or suspicion" that the machine could be an imposture.

The Landgrave seems to have acquiesced in Orffyreus' view that he had a right to keep the structure of his machine secret until he had derived some pecuniary benefit from it. But the inventor's efforts towards this end do not seem to have been prolonged or well-judged, and they were certainly unsuccessful. His proposals, such as they were, are outlined in the concluding portion of Fischer's letter to Desaguliers. It will be noted that

---

* He executed, in 1716, that copy of Graham's original planetary machine (1715) to which, at Steele's suggestion, the generic name of "Orrery" was given. It now belongs to Admiral of the Fleet the Earl of Cork and Orrery. I had the pleasure of cleaning and repairing it in 1937. See *I.L.N.*, 18-XII-37.

he looked to England as the nation most likely to reward him; possibly because our country had, in 1714, offered an official reward of £20,000 for a method of finding longitude at sea—and had, in consequence, become the target of every projector, crank, swindler, and lunatic in Europe and/or Bedlam.

(*Fischer to Desaguliers.*)

"I said to His Highness that I had no doubt a company might be formed in London to purchase the secret. The Prince would be exceedingly happy if such a company would consign into his or other hands £20,000 in favour of the Inventor—then the machine should be examined and the secret communicated. If the movement were found to be a perpetual one, the £20,000 would be given up to the inventor; and, if not, the money would be returned. This would be stipulated by proper legal documents.

"I told His Serene Highness that no one could institute such a company better than yourself, for you are always working for the instruction of the public. Consider under what obligation you would lay the most enlightened nation in Europe, if you procured for it the knowledge of the principle of this perpetual motion. . . .

"As I shall not long remain here, I must beg of you to correspond with Mr. Roman, Superintendent of Works to His Highness. He will show all your letters to the Prince, and will come to an understanding with you touching this matter, which well merits your highest consideration, as it is not well to leave this treasure buried. Will you also communicate with your friend Mr. Newton, and tell him my opinion of the machine? I hope that you will soon hear from our friend M. 's Gravesande, of Leyden, who is soon expected here by His Highness. . . ."

It is very doubtful whether Desaguliers took any steps to further this rather cool proposition. In any event Orffyreus soon afterwards put a stop, by his own act, to any such negotiations. In a fit of passion he destroyed his wonderful machine. He was, apparently, driven to this insane act by misapprehending 's Gravesande's motives for the careful examination which that savant had made of the axle and bearings of the wheel—an examination which had been conducted with the sole object of establishing that it was not connected in any way with an external source of power. If Orffyreus had only waited a few hours (he smashed the wheel on the day following that examination) he would have learned from the written report which 's Gravesande handed to the Landgrave, that the self-moving character of his machine was satisfactorily established. 's Gravesande tells the story himself, in a letter written in 1729 to one M. Crousaz, a sceptic who had seen the machine when in working order.

"My Lord the Landgrave, in the presence (at my request) of the Baron

Fischer, Architect of the Emperor, and other persons, showed the supports of the machine; *we saw the axles uncovered; I examined the plates or brasses on which the axles rested, and, in that examination, there did not appear the slightest trace of communication with the adjoining room.**I remember very distinctly the whole of the circumstances of that examination which put Orffyreus in such a rage with me that, the day after, he broke his machine in pieces, and wrote on the wall that it was the impertinent curiosity of Professor 's Gravesande which was the cause. . . ."

After this débâcle, the history of Orffyreus and his famous wheel becomes vague and shadowy. According to a letter from Roman to 's Gravesande, dated Cassel, May 18, 1727, Orffyreus was then engaged in rebuilding the machine. He hoped to have it ready within a month, and 's Gravesande would then be invited by the Landgrave to make a fresh examination of it. Whether this examination was to include the mechanism of the wheel does not appear—it is difficult to believe that 's Gravesande would have consented merely to repeat his former scrutiny of the exterior. There is no further record of any trial or exhibition of the machine. Orffyreus died in November 1745.

It was not given to him to say, as Bacon truly and proudly said, ". . . For my name and memory, I leave it to men's charitable speeches, and to foreign nations, and to the next age". Generally regarded in his lifetime as an impostor, he met the same fate at posterity's hands. For example, that repository of accurate information, *Chambers's Encyclopædia*,† in its article "Perpetual Motion", remarks, after describing the tests of his wheel, ". . . We must, of course, assume the existence of some imposition in this. . . ."

Long after his death, one man arose to defend his memory. Unfortunately, that man's character and writings made him certain to do it more harm than good. He was one Dr. William Kenrick, originally a rulemaker, who took to literature and became a hack employed by Strahan, the London bookseller, for whom he edited *The London Review* from 1775 until his death in 1779. He is remembered now, if at all, only by Johnson's sarcastic reference to him: "Sir, he is one of the many who have made themselves *public*, without making themselves *known*".

Kenrick, who seems to have greatly resembled Orffyreus in his union of a turgid style with a quarrelsome disposition, published in 1770 a pamphlet entitled *An Account of the Automaton constructed by Orffyreus*, in

---

*My italics. The point is important, as will appear.

† Many years ago I read through both *Chambers's Encyclopædia* and *The Encyclopædia Britannica*. Candidly, I greatly prefer the former—not merely because it is shorter but because, in my opinion, it is planned on far sounder lines, and with a much better sense of proportion.

which he gave a not very accurate account of his hero's life, mixed up with comments and absurdities of his own. In the same year he published *A Lecture on the Perpetual Motion* (which he professed to have discovered). He proposed to give, in this pamphlet, a clear demonstration that "perpetual motion" must be "the necessary consequence of the known and established laws of nature".

The pamphlet is practically unreadable, chiefly on account of its extraordinary style. He remarks, for example:

"I could almost as readily impute ingenuity to vegetables and fossils—to the sensitive plant and the loadstone—as meditation to muscles (*sic*), or cogita bundity to cockles, periwinkles, and rock oysters!"

In addition, it is verbose, dull, and stupid. He issued proposals for constructing, by subscription, a machine similar to that of Orffyreus, which he termed a "Rotator". These, naturally enough, met with no attention. He petitioned, on May 19, 1779, for a patent in connection with his machine, but died on June 13th following, "less lamented than he might have been, owing to his generally malignant and vituperative style of writing".

But the aberrations of fools like Kenrick, and knaves like the many detected impostors who, from time to time, have attempted to hoax the public with false "perpetual motions", should not be allowed to obscure the real issue. It is this. There exists a considerable and impressive body of testimony, subscribed by most competent witnesses, as to the self-moving character of Orffyreus' wheel at Weissenstein. If we reject this testimony, *cadit quæstio*—but we must then give up attempting to write history from contemporary documents. Yet, if we accept it, how is it to be explained?

In view of Orffyreus' reputation (whether merited or otherwise) it is natural to begin by supposing that the machine was a pure fraud. The arguments in favour of this view are summed up in a letter from de Crousaz to 's Gravesande.

(*Extract*)   *February* 3, 1729.

". . . Firstly, Orffyreus is mad.

"Secondly, it is impossible that a madman can have discovered what such a number of clever persons have searched for without success.

"Thirdly, I do not believe in impossibilities.

"Fourthly, we can easily imagine that persons keep a secret from which they are to receive benefit; but this fellow, hoping only to gain reputation, allows this to be tarnished by an accusation which he has it in his power to disprove, if false.

"Fifthly, the servant who ran away from his house, for fear of being strangled, has in her possession, in writing, the terrible oath that Orffyreus made her swear.

"Sixthly, he only had to have asked, in order to have had this girl imprisoned, until he had time to finish his machine.

"Seventhly, they publish that the machine is going to be exhibited, when suddenly those who advertise it become silent.

"Eighthly, it is true that there is a machine at his house, to which they give the name of perpetual motion; but that cannot be transported, it is much smaller, and it differs from the first, in that it only turns one way. ..."

It is significant that 's Gravesande, who certainly had no cause to love Orffyreus, and who had suffered much undeserved ridicule for having asserted his belief in the possibility of perpetual motion,* stuck to his guns in his reply.

"I have deferred replying to you, until I had found a paper which I wrote the day after I examined Orffyreus' machine; for although I remember well all that passed, I believe that a paper, written the day after the examination, and communicated to my Lord and all those who were with him, must have more weight.

"This is what I heard; they say, that a servant under oath, turned Orffyreus' machine, (she) being placed in an adjoining room.

"I know well that Orffyreus is mad; but I have no reason to think him an impostor; I have never decided whether his machine is an imposture or not; but this I know, as certainly as anything in the world, that if the servant says the above, she tells a great falsehood. ..."

's Gravesande's correspondence on the subject of Orffyreus' wheel with Newton and de Crousaz was printed in the collected edition of his scientific works.† His editor, Professor Allemand, made some very sensible comments on the foregoing.

"Examining minutely the pros and cons, we can come to these conclusions. 1. That Orffyreus was evidently mad, as M. 's Gravesande and M. de Crousaz both affirm; his breaking his machinery at different times without either reason or necessity proves this. But his was a sort of madness we do not often see; a mania fixed only on certain objects, which merits more the name of fantasy or whimsy—this kind of mania is often accompanied by much genius, and when persons of this disposition apply themselves solely to one subject, as it appears he did, it is not surprising to find them making discoveries which have escaped the sagacity of wiser people.

* He explicitly asserted this belief in a work on Newton's *Principia*, which he published in 1720. He attempted to defend it by a demonstration, which he unfortunately based on the supposition that the kinetic energy of a body m moving with a speed v is proportional to mv (instead of $\frac{1}{2}mv^2$). He admitted this error in his second edition (1725).

† *Œuvres Philosophiques et Mathématiques de M. G. J. 's Gravesande, rassemblées et publiées par Jean Nic. Seb. Allemand* (Amsterdam, 1774, 2 vols. 4to).

"Thus I do not agree with M. de Crousaz, that it is incredible that a madman, such as Orffyreus, should have found out something that learned men have searched for unsuccessfully. . . .

"2. No exterior agent moved the machine; if it were a servant that moved it, would this not have been apparent to eyes so searching as those that made the examination, or to the Landgrave, who had seen the interior of the machine? Besides, how can one assume that a wheel of so great a volume could have been moved by such a cause, a cause which would act only on the axle crossing the supports, and which must have been so small as to have excaped the most rigorous examination?

"3. Supposing that the servant has not been bribed to depose against Orffyreus, what does her testimony prove? Only that her master made her believe that, by turning a little wheel, she moved the whole machine —and we can fancy a singular character such as he was might have done this to baffle the curiosity of those who sought to penetrate his secret. . . ."

The theory that the machine was moved by external power provides, of course, a ready explanation of the mystery. Moreover, this plan is definitely known to have been used in at least one fraudulent "perpetual motion"—Redhoeffer's, exhibited (and exposed) at New York in 1813. At the instance of Robert Fulton, some of the onlookers demolished a few very thin struts running from the frame of the machine to the wall of the room. This exposed a thin catgut line, encircling the axle and led away, under the floor-boards, to a distant loft, in which sat an old man turning a crank!

If we assume that Orffyreus had a free hand to install his wheel at Weissenstein in circumstances of profound secrecy—and, also, that 's Gravesande's examination of its bearings was perfunctory—it then becomes quite conceivable that he adopted some plan of this kind, running his gut line up one of the wheel's supports, and so turning a built-in friction-wheel on whose rim the axle of the wheel rested. There would be quite enough friction between the two surfaces to transmit a torque adequate to keeping the wheel in motion, and even accelerating it, once it had been started by hand—as it always was. Orffyreus need not have employed a confederate—the power might have been derived from a falling weight, and "clutched in" (on the lines of the modern self-starter pinion) by a system of selective ratchets, so arranged that whichever way the wheel was set in motion, the weight would take up the drive.

And, as Plate III shows, there is a slightly suspicious feature about one of the wheel's supports—the one with a hole in it, through which a rope is led. Mechanically this plan is both unnecessary and objectionable: exactly the same end would have been better served by leaving the support unweakened, and taking the rope through a leading-block close to its foot.

On the other hand, Orffyreus' plan might well serve to lull any suspicion that the support was pierced from top to bottom, and had a double line running through it. But against all this must be set two very weighty considerations. Orffyreus might easily have fitted up a deception of this kind in his own house—but to do this at Weissenstein would involve various architectural problems; and, both then and later, the gravest risk of detection. And, secondly, by 's Gravesande's own account he fully satisfied himself that he had examined the actual "plates or brasses on which the axles rested". If he did, no concealed friction-wheel or other device could, one would think, possibly have escaped his scrutiny*—his competence, and his honesty, are beyond question—had he discovered the slightest indication of fraud he would at once have exposed it, for he had no conceivable motive for shielding Orffyreus—and, after all, he was there and we were not.

If then we reject the theory that external power drove the wheel, we must conclude that its rotation was due to some source of power inside the wheel itself. What was that source?

The most obvious answer is that there was a man in it.† Either straddling the axis, or sitting on some form of saddle below this, he could easily have provided the power to rotate the wheel and to perform the comparatively light work (raising water by an Archimedean screw) expected of it at intervals. He could apply his weight either through some form of pedalling-gear or directly, as in a treadmill—and there would have been no difficulty in so designing this that he could rotate the wheel in either direction with equal ease.

Unfortunately, this solution creates more difficulties than it removes. It is true that the dimensions of the Weissenstein wheel—12 feet in diameter and 15–18 inches thick—would allow of a man being housed in it, although he would have been scarcely more comfortable than were prisoners in the mediæval "Cells of Little Ease", whose dimensions were so cunningly planned that there was not room either to stand, sit, or lie. But, on this assumption, what is one to make of the three earlier wheels? The Merseburg wheel was only a foot thick over all—say 10 inches

---

* All the same, I was once shown a bogus "perpetual motion" wheel (actually driven by concealed clockwork) which a competent watch-repairer took to pieces, cleaned and reassembled *without discovering the fraud*. This, however, was a wheel about one-twelfth the size of Orffyreus', and needed extremely little power to keep it moving.

† Philip Thicknesse, writing in 1785, gives a sarcastic account of a deception of this kind, exhibited in London:—

"The wheel was stated to be a pure mechanism: but a small paper of snuff put into the wheel soon convinced all round that it could not only move, but sneeze too, like a Christian."

internal clearance (for the spokes must have had some thickness, and presumably the man did not go round with the wheel). This would be an impossible housing for anybody but a dwarf or a child—and the wheel was well attested to be self-moving. The machine at Draschwitz was only 6 inches thick, and that at Gera 4 inches—in such wheels any concealed human agency would be out of the question.

Again, granting that there was a man in the Weissenstein wheel, how did he manage to exist for two months in a sealed room and yet leave no indication of his presence at the end of that time? There is no need to go into the details of such an enquiry.

But, finally, there is the testimony of the one man, apart from its maker, who ever saw the mechanism of the fourth wheel—the Landgrave of Hesse-Cassel. It is improbable that he would have countenanced a fraud from which he could derive no benefit, and whose exposure would be sure to involve him in undignified recriminations, merely to serve a man who was generally suspect and unpopular, and whom he must on this supposition have known to be a cheat. Yet here are the statements of 's Gravesande and Fischer.

('s Gravesande.)

". . . The Landgrave being himself present on my examination of this machine, I took the liberty to ask him, as he had seen the inside of it, whether, after being in motion for a certain time, no alteration was made in the component parts; or whether none of those parts might be suspected of concealing some fraud; on which His Serene Highness assured me to the contrary, and that the machine was very simple."

(Fischer.)

". . . His Highness, who is a perfect mathematician, assured me that the machine is so simple that a carpenter's boy could understand and make it after having seen the interior."

John Phin, in his *Seven Follies of Science** (an able book of the *nil admirari* kind) has suggested another solution.

"I have no doubt that this was a clear case of fraud, and that the wheel was driven by some mechanism concealed in the huge axle. As already stated Orffyreus was at one time a clock-maker; now clocks have been made to go for a whole year without having to be rewound, so that forty days was not a very long time for the apparatus to keep in motion."

Actually, the period of the test at Weissenstein was fifty-four days. That, however, although casting a shade of doubt on Phin's general accuracy, does not affect his argument. He might have made it even more

* *The Seven Follies of Science*, John Phin (New York, 1906).

striking if he had known that Jean Romilly, a Parisian watch-maker (1714–96), had produced, about 1750, a *watch* capable of going for a year with one winding. But, really, it is no argument at all.

It is perfectly true that both weight-driven and spring-driven clocks have often been made which will go for a year without re-winding. But it is equally true that the stored power has necessarily to be doled out to their mechanism in such infinitesimal doses that all the moving parts have to be kept as light and frictionless as possible; and hence such clocks are utterly incapable of doing any more work than that involved in keeping themselves going. In consequence, they are not good timekeepers. The modern spring-clocks of the kind are beneath contempt; but the twelve-month weight-driven clock made by Daniel Quare about 1700, which was for a long time at Hampton Court, near Leominster,* is a good specimen. This was examined in 1873 by Mr. H. P. Palmer, a clock-maker of Leominster, who found that the driving weight of the clock weighed 81 lb. and, with a fall of 4 feet 6 inches, had to drive the clock for 403 days. If we assume that Orffyreus' wheel weighed no more than a couple of hundredweight (which is probably a long way below the truth), such a store of power would not have kept it turning, in its bearings, for a single day at twenty-six turns a minute. In fact, I question whether, if Orffyreus had contrived to fill the whole of his immense drum with stored power in the form of weights or springs (and it must be remembered that no other ways of storing power were then known), he could, bearing in mind the great weight thus involved, have kept it turning for fifty days in 1-inch plain bearings.

Even if we grant the possibility of his having done so, there are two further objections, both of which are fatal. The power available would have been so slight that the wheel certainly could not have done work: the application of the cord connecting it with the water-raising plant would not have merely reduced its speed by a few revolutions—it would have slowed down gradually and steadily until it stopped altogether. And secondly, and for the same reason (the very slight power available), the wheel would, if it accelerated at all, have taken hours, or even days, to work up to a speed of twenty-six revolutions a minute—whereas it is attested to have actually done so, after being barely started, in a few turns.

This second objection—the very slow acceleration of the wheel if driven by clockwork—also disposes of the suggestion that it might possibly have been contrived, in some manner, to stop itself after the room was sealed and restart itself as the latter was being opened. I mention this point because I believe that some such contrivance was at the bottom of a

---

* Rather confusingly, there is another twelve-month clock, also by Quare, at Hampton Court Palace. My friend Mr. Courtenay Ilbert possesses a third specimen.

curious paragraph which appeared in the *Horological Journal* for November 1881.*

"A veteran watch-maker at Vouvry, Switzerland, claims to have invented a process (*sic*) by which watches will go for years without winding up.† A sealed box containing two watches, entrusted to the municipal authorities on the 19th of January, 1879, has just been opened, and the watches were found going.—*The Times*."

It is scarcely credible that Orffyreus could have been able to determine beforehand, within an hour or so, the exact time of either the intermediate or final openings of the sealed room; in consequence, the restarting mechanism could not have been worked by, say, a two-month clock, but must have been set in action by the actual breakage of the seals or the opening of the door. The wheel, therefore, would have had only a few seconds to accelerate from rest to its maximum speed.

In addition, there is the Landgrave's direct statement, in the certificate which he gave to Orffyreus, that the construction of the machine was not such that it required winding up.

It would almost seem, then, that we must assume the mechanism of the wheel to have been such as to enable it to tap some natural source of power —unless, indeed, we prefer to believe that Orffyreus was generations ahead of his time, and fitted his machine with an electric motor, driven by current supplied either from accumulators inside the wheel or, *via* the pivots and bearings, from some external source. With regard to the latter hypothesis, *credat Judœus Apella*—I do not propose to discuss it.

However repugnant the notion may be to modern theories of dynamics and mechanics, contemporary accounts agree in stating that the machine was moved by the force of gravity. Thus, the account given in the *Acta Eruditorum* remarks: ". . . Orffyreus did not attempt to conceal that his machine was set in motion by weights," and Fischer, as already quoted, remarks: ". . . At every turn of the wheel can be heard about eight weights, which fall gently on the side towards which the wheel turns."

There is still stronger evidence (of a kind) to this effect—Orffyreus' own statement. I say "of a kind" because, as will be seen presently, his account of his own invention is entirely inconsistent with what we know of mechanics—from which it follows that he either did not understand himself how the machine worked, or deliberately gave a wrong explanation of its action. In either event, his evidence goes for little.

---

* It was taken from *The Times* of Oct. 27, 1881. The box was probably opened on or about Oct. 15, which would make the period of the test 1000 days.

† It is, however, possible that these watches were self-winding. Such a watch, wound by the force exerted by the expansion and contraction (in heat and cold) of a small quantity of glycerine, was brought out in Switzerland about 1926.

His account, which is short and obscure, is embodied in his pamphlet of 1719, in German and Latin, whose title may be translated as follows:

"The Triumphant Orffyrean Perpetual Motion, dedicated in humble submission to all Ambassadors, High Heads, and Magistrates, and all ranks of the world. Presented for purchase and an offer projected by the Inventor Orffyreus. Printed in Cassel, October 1719, and published by the inventor himself; bound copies to be had of him at the Castle of Weissenstein."

It is a small octavo, set in rather battered type; the text, in German and Latin, appearing in parallel columns on the same page. Its style and contents certainly go far to justify the opinions of 's Gravesande and de Crousaz as to its author's mental condition.

It contains, for example, no less than four dedications occupying, in all, not much less than half the book. The first is to God, the second to the general public, the third to men of learning, and the fourth to himself. It is full of windy rhetoric, of which the following specimen, from the Introduction, will serve:

". . . When I, at last, an unworthy man, was made an instrument in God's hands to solve this long-sought-for and valuable secret, and to give a representation, proposition, and instruction on this rare invention, no longer do I doubt, nay I presume, that as the discoverer I possess it, after many years of scrupulous doubts, much calumny, and exasperation from all my enemies....."

Such account as he gives of the machine is ensconced in the Introduction. After citing and acknowledging the various benefits which he has received from the Landgrave of Hesse-Cassel, he continues:

". . . In gratitude for all these gracious acts, I consented to make another example of my Perpetuum Mobile machine. I put all in fresh order, and began work in all possible haste, doing everything in the manner of those I had already made and destroyed, with only a few changes in the dimensions of the so-called turning-wheel. For as a grindstone may be called a wheel, so may the principal part of my machine be named.

"The outward part of this machine is drawn over, or covered, with waxed linen, and is in the form of a drum. This cylindrical basis is 12 Rhenish feet in diameter, the thickness from 15 to 18 inches, the middle axis 6 feet long and 8 inches in thickness. It is supported in its movement on two pointed steel pivots, each 1 inch thick; and the wheel stands vertical. The movement is controlled by two pendulums, as shown in the engraving at the end of this book.*

"The internal structure of the machine is of a nature according to the

*See Plate III.

laws of mechanical perpetual motion, so arranged that certain disposed weights, once in rotation, gain force from their own swinging, and must continue this movement as long as their structure does not lose its position and arrangement.

"Unlike all other automata, such as clocks or springs, or other hanging weights which require winding up, or whose duration depends on the chain which attaches them, these weights, on the contrary, are the essential parts, and constitute the perpetual motion itself; since from them is received the universal movement which they must exercise so long as they remain out of the centre of gravity; and when they come to be placed together, and so arranged one against another that they can never obtain equilibrium, or the *punctum quietus* which they unceasingly seek in their wonderfully speedy flight, one or other of them must apply its weight at right angles to the axis, which in its turn must also move."

It must be confessed that if it were not for the attested performance of the wheel which Orffyreus thus describes, one would be tempted, at this point, to shut his book gently but firmly, and to clothe one's self with cursing, as with a garment,* at having wasted time in reading it. For by his account his mechanism was nothing more than a form of the "over-balancing wheel"—a hoary fallacy as old as the hills and as exploded as the Gunpowder Plot.

The idea (one cannot dignify it with the title "theory") of the over-balancing wheel has been (strange to say) well expressed by the Marquess of Worcester in his *Century of Inventions*,† as follows:

"56. To provide and make that all the Weights of the descending side of a Wheel shall be perpetually farther from the Centre, than those of the mounting side, and yet equal in number and heft to the one side as the other. A most incredible thing, if not seen. . . ."

In the history of "perpetual motion", nothing is more remarkable than the persistency with which this idea has been stumbled upon, over and over again, by inventor after inventor. Hundreds of these have wasted their time, money, and patience in the full persuasion that such an arrangement of weights has never been produced; but that, if it could be evolved, it would infallibly give perpetual motion.

Neither of these ideas is sound. The thing has been done over and over again—Worcester, in the same section of his book, asserts that he himself accomplished it, and there is no reason to doubt his statement. There are

---

* ". . . He clothed himself with cursing like as with his garment" (Ps. cix. 18). Theodore Hook's explanation of this remarkable phrase was, that the person referred to had a habit of swearing.

† "*A Century of the Names and Scantlings of such Inventions as at present I can call to mind to have tried and perfected. . . .*" (London, J. Grismond, 1663).

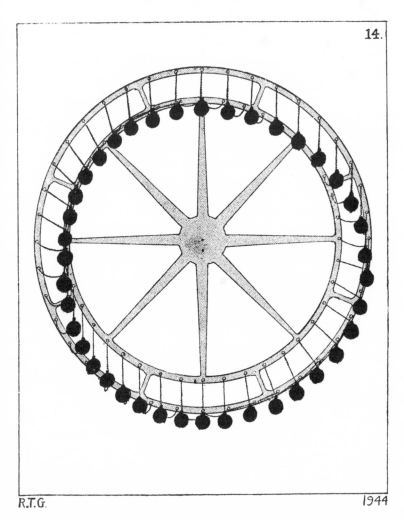

14.

R.T.G.   1944

FIG. 14.—An "overbalancing wheel", designed by H. Dircks, C.E., as a re-
construction of the Marquis of Worcester's wheel, in which the weights
on one side were always a foot farther from the centre than those on the
other.

The wheel has no tendency to rotate. It will be noted that two weights
are vertically in line with the centre of the wheel, and that of the remainder 20 on the left side, nearer the centre, counterbalance 18, farther
from the centre, on the right,

many ways of performing the feat (two are shown in Figs. 14 and 15, both invented by Dircks, author of the only work in English on "perpetual motion"),* but none of them brings us any nearer achieving "perpetual motion".

Consider the case of the common letter-balance; not the "bent-lever" form, but the older kind like a pair of scales. On one side is a small pan for the weights—on the other a large flat plate for the letter to be weighed. It makes no difference whereabouts on that plate you lay the letter—it may be as close as possible to the fulcrum, or almost falling off at the far-side of the plate. The same weight in the pan will counterbalance it, wherever it is.

That is because the "parallel-bar" arrangement of the links of the balance compels one scale to sink exactly as far as the other rises. It is true that the centre of gravity of the combined weights may be to one side of the fulcrum; but owing to the link-motion its position remains unaltered by any tilting of the beam. There is, therefore, no reason for the latter to tip.

So it is with the "overbalancing wheel". Even if its mechanism does what it sets out to do—even if it keeps all the weights on one side of the wheel farther from the centre than those on the other side—the wheel has no tendency to turn. Most of such wheels, however, are as defective in design as in theory; there is not one in a hundred which really keeps the preponderance of weight on one side of the centre throughout a complete revolution.

Was Orffyreus honestly deceived when he wrote down such an incorrect description (for so we must regard it)† of his own mechanism? The thing is unlikely—but it is possible, as a later case has sufficiently shown.

Towards the end of the last War, public attention in the United States became focused, for a short time, upon an inventor bearing the perfectly incredible name of Giragossian. He appears to have been an honest but misguided man. He had evolved a project for obtaining what he called "free power", and which proved, in reality, to be a "perpetual motion" fallacy of an interesting kind. It attracted more attention than most, partly because of its novelty and partly because its inventor considered it to be of

* *Perpetuum Mobile, or Search for Self-Motive Power.* Henry Dircks, C.E. London, 1861 (second series, 1870). There is a German work of the same name by A. Daul (Leipzig, 1900).

† The supposition that the wheel was kept going by external power does not, of course, exclude the possibility that it also contained "overbalancing" mechanism. If well made, this would *waste* very little power, though it could not generate any: and it would certainly impress an amateur mechanic like the Landgrave—the only man who ever saw it.

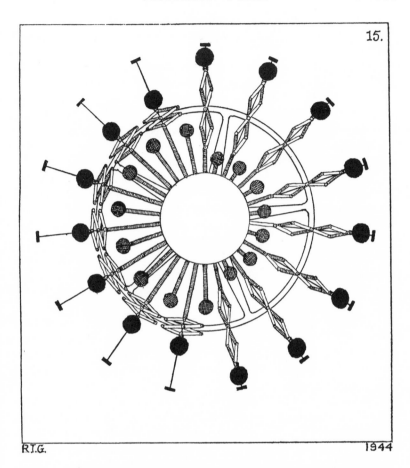

RT.G.   1944

FIG. 15.—Another "overbalancing wheel", also designed by Henry Dircks, C.E., to show the fallacy of all such constructions.

The weight of each smaller ball and its attached rod slightly exceeds that of the larger ball; in consequence, it extends or contracts the lazy-tongs when the rod is vertical (in other positions the rod is prevented from sliding by stops inside the hub).

In spite of the fact that the larger balls on one side of the wheel are much farther from the centre than those on the other, the wheel has no tendency to rotate.

such far-reaching importance that it could scarcely be secured from piracy by an ordinary patent. An attempt was therefore made to attain this end by means of a special Act of Congress.

It may be noted that the U.S. Patent Office does not follow the precedent set by the French Académie des Sciences in 1775 when that body passed its celebrated resolution declaring, *inter alia*, that it would not consider, in future, "any machine announced as showing perpetual motion". But it sometimes has recourse to its legal right of requiring the patentee of such a machine to deposit a *working model* of his invention. Its Museum, I believe, has not yet acquired a model of this kind.

A committee appointed to examine the Giragossian machine had little difficulty in classifying it. Broadly speaking, its operation was as follows:

A very large and heavy flywheel was set in motion, and gradually accelerated, by means of a very small electric motor of (say) one-quarter horse-power. The process of "speeding-up" the flywheel may have taken a fortnight. The motor was then disconnected, and the flywheel brought to rest by the application of a brake. A horse-power test made during the stopping process indicated that the flywheel was then developing several hundred horse-power. It was pointed out that the original source of this power was a one-quarter horse-power motor; and it was claimed that, since the accepted horse-power formula takes account of time, there could be no doubt that "free power" had been generated to the amount of the difference between the horse-power required to spin the wheel and that needed to stop it.

A simple analogy will prove the fallacy of this reasoning. If the electric motor had been made to pump water into a reservoir for the same length of time, and the whole contents of the reservoir then run through a suitable turbine in the time taken to stop the flywheel, the horse-power developed by the turbine would probably have been much the same as that exerted at the brake around the flywheel. The parallel would have been complete; and the fact would have become obvious that, neglecting the inevitable losses by friction, etc., the power stored by the motor was equal to that given out by the turbine, the only difference being that the power was given out much faster than it had been stored. In the same way a man earning two hundred a year might, say, save half of this for two years and then dissolve the proceeds in the course of a very pleasant week in Paris, or even nearer home. During that hectic period he would certainly be spending at the rate of something over ten thousand a year; but if he had any lucid intervals he would surely not delude himself into thinking that he had permanently raised his salary to that figure.

All that Mr. Giragossian had really done was to evolve a form of leverage depending on time instead of space. Yet I have no doubt that he believed (and, for all I know, still believes) that his machine was capable of creating power.

In view of this case, it is not to be denied that Orffyreus may have been misled as to the action of his machine. It worked—so, in its way, did Giragossian's. Its results may have been equally fallacious. But the puzzle of its actual mechanism remains unsolved.

In one minor point Orffyreus certainly showed great ingenuity. That is, the arrangement of pendulums by which he controlled his machine. Incidentally, nearly all of the writers who have attempted to describe his wheel have omitted all mention of these pendulums—although the latter explain several obscure points in connection with the whole story.

Judging by the engraving in his book (Plate III) they were connected by links to two opposed cranks on the axle of the wheel, their effects being thus balanced, so that they did not, in any position, oppose the rotation of the wheel, even when it was being started from rest. They appear to have been about 11 feet long, and would therefore have had a period, if they were simple pendulums, of some 1·8 seconds, corresponding to a wheel-speed of roughly thirty-three revolutions per minute. But, as shown, they were not simple pendulums by any means, since they had three "bobs", two being at their upper ends. In consequence, their period would have been lengthened, and might easily have coincided with a wheel-speed of twenty-six turns a minute, which was that observed by 's Gravesande and Fischer. It would have been difficult to use an escapement to control the wheel, and these pendulums probably formed a very efficient substitute —although a fan, one thinks, would probably have been better.

It will be noticed that I am assuming that the wheel possessed inherent power of rotation sufficient to require some form of control. I regard this as strongly suggested by the evidence—although I can offer no indication of its real source.

It is certain that power cannot be generated by any form of "over-balancing wheel". It is almost certain that it cannot be generated by any mechanical means whatsoever. I qualify this second statement, because of what was once written on the point by a man well equipped to judge.

Sir George Airy was one of the most outstanding scientific figures of the past century. He was, to begin with, a Senior Wrangler and Smith's Prizeman—and, contrary to the prevailing impression, these distinctions did not handicap him in after-life. He was subsequently Director of the Cambridge Observatory for eight years, and Astronomer Royal for forty-six. He was a first-class mathematican and a clear-headed thinker, with a pronounced bent for original investigation.

In 1830 he published, in the *Cambridge Philosophical Transactions*, a paper with the somewhat surprising title "On Certain Conditions under which a Perpetual Motion is Possible". It is very short—and, by omitting most of the mathematics, can be condensed still further. It opens as follows:

"It is well known that Perpetual Motion is not possible with any laws of force with which we are acquainted. The impossibility depends on the integrability *per se* of the expression $Xdx + Ydy + Zdz$: and as in all the forces of which we have an accurate knowledge this expression is a complete differential, it follows that perpetual motion is incompatible with these forces."

(I may point out that the second sentence above is a statement, in mathematical language, of the fact that the hypothesis of the Conservation of Energy holds for any three-dimensional field of force—i.e. for our space as we know it.)

"But it is here supposed that, the law of the force being given, the magnitude of the force acting at any instant depends on the position, at that instant, of the body on which it acts. If, however, the magnitude of the force should depend not on the position of the body at the instant of the force's action, but on its position at some time preceding that action, the theorem that we have stated would no longer be true. It might happen that, every time that the body returned to the same position, its velocity would be less than at the preceding time: in this case the body's motion would ultimately be destroyed. On the contrary it might happen that the body's velocity in any position would be more rapid every time than at the time previous. In this case the velocity would go on perpetually increasing: or the velocity might be made uniform if the machine were retarded by some constantly acting resistance: or in other words, the machine might move with uniform velocity, and might at the same time *do work*, which is commonly understood to be the meaning of the term *perpetual motion*. If the machine had no work to do, the increasing friction, etc., would operate as an increasing work, and the velocity would be accelerated till the acceleration caused by the forces was equal to the retardation caused by the friction; after which it would remain unaltered.

"For this idea I am indebted to the admirable account of the organs of voice given by Mr. Willis. The phenomenon to be explained was this.

"When two plates are inclined at an angle greater than a certain angle, it is found that the effect of a current of air passing between them is to give a tendency to open wider. When they are inclined at any angle smaller than that certain angle, the effect of the current is to make them collapse. If, then, the plates be supposed to vibrate through the position corresponding to that angle, the tendency of the forces is at all times to bring them to that position. Each plate is in the state of a vibrating pendulum: and whatever be the law of force which acts upon it, it is certain that if the force be the same when the plate is in the same position, this force will have no tendency to increase the velocity. The retardation arising from friction, etc., will, therefore, soon destroy the motion.

"But it is found, in fact, that the motion is not destroyed. What, then, is the accelerating force which keeps up the motion?

"Mr. Willis explains this by supposing that *time* is necessary for the air to assume the state and exert the force corresponding to any position of the plate: which is nearly the same as saying that the force depends on the position of the plate at some previous time. In this paper, which is intended to investigate the mathematical consequences of an assumed law, I shall not discuss the identity of these suppositions: I shall only remark that the general explanation appears to be correct, and that it clears up several points which have always appeared to be in great obscurity."

And this he proceeds to do, mathematically, with a profusion of symbols a little alarming to the casual reader. He concludes by modestly remarking:

"My object is gained if I have called the attention of the Society to a law hitherto (I believe) unnoticed, but not unfruitful in practical applications."

Like many another paper read before a "learned Society", this of Airy's was printed—and forgotten. For his own sake—for the sake of his peace of mind and reputation—this was probably as well. If it had become widely known, it would at once have been seized upon by the perpetual-motion cranks—who, as is their cheerful custom, would probably have paraded the authority while deriding the author. I can find no record of Airy having altered his views on the subject; but he did not recur to it in any of his later writings.

There are one or two phrases in his paper curiously reminiscent of those used by Orffyreus . . . and I return to that singular man. Was he charlatan, or monomaniac—or both? Did he deliberately carry out, through many years, a campaign of imposture which gained him no money, no repose, no reputation—nothing but enmity and obloquy? He may have done so. There are some perverted minds that will endure much to gain even an evil reputation. Many an old crone in a country village has found solace for her declining years in hugging the thought that her neighbours, while openly deriding her, secretly dread her powers of witchcraft—many such have deliberately encouraged this impression. Orffyreus may have done the same.

Or was he only a harmless crank, pursuing a mechanical *ignis fatuus* with an intensity which produced, or was itself produced by, monomania? Did he fall at odds with the world because he thought its concerns trivial by comparison with his own—a feeling heartily reciprocated? If his labours were systematic and prolonged—if he consecrated his life to the attainment of a single object—did he, really, win some reward? And was that reward the secret of a genuine discovery which perished with him, or only that of a most marvellous deception? Did he deceive others, or only himself—or neither?

Still offering an unsolved problem, he passes from our sight, an exasperating and yet pathetic figure—morose, self-centred, childishly passionate, vacillating and yet tenacious, his own worst enemy, forgetting the duties of ordinary human intercourse in his passion for mechanism and wrecking his life as the result. *Non deficit alter.*

VI

CROSSE'S ACARI

Until 1836 the English public had never heard of Andrew Crosse. A small circle of friends knew that he lived at a rather dilapidated country-seat in the Quantock Hills, where he spent his time, and what money an encumbered estate allowed him, in electrical experiments. His rustic neighbours spoke of him as "the thunder and lightning man", and shunned his house like the plague, especially after nightfall, it being the subject of a legend that devils, surrounded by lightning, were then to be seen dancing upon wires encircling its grounds.

By the end of 1837 he was reviled from one end of England to the other. He was an atheist, a blasphemer, "a reviler of our holy religion", "a disturber of the peace of families", a modern Prometheus, a would-be Frankenstein, a man who had presumptuously attempted to rival the God that made him—and many other of those flowers of speech which generally spread themselves about like leaves in Vallombrosa during the progress of religious or quasi-religious controversies.

Who was this dreadful person, and what had he done?

He was a simple, honest, and God-fearing man, belonging to a class very common in the last century but increasingly rare in this. In other words, he was a scientific amateur, having the time and money for prolonged experimental work, but gravely handicapped by lack of scientific training and by an almost complete ignorance of the work of other men in the same field.

His offence—which, incidentally, he had not committed—was of an unusual kind. He was accused of having attempted to create living creatures, by an electrical process, from dead matter. Indeed, it was further laid to his account that he had succeeded in doing so—that he had evolved, in poisonous solutions fatal to all normal animal life, numbers of insects of the species *Acarus* (mites), which insects lived, moved, and bred.

Actually, he had done this. But he had not done it designedly, and whether what he had done was, in effect, an artificial production of life, re-mained and remains an open question, which he did not attempt to answer.

Here are his own words on the subject:*

"As to the appearance of the acari under long-continued electrical action, I have never in thought, word, or deed, given any one a right to suppose that I considered them as a creation, or even as a formation,

---

* In a letter, dated 12.8.1849, to Harriet Martineau.

117

from inorganic matter. To create is to form a something out of nothing. To annihilate, is to reduce that something to a nothing. Both of these, of course, can only be the attributes of the Almighty.

"In fact, I assure you most sacredly that I have never dreamed of any theory sufficient to account for their appearance. I confess that I was not a little surprised, and am so still, and quite as much as I was when the acari first made their appearance. Again, I have never claimed any merit as attaching to these experiments. It was a matter of chance. I was looking for silicious formations, and acari appeared instead. . . ."

The obloquy so freely showered upon Crosse left him unmoved: knowing it to be undeserved, he could afford to despise it.* It affected neither his life nor his temper. But it had one definitely evil effect—the natural result of all such persecutions. It prevented Crosse from publishing, or even communicating, his further work on the same subject. Extensive though that work was, very little record of it, or of the original experiments, has survived—and in consequence it is not easy to put together a clear account of what Crosse did and what he observed.

However, two short papers written by Crosse in 1837 are extant: one in the *Transactions of the London Electrical Society* (for 1838) and the other in the *Annals of Electricity* (Oct. 1836–Oct. 1837). In addition, his wife's *Memorials of Andrew Crosse* (1857) reproduced the substance of the former paper, together with a letter written by Crosse to Harriet Martineau for publication in her *History of the Thirty Years' Peace* (1849). The following account is compiled from these sources.

In the year 1837 Crosse was making certain experiments upon the artificial formation of crystals by means of weak and long-continued electric currents. The acari first appeared in the course of an attempt to make crystals of silica by allowing a suitable fluid medium to seep through a piece of porous stone (oxide of iron, from Vesuvius) kept electrified by means of a battery. The fluid used was a mixture of hydrochloric acid and a solution of silicate of potash.

"On the fourteenth day from the commencement of this experiment I observed through a lens a few small whitish excrescences or nipples, projecting from about the middle of the electrified stone. On the eighteenth day these projections enlarged, and struck out seven or eight filaments, each of them longer than the hemisphere on which they grew.

"On the twenty-sixth day these appearances assumed the form of a *perfect insect*, standing erect on a few bristles which formed its tail. Till

---

* I have only found him complaining once. In a letter to Dr. Noad (whose *Lectures on Electricity*, published in 1849, contain a short account of Crosse's work), he says: ". . . (I) met with so much virulence and abuse . . . in consequence of the experiments, that it seemed as if it were a crime to have made them".

this period I had no notion that these appearances were other than an incipient mineral formation. On the twenty-eighth day these little creatures moved their legs. I must now say that I was not a little astonished. After a few days they detached themselves from the stone, and moved about at pleasure.

"In the course of a few weeks about a hundred of them made their appearance on the stone. I examined them with a microscope, and observed that the smaller ones appeared to have only six legs, the larger

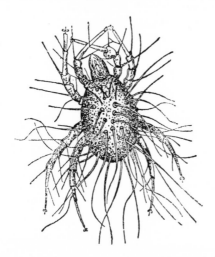

FIG. 15A.—The *Acarus electricus*. From a drawing in H. M. Noad's *Lectures on Electricity* (London, 1849).

NOTE.—The exact scale of the drawing, here reproduced in facsimile, is not stated. It probably represents a magnification of 100-150.

ones eight. These insects are pronounced to be of the genus *acarus*, but there appears to be a difference of opinion as to whether they are a known species; some assert that they are not.*

"I have never ventured an opinion on the cause of their birth, and for a very good reason—I was unable to form one. The simplest solution of the problem which occurred to me was that they arose from ova deposited by insects floating in the atmosphere and hatched by electric action. Still I could not imagine that an ovum could shoot out filaments, or that these filaments could become bristles, and moreover I could not detect, on the closest examination, the remains of a shell. . . .

"I next imagined, as others have done, that they might originate from the water, and consequently made a close examination of numbers of

* See Fig. 15A.

vessels filled with the same fluid: in none of these could I perceive a trace of an insect, nor could I see any in any other part of the room."

In subsequent experiments Crosse discarded the porous electrified stone, and for the most part produced the acari in glass cylinders filled with concentrated solutions of such substances as copper nitrate, copper sulphate, and zinc sulphate. The acari generally made their appearance at the edge of the fluid surface, but he remarks:

"In some cases these insects appear two inches *under* the electrified fluid, but after emerging from it they were destroyed if thrown back."

In one case the acari appeared on the lower part of a small piece of quartz, immersed to the depth of two inches in fluoric acid holding silica in solution.*

"A current of electricity was passed through this fluid for a twelvemonth or more; and at the end of some months three of these acari were visible on the piece of quartz, which was kept negatively electrified. I have closely examined the progress of these insects.

"Their first appearance consists in a very minute whitish hemisphere, formed upon the surface of the electrified body, sometimes at the positive end, and sometimes at the negative, and occasionally between the two, or in the middle of the electrified current; and sometimes upon all. In a few days this speck enlarges and elongates vertically, and shoots out filaments of a whitish wavy appearance, and easily seen through a lens of very low power.

"Then commences the first appearance of animal life. If a fine point be made to approach these filaments, they immediately shrink up and collapse like zoophytes upon moss, but expand again some time after the removal of the point. Some days afterwards these filaments become legs and bristles, and a perfect acarus is the result, which finally detaches itself from its birthplace, and if under a fluid, climbs up the electrified wire and escapes from the vessel. . . .

"If one of them be afterwards thrown into the fluid in which he was produced, he is immediately drowned. . . . I have never before heard of acari having been produced under a fluid, or of their ova throwing out filaments; nor have I ever observed any ova previous to or during electrization, except that the speck which throws out filaments be an ovum; but when a number of these insects, in a perfect state, congregate, ova are produced."

The acari thus produced lived, generally, until the first frost, which was invariably fatal to them.

In a later experiment, Crosse succeeded in producing an acarus in a closed and airtight glass retort filled with an electrified solution, one wire

* H_2SiF_6.

being led in through the wall of the retort and the other through a cup of mercury at its beak. The solution was a silicate one, prepared as for the first experiment, and was put in hot. On connecting up the battery:

"An electric action commenced; oxygen and hydrogen gases were liberated; the volume of atmospheric air was soon expelled. Every care had been taken to avoid atmospheric contact and admittance of extraneous matter, and the retort itself had previously been washed with hot alcohol. This apparatus was placed in a dark cellar.

"I discovered no sign of incipient animal formation until on the 140th day, when I plainly distinguished *one* acarus actively crawling about *within* the bulb of the retort.

"I found that I had made a great error in this experiment; and I believe it was in consequence of this error that I not only lost sight of the single insect, but never saw any others in this apparatus. I had omitted to insert within the bulb of the retort a *resting-place* for these acari (they are always destroyed if they fall back into the fluid from which they have emerged). It is strange that, in a solution *eminently caustic* and under an atmosphere of *oxihydrogen gas*, one single acarus should have made its appearance."

Crosse also succeeded in producing acari in "an atmosphere strongly impregnated with chlorine"; but while these assumed the form of perfect insects, and remained undecomposed until the apparatus was taken apart over two years later, they never moved or showed any signs of life.

His experiments were repeated and extended by another enthusiastic amateur, Weeks of Sandwich, who took a number of precautions to ensure, as far as possible, that no animal life was already present at the start of the experiments. For example, he baked his apparatus in an oven, used distilled water, filled his receivers (inverted over mercury troughs) with manufactured oxygen instead of air, and super-heated his silicate solutions. After about a year and a half of electrification, acari invariably made their appearance. Control experiments, made in exactly the same manner and with the same apparatus, but omitting the electric current, gave uniformly negative results—no acari appeared. He also made quantitative experiments, and found that the number of acari electrically produced varied, roughly, with the percentage of carbon in his solutions.

Weeks's experiments, although most intelligently conducted, seem to have attracted little attention. He communicated a summary of his results to the Electrical Society, but does not appear to have published a complete account of them. In view of the precautions which he took, it is interesting to note that at the height of the Crosse furore (1837) no less an authority than Faraday stated, in a paper read at the Royal Institution, that similar appearances had presented themselves in the course of his own electrical experiments, but that he was doubtful whether they should be regarded as a case of production or revivification.

Should anyone in Tennessee or elsewhere be brave enough, in the face Crosse's experience, to repeat his experiments, it may be useful to record here a caution noted by Crosse himself.

". . . I must remark, that in the course of these and other experiments, there is considerable similitude between the first stages of the birth of acari and of certain mineral crystallizations electrically produced. In many of them, more especially in the formation of sulphate of lime, or sulphate of strontia, its commencement is denoted by a whitish speck: so it is in the birth of the acarus. This mineral speck enlarges and elongates vertically: so it does with the acarus. Then the mineral throws out whitish filaments: so does the acarus speck.

"So far it is difficult to detect the difference between the incipient mineral and the animal; but as these filaments become more definite in each, in the mineral they become rigid, shining, transparent six-sided prisms; in the animal they are soft and waving filaments, and finally endowed with motion and life."

If the foregoing passage were all that we knew of Crosse's work, it might be permissible to suppose that he had simply been misled by appearances. It is quite possible to "grow" artificial forms, from dead matter, which simulate living bodies in a positively uncanny way. Artificial "plants", for example, can be grown (in certain solutions) which, although formed by a purely mechanical process—osmosis—have every appearance of life, and can even imitate the properties and movements of organic cells. The "osmotic growths" produced by Dr. Stéphane Leduc of Nantes not only present the cellular structure of living matter, but reproduce such functions as the absorption of food, metabolism, and the excretion of waste products.

In spite of the precautions taken by Crosse and Weeks, it is, of course, impossible to disprove the assertion that their acari were hatched in the course of their experiments, having found their way into the apparatus as ova—the same cry of "faulty technique" that has been raised (in my submission with more force) against such experimenters as Bastian. Like Crosse, I offer no opinion.

Andrew Crosse died in the room in which he was born on July 6, 1855. He was seventy-one. For many years he had lived the life of a recluse in his Quantock eyrie, shut off from society, but happy in his marriage and his work. He died as he had lived, an honest man who would make no concession of any kind to popular clamour, but sought truth wherever he might find it. Such men are the true salt of the earth.

POSTSCRIPT

An authority upon acari, Dr. A. C. Oudemans of Arnhem, informed me in 1934 that, in his opinion, Crosse's were quite certainly the common *Glycophagus domesticus*, which is very tenacious of life and capable of getting into tins which appear to be hermetically sealed.

I hardly felt competent to argue the matter, at the time; but I have since come to the conclusion that this hypothesis, while very plausible, does not go quite far enough to cover all the reported facts.

VII

THE AURORAS, AND OTHER DOUBTFUL ISLANDS

At the beginning of last century the existence of the three Aurora islands, lying to the south-eastward of the Falklands, was as little doubted as that of Australia. Originally discovered by the *Aurora* in 1762, they were reported again by the *Princess*, Captain Manuel de Oyarvido, in 1790, and by other vessels at various dates, while in 1794 the Spanish surveying-vessel *Atrevida* surveyed and charted (so she imagined) all three islands, as well as determining their position by astronomical observations. Lying in the track of sailing vessels bound round Cape Horn, they were, of course, much too important to omit from even small-scale charts; consequently every chart-maker who valued his reputation and his sales proceeded to embellish his charts of the South Atlantic with a "new and correct delineation" of the group, frequently adding the track of the *Atrevida* in their vicinity—presumably as "corroborative detail" in the Pooh-Bah style, although that vessel's narrative was neither bald nor unconvincing.

But while the cruise of the *Atrevida* certainly contributed to human knowledge, that contribution was not an exact survey of some newly-discovered islands, but a very striking illustration of a previously unsuspected fact; namely, that even surveyors are human, and sometimes capable of giving

> . . . to the airy nothing
> A local habitation and a name.

It is a known fact that the Auroras do not exist; and it seems to be perfectly well-established that they never did exist.

Their case is not unique. Similar non-existent islands have often been reported, in all good faith, both before their time and since—although no others have successfully survived the ordeal of examination by a properly equipped surveying-vessel. They were not the first of their kind—and in all human probability they will not be the last. Until we know considerably more about the geography of our planet than we do now, there will always be "doubtful islands", distinguished on the Admiralty charts by the sceptical affix "E.D." ("existence doubtful") or "P.D." ("position doubtful").

It may seem curious, in these days of over-civilization, that we should still be in this state of uncertainty. But, in sober fact, we still know much less about the "round world" than is generally supposed, and a small departure from the beaten track may still, in certain parts of the great oceans, and even nearer home, transform the ordinary mariner into a discoverer. An excellent example of this neglected truth is the case of the Belcher Islands in Hudson Bay.* Hudson Bay has been known and traversed ever since 1610, and that famous, if somewhat retiring, corporation the Hudson Bay Company has maintained trading-posts on its shores for centuries past; yet in quite recent times (1915) a group of unknown islands was discovered within the Bay (or rather, inland sea) itself, and almost within sight of land. They are quite large islands—several are more than seventy miles long—and they have a total area of about five thousand square miles.

Strictly speaking, they were not absolutely a new discovery. Old charts showed, in their vicinity, one or two little clusters of tiny islets, proving that in times gone by some vessel or vessels had sighted them; but their actual size, extent, and position had remained unknown and unguessed at. Obviously, they are not of recent formation; they merely happen to lie off the ordinary trade-route of vessels navigating the Bay, and in a region which, until 1915, had never been properly examined.

In the early days of cartography—say until the beginning of the seventeenth century—it was not much more than an even chance that any particular island shown on a chart had any real existence. It was just as likely to have come there direct from the draughtsman's imagination; or through a misreading or miscompilation of old and irreconcilable authorities; or as a compliment to a patron of either sex; or in consequence of some political exigency. If it did exist, the only real information which the chart afforded concerning it was that its topography and position quite certainly differed in a very marked degree from their representation on the paper. Yet some of the non-existent islands, especially if they were charted in unfrequented parts of the ocean, held their place on the charts for what seems an amazing length of time; their vitality is as remarkable as the longevity of the invalid, now recognized by most medical men. Such, for example, was the island of Hy Brasil, the mythical island supposed to be visible in the sunset from a wide range of places on the West Coast of Ireland. *Ichabod!* Its charted position (in so far as it can be said to have had any accepted position on the charts) is now occupied by a shoal with the comparatively prosaic name of "Porcupine Bank".

St. Brandan's Isle, too, was long charted as the westernmost of the Azores; while Mayda, another mythical island which was probably a distorted version of Bermuda, and was long a source of puzzlement to

* See Fig. 13.

cartographers in general, turned up smilingly, in the middle of the Bay of Biscay, on a map published at Chicago as recently as 1906.

Between these entirely mythical islands and the "doubtful" islands of the Admiralty charts, brief mention may be made of another class of island, apparently created for the sole purpose of irritating the map-maker; who may justly observe, with Fuseli the painter, that "Nature is always putting me in the wrong". These are the islands which appear and disappear, generally as the result of volcanic disturbances. Actual "floating islands" the cartographer severely, and justly, neglects. The best-known specimens, such as those in Lake Orion and the famous island in Derwentwater, can never form a menace to shipping, and may safely be left to the care of the Ordnance Survey and similar bodies; although it is worth noting that the Derwentwater island, which usually, but not always, comes up for a few weeks in summer (always in the same place)* and then sinks again, was surveyed in 1887 by no less distinguished a cartographer than the late Admiral W. J. L. Wharton, then and for seventeen years afterwards Hydrographer of the Navy. A remarkable feature of this little island, as of the similar specimens in L. Ilfung (Latvia) and L. Victoria (Australia) is that when above water it rises and falls with the level of the lake, as though it were a raft. The flotation is due to the temporary trapping of marsh-gas in the layer of peat composing the bulk of the island. When "up", it is perfectly firm: on one occasion the Keswick town band landed on it and gave a concert—and even then it didn't sink.

At sea, the mariner is almost as likely to fall in with a sea-serpent as with a floating island; practically the only hunting-ground for such phenomena is the Indian Ocean, where small islets formed of decayed vegetation, and sometimes bearing young trees, are occasionally blown out to sea at the changing of the monsoon. If we class some of the enormous Antarctic icebergs as islands, of course, the case is altered; and certainly, in dimensions, some of them could give points to many real islands. For example, an L-shaped berg sixty by forty miles in length was seen in the South Atlantic in 1865 and 1866, and one unfortunate vessel which got embayed between the two arms of the L was wrecked and destroyed on its shore quite as rapidly and efficiently as if she had blundered against Ushant in a fog. Even this is not a record (or, as *The Times* used to print it, a "record") for size, for in 1927 a Norwegian whaler, the *Odd I*, sighted off the South Shetland Islands an ice-island about a hundred miles long and wide, thus covering some 10,000 square miles.

But while floating islands are outside the purview of the cartographer, those irritating volcanic islands which periodically appear and disappear

* In 1877 this site was sounded-out (the island being then submerged), and its position accurately determined, by Sir George Airy, Astronomer Royal.

are not; and there have been many such cases. Falcon Island, near the
Tonga group, is a good example of the class (it was "doing its stuff" quite
recently), and there have been one or two instances nearer home.

For example, in the year 1831 an islet emitting smoke and fire
appeared, like Venus Anadyomene, some miles off the south-west coast of
Sicily and rose gradually to the height of over a hundred feet above sea-
level, with a diameter of about half a mile. At the end of the year, however, it found itself unable to support the honour of having been named
"Graham Island",* after Sir James Graham ("Peel's dirty boy"), then
First Lord of the Admiralty. In consequence, it modestly effaced itself,
sinking back towards the bed of the Mediterranean, and has ever since
remained covered by several fathoms of water. It is, however, quite
possible that one day it will emerge again, and change its name a second
time from "Graham Shoal" to "Graham Island". The Italian Government is taking no chances in the matter; the position of the shoal was
carefully surveyed in 1926, and several slight changes of depth noted.

As the island lies reasonably near the route between Tunis and Milan,
I have a private suspicion that it once was inhabited by Caliban, and that it
owes its mysterious activity to the still-potent influence of Prospero's
spells—perhaps his book may lie there. I commend this theory to students
of Shakespeare; but on account of its extreme improbability it may perhaps
find more favour in the eyes of those earnest people whom the late Sir
Edward Sullivan so aptly dubbed "Verulamaniacs".

Apart from this, the island is not without literary associations. Sir
Walter Scott landed on it from H.M.S. *Barham* (20-XI-1831) in the
course of that last, tragic voyage, in vain search of physical and mental
health, from Portsmouth to Naples. And readers of Jules Verne will
remember that a treasure deposited on it by an exiled Pasha forms the
central feature of his novel *Captain Antifer*. Like all, or nearly all, Verne's
works, the book is put together with wonderful skill; although the
ordinary cartographer cannot but rub his eyes when he comes to the
passage where Antifer's gifted son-in-law, having as his only data the
positions of three other islands forming a triangle with sides several
thousand miles in length, succeeds in determining the location of the
(sunken) treasure-island by means of a direct geometrical construction
performed on a twelve-inch globe.

The subsidence of another volcanic islet, off the south-west corner of
Iceland, was the cause of the extinction of a very famous bird—the Great
Auk. The last colony of these rare birds had made a secure aukery on a
rock, named after them the "Geirfuglaskeir" (Garefowls Rock), about

* It was also known, during its short lifetime, as "Julia Island" and Ferdinandea
Island".

fifteen miles from the land. The rock was precipitous—in fact, practically inaccessible to man. Here they bred in security. It might have been said of the Geirfuglaskeir, as it was once said of Beachy Head:*

> Here the Great Auk, a bird with hairy legs,
> Arrives in early Spring, and lays its eggs.

But Nature herself seems to have been in·league with Man against these doomed birds, and (as was so feelingly related to Tom by the Last of the Gare-fowl†) the Geirfuglaskeir, shaken by a volcanic convulsion, sank in 1830, compelling them to remove to another islet named Eldey, nearer the coast and far more accessible. Here, in obedience to that law of (museum) supply and demand which enacts that the rarer a species becomes the more rapidly it shall be exterminated, their numbers were rapidly depleted by the hardy Icelanders, who dared not only the perils of a six-mile voyage, but also the grave risk of getting quite a sharp nip in the slack of their trousers before they could safely knock their formidable quarry on the head. Rabbit-shooting itself could scarcely offer more thrills and dangers. It was on Eldey, in 1844, that the last known pair of Great Auks‡ were murdered by two heroes named Jón Brandsson and Siguror Islefsson, both natives of Iceland. It is permissible to hope that by now they are experiencing a much hotter climate.

But the "doubtful islands" of the Admiralty and other modern charts are neither floating nor, in general, actively volcanic. They are situated chiefly in the South Atlantic and South Pacific Oceans, and most of them lie on the fringes of the Antarctic regions proper. It is a singular fact that we know much more about a considerable part of the Antarctic than we do about such islands, although they lie much farther northward. There used, it is true, to be charted off the coast of Victoria Land, in the far South, an island actually named "Doubtful Island" by Sir James Ross, its discoverer; since, as he said, it was quite impossible, at his nearest approach, to tell whether it was an island or an iceberg. But it is now known to have been the latter—and, in consequence, it is no longer shown on the charts.

Actually, a similar fate has also overtaken one or two of the islands whose stories ". . . as you have not heard, I shall now proceed to relate". In fact, the specimens here exhibited may be divided into three classes— never-existing islands which have been removed from the charts in recent times, long-doubtful islands which have recently been proved to exist, and islands whose existence is still an open question. The facts in connection

* Mr. Hilaire Belloc is my authority for this statement. See his *Four Men*, p. 241.

† See Kingsley's *Water Babies*.

‡ In 1929 it was claimed that a bird, definitely identified as a Great Auk, had been observed swimming about under a wharf at one of the Lofoten Is., Norway. See *Bird Notes and News*, No. 7, Vol. XIII (London, 1929).

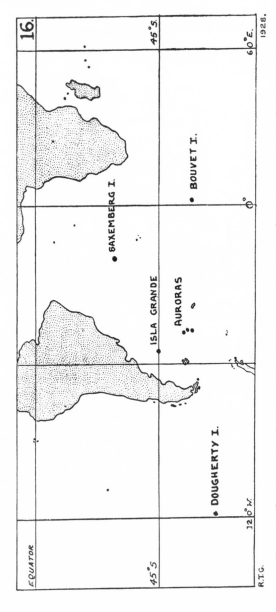

FIG. 16—Sketch-map showing (approximately) the reported positions of the Auroras and other doubtful islands.

with them show that the existence of an imaginary island may be attested by the clearest and most consistent testimony of entirely independent witnesses; while, on the other hand, an island which has been searched for unsuccessfully on many occasions may, after all, prove to be a very concrete reality. In conjunction with such data, the enigma of the Aurora Islands may then be found a little less baffling.

Isla Grande (see Fig. 16).

In 1675 Antonio de la Roché, who was either the discoverer or the rediscoverer of South Georgia, fell in, so he believed, with a previously undiscovered island in the South Atlantic. He described it as "a very large and pleasant island, with a good harbour towards the Eastward", and gave its latitude as 45° S., leaving its longitude unspecified—and its position, in consequence, quite uncertain.

It should be remembered that while seamen in all ages have been able, when out of sight of land, to find their latitude more or less accurately by means of astronomical observations, the finding of longitude at sea remained an unsolved and apparently insoluble problem until the eighteenth century was more than half gone by. It was no academic problem; it overshadowed the life of every man at sea and the safety of every ship and cargo. Scientific men and practical navigators alike found themselves baffled by it, even with the stimulus provided by various large Government rewards, of which the most famous is the £20,000 offered by the British Government in 1714, and won, after a long struggle, by John Harrison, the Yorkshire carpenter.

It is, perhaps, in the fitness of things that our own country should have led the way in the matter. Our legislators have generally shown themselves (except, originally, in the case of the Plimsoll line) sympathetic towards the needs of British seamen—even if in some of the resulting legislation those seamen have, not altogether unreasonably, been classed with children and lunatics. In view of our predominant shipping interests. it would have been a standing reproach to this country if we had not done more than any other towards solving the problem of finding longitude at sea. Happily, we have no such blot on our 'scutcheon. Governments, as we all know, are not usually over-clever at solving problems—but what the British Government could do in the matter it did. It offered a reward, for any practical method of finding longitude at sea, far larger than that offered by any other nation—and differing yet more widely from the latter in that it was actually paid. And we got our money's worth—Harrison's marine time-keeper, incalculable benefit to shipping, and the bulk of the world's chronometer trade, which we still retain.

But in De la Roché's time, and for long after, there were no chronometers, and while an adept in the art and mystery of navigation could find his latitude at sea, his longitude was a matter of guess-work. Like the Bristol merchants of whom Thackeray sings, he could scarcely tell, on sighting land, whether it were Jerusalem or Madagascar, or haply North or South Amerikee. All that he could do was to keep a reckoning, called the "dead-reckoning", of the various courses and distances run by his ship, and make such allowances as he thought most suitable for errors of steering, errors in estimating the speed, leeway, the effect of tides and currents, the variation of the compass, and the innumerable other perplexities which combine to make the way of a ship in the sea, as Solomon has acutely remarked, no less mysterious than that of a snake on a rock, or of a man with a maid.

In short, he guessed his way across the ocean, and he might well have taken for his slogan the refrain of the once-famous coster ditty ". . . 'E dunno where 'e are". So late as 1750 he might still easily be as much as 10° wrong in his longitude at the end of a six weeks' voyage—in other words, if running up-Channel in thick weather he might imagine himself a hundred miles west of Land's End when he was actually off Brighton. It follows that none of the early navigators can truly be said to have made "discoveries" in the modern sense; all that they really "told the world" was that they had fallen in with new land on a certain parallel of latitude and between certain wide limits of longitude. The only way to revisit such discoveries was to get into their latitude a long way to the eastward or the westward, and run along it; and, as will be seen in the case of Bouvet Island, even this plan was not infallible in its results.

After De la Roché, many competent navigators did their best to rediscover his "Isla Grande" without success. Disbelief in its existence, however, was a plant of slow growth. It was natural to suppose that the difficulty in finding this "large and pleasant island with a good harbour" was due solely to the uncertainty attaching to its longitude. Not until the turn of the nineteenth century did doubt grow into scepticism, and scepticism swell into unbelief, as the result of long and exhaustive searches* along the parallel of latitude 45° S. from the South American coast to the middle of the South Atlantic. It seems quite clear that "Isla Grande" never existed at all. Cartographers in general appear to have reached this conclusion—and accordingly to have expunged the island from their charts—somewhere about 1820. As Mayda did, however, it may yet reappear—possibly, in view of the Bolshevik penchant for enunciating scientific "novelties" long discarded by less progressive nations, in the next Russian chart of the South Atlantic.

* As late as 1795 Vancouver, on his way home after rounding C. Horn, thought it worth his while to make a detour in order to search for Isla Grande.

It is not necessary, however, to write De la Roché down as either an ass or a liar. He may have thought, quite sincerely, that he had discovered a new island, and done his best to ascertain its position. But he neglected to take an obvious precaution. It cannot be too strongly impressed upon all young explorers who may read this book that if they find a new shoal they should always take a sounding thereon—and that if they discover a new island they should sail round it. If De la Roché had tried the latter plan he would probably have found that "Isla Grande" was part of the South American mainland. A little northward of the Gulf of St. George, in approximately 45° S., there are two projecting headlands, either of which can easily be mistaken for an island. A single day spent in attempting to circumnavigate his discovery would have saved much time, trouble, and profanity fruitlessly expended by navigators during the succeeding century and a half.

"Isla Grande", then, probably owes its long span of fictitious existence to the fact that De la Roché did not stop to examine his "discovery". But the next example is not so easy to explain away.

Saxemberg Island.

In the year 1670, Lindeman, a Dutch navigator, reported the discovery of an island, which he named Saxemberg Island, in the South Atlantic. He gave as its position lat. 30° 40′ S., long. 19° 30′ W. If we assume for the moment that his longitude was correct, Saxemberg Island would then have been situated about six hundred miles north-west from Tristan da Cunha, remarkable for the seclusion and (judging by photographs) acromegaly of its inhabitants. Lindeman made a sketch of his discovery, which shows a low island with a remarkable high peak rising from its centre.

The position given for the island is remote from the ordinary sailing-ship routes, and I have not been able to trace details of the searches which must, one would think, have been made for it during the next fifty years or so. In view, however, of the absence of any mention of the island in such of the instructions issued to the celebrated explorers of the eighteenth century as I have been able to examine, there can be little doubt that by 1730 or so doubt of the gravest kind had already attached to the accuracy of Lindeman's report.

At the very end of the century James Horsburgh, afterwards Hydrographer to the East India Company, made two attempts to find Saxemburg Island, following the rather unsatisfactory plan of assuming an error in Lindeman's *latitude*, while accepting his longitude! He twice crossed the meridian of 19° W.; on one occasion a few miles southward, and on the other a few northward, of lat. 30° 45′ S. He saw no land.

A careful search, planned on much sounder lines, made in October, 1801 by Capt. Matthew Flinders, R.N., on his way out to Australia, did nothing to dispel the doubt surrounding the island's existence. He ran from 31° 02′ S., 26° W., to 30° 34′ S., 20° 28′ W., and thence E.S.E., passing very close to Lindeman's position. He saw some birds and a turtle —in themselves, indications of land—but nothing else.

In 1804, however, confirmatory evidence of the most satisfactory nature was received from an American source. Captain Galloway, of the ship *Fanny*, reported that he had been in sight of the island for four hours, and that it exhibited a peaked hill in the centre. He agreed with Lindeman, also, as to its latitude, but made its longitude some two degrees farther eastward—a discrepancy of no moment.

On the other hand Mr. Long, master of the sloop *Columbus*, who reported sighting the island in 1809, stated that it lay somewhat northward, and nearly 9° *westward*, of Lindeman's position. Here is an extract from his log:

"September 22nd, 1809, at 5 p.m., saw the island of Saxonburg, bearing ESE . . . found it to be in the latitude of 30° 18′ S., longitude 28° 20′ W., or thereabout.*

"The island of Saxonburg is about four leagues in length, NW and SE., and about 2½ miles in breadth. The NW end is a high bluff of about 70 feet, perpendicular form, and runs along to the SE about 8 miles. You will see trees at about a mile and a half distance, and a sandy beach."

Whatever its true position might be, no further confirmation of the island's existence would appear necessary—yet such was shortly forthcoming. In 1816 Captain Head, of the English ship *True Briton*, reported that he had spent six hours in sight of the island. He described it as having the same high peak in the centre which had previously been seen by Lindeman and Galloway,† while his position for it agreed exactly with that given by the latter.

Bearing in mind the isolated position of the island (six hundred miles from the nearest land) and its remoteness from the trade-routes, one would undoubtedly think that its existence, position, and appearance had been established beyond possibility of question; yet, from the repeated

* Flinders, discussing this report in his *Voyage to Terra Australis* (Vol. I, pp. 34, 35) notes that on Sept. 28, 1801 his ship, the *Investigator*, saw many birds when about 80 miles from Long's position. He accepted this, as explaining why so many ships had previously missed the island. On the other hand Purdy, in his *Oriental Navigator* (1816) showed that it must be in error, since it fell almost exactly upon Capt. Cook's track in "1774" (a misprint for 1776. R.T.G.)—and Cook certainly saw no land in the vicinity.

† But not, it will be noted, by the *Columbus*.

searches which have since been made for it, and the soundings of over two thousand fathoms taken in the vicinity of its reported position, one is driven to conclude that, in all probability, it never had any real existence.

One of the searchers, the notorious American sealer Benjamin Morrell (popularly known in his day as "the biggest liar in the Pacific"), gives an amusing account of his endeavours.*

". . . On Saturday, August 23rd (1828) we were roused by the cheering cry from the masthead of 'Land ho, land ho, about six points off the starboard bow.'

"We now had the wind from west-by-south, which permitted us to haul up for it; but after running in that direction about four hours, at the rate of eight miles an hour, our tantalizing land took a sudden start, and rose about ten degrees above the horizon. Convinced that we could never come up to it in the ordinary course of navigation, we backed and stood to the northward."

This extract provides us with a useful clue in a complicated maze. If we regard the accounts of Lindeman, Galloway, and Head as absolutely independent, their remarkable agreement both as to the position and the appearance of "Saxemberg Island" would be inexplicable except on the supposition that all three saw the same real island.† But we are not entitled to say that they were actually independent—i.e. that Galloway knew nothing of Lindeman's account, and Head nothing of either's— and the strong probability is that they were not. If we assume that Lindeman was originally deceived by some such cloud-effect as that encountered by Morrell, and that, unlike the American, he did not close it sufficiently to discover his mistake—and if we further assume that Galloway and Head were acquainted with the reports made by their predecessors—the matter becomes fairly clear.

The doctrine of "expectant attention" is familiar to psychologists. Broadly speaking, if you impress upon a person that he is to look for something, and that he will probably see it—or even if he makes a suggestion of this kind to himself—the chances are that he will ultimately come to imagine that he has seen what he is looking for. This result may come about as a pure effort of imagination—or, more probably, he will unconsciously graft on to some object which he really sees the qualities and appearance of the thing which he is expecting to see.

* A Narrative of Four Voyages to the South Sea, by Captain Benjamin Morrell, Junr., pp., 276, 277 (New York, 1832).

† What the Columbus saw, or thought she saw, is a mystery. She was too near, one would imagine, to be misled by a mirage, a cloud-effect, or an iceberg—which last, also, could scarcely be met with in 30° S.

For example, those naval officers who were serving with the Grand Fleet in the early days of the War are familiar with the remarkable but little-known Battle of Scapa Flow, which was fought in September 1914. One afternoon sounds of gunfire came from the light cruiser *Falmouth*, guarding the eastern entrance of that admirable, if scarcely exhilarating, anchorage. She signalled that she had shelled and sunk a German submarine (revealed by her periscope) in the act of entering the harbour.

As it was quite possible that the submarine might not have been sunk, and that there might be more than one about, the harbour was soon black with destroyers dashing about at full speed, and hoping either to ram the U-boats or at least confuse their aim. One is reminded of the old lady whose custom it was, during air-raids, to perambulate the streets at a jog-trot, on the theory that a moving target is notoriously difficult to hit. The remarkable scene was further enlivened, every now and then, by the discharge of a four-inch gun from some battleship which imagined that she had sighted a periscope.

In all probability, no U-boat had actually been within several hundreds of miles of Scapa Flow on that particular occasion.* "Expectant attention" provides the key both to the *Falmouth's* initial error and to the succeeding developments.

Similarly, with regard to the case of Saxemberg Island, it is easy to see that if Galloway and his crew, knowing of Lindeman's report and being in the vicinity of his "discovery", had been scanning the horizon hoping to see a low island with a peak in the centre, they would quite easily (and, in actual fact, willingly) have been deceived by a cloud-effect of the kind that Lindeman probably saw in the first place. Given the necessary (but not absolutely indispensable) cloud, precisely the same thing was likely to happen in Head's case—more likely, in fact, for while it is by no means certain that Galloway knew of Lindeman's report, there can scarcely be much doubt, in view of the much shorter interval, that Head knew of Galloway's. It is not suggested in any of the three accounts that the "island" was approached more closely than, say, ten miles; and, in all probability, it was on the horizon most of the time. One can see a very long way from a ship's masthead in clear weather. Assuming that Morrell's masthead height was 70 feet, which is probably not far from the truth, the cloud which he at first took for the island must have been about forty miles distant when sighted, and about ten when he discovered its true nature.

Summarizing, then, we may say that in all probability Lindeman,

* I am not losing sight of the fact that in 1939 the *Royal Oak* was torpedoed and sunk, in Scapa Flow, by a U-boat.

Galloway, and Head were all three deceived by cloud-effects; and that the remarkable similarity in their accounts, inexplicable otherwise, is due to "expectant attention", based upon knowledge of previous reports, and producing two successive cases of unconscious plagiarism.

Bouvet Island.

Bouvet Island, about fifteen hundred miles south-westward from the Cape of Good Hope, is a real island which was long regarded as apocryphal. It came into prominence in 1928 owing to a dispute as to its ownership between this country and Norway—amicably settled in Norway's favour. Although of exceedingly slight value as a territorial acquisition, there is one respect in which it is unique among islands. It is the most isolated spot in the whole world—a fact which anyone who cares to spend an instructive five minutes with a pair of dividers and a good globe can easily verify. Around Bouvet Island, it is possible to draw a circle of one thousand miles radius (having an area of 3,146,000 square miles, or very nearly that of Europe) which contains no other land whatever. No other point of land on the earth's surface has this peculiarity.

Bouvet Island was discovered on January 1, 1739, by J. B. C. Bouvet de Lozier, a Frenchman who has a clear title to be regarded as the first Antarctic explorer on record. At the time an employee of the "Compagnie des Indes", he afterwards became Governor of Mauritius, and seems to have been a man of fine character. Following the very useful custom of the early navigators, he christened his discovery, from its date, "Cap de la Circoncision".

Like De la Roché, he failed to circumnavigate his new land (he was greatly hampered by fog), and after ten days spent off-shore in weather uniformly too bad to permit of landing he quitted it under the impression that he had at last discovered a promontory of the long-sought Southern Continent. In his time, and much later, geographers believed most firmly, on *a priori* grounds such as the necessity for balancing the known preponderance of land in the Northern Hemisphere, in the existence of a huge Southern Continent, extending northward into quite low latitudes. For example, Staten Island (east of the Horn), the Solomon Islands, Easter Island, and Kerguelen were all in turn taken, when first discovered, for promontories of such a Continent. It was not until Cook's second voyage round the world (1772–5) that clear proof was given that such a continent, if it existed (we know now, of course, that it does) must lie southward of about lat. 60° S. It is a significant comment on the geographical knowledge of Cook's time that, shortly before he sailed, his inveterate enemy Alexander Dalrymple (afterwards the first Hydrographer of the Navy) roundly asserted his belief in a temperate, fertile, and wealthy Southern Continent, inhabited by *at least* fifty millions of people.*

If Bouvet had only known it (perhaps, for his own peace of mind, it was as well that he was spared the knowledge), his "Cape Circumcision", instead of being the Cape North of the Southern Continent, was the northwest extremity of a tiny island about five miles in diameter. That he should have succeeded in falling in with this microscopic and isolated spot of land in the course of a brief excursion southward of his normal course is one of the most remarkable "lucky dips" in the whole history of exploration.

Like the skilful navigator that he was, he did his best, with the means at his disposal, to fix the position of his discovery. He made its latitude about 54° S. (it is actually 54° 26′ S.) and its longitude about 9° E. of Greenwich, with a "probable error" of certainly not less than 5°.

The greatest of all navigators, Captain James Cook, R.N., F.R.S., now takes up the tale. In 1772, commanding H.M.S. *Resolution*, he searched unsuccessfully for Cape Circumcision in the position assigned to it by Bouvet, and by running some five hundred miles from east to west and back again in a considerably higher latitude he showed that, if it existed, it was in all probability situated on a comparatively small island.

In 1775, on his way homeward to civilization from the second† circumnavigation of the Antarctic, Cook resumed his search, on the standard plan of getting into the latitude of Bouvet's discovery a long way to the westward, and then running it down along the parallel. He made a careful but unavailing search along lat. 54° S. from 6° E. to 22° E. and concluded, rather unjustly, that what Bouvet had really seen was an enormous iceberg.

Although Cook did not know it at the time, his colleague Furneaux, H.M.S. *Adventure*, had made a similarly unsuccessful, but not so thorough, search for the Cape in the previous year. He had explored the region between 19° W. and 11° E., but in a latitude varying from 54° S. to 53° S., so that he might easily have passed to the northward of Bouvet's discovery without sighting it.

As the result of the view so definitely expressed by the one man in all the world best qualified to give an opinion, the existence of Bouvet's "Cape Circumcision" became, except in France, generally discredited. But not for very long.

* He expressed this remarkable opinion in two letters which he addressed to Lord North in 1772.

† The first, technically, was made more or less independently by the *Resolution's* nominal consort, the *Adventure*, under Furneaux, in 1772-1774. She parted company during a gale (Oct. 1773), and was not seen again throughout the voyage.

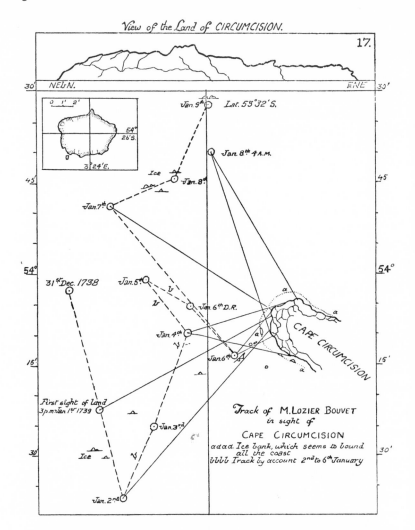

Fɪɢ. 17.—"Cape Circumcision" (Bouvet island) as originally charted from the data recorded in Bouvet's journal. Copied from a plate in Alexander Dalrymple's *Collection of Voyages, chiefly in the Southern Atlantick Ocean* (London, 1775).

Inset: Bouvet I., from a running survey by Capt. Harold Horntvedt, S.S. *Norvegia*, Dec. 1927.

Nᴏᴛᴇ. The linear scale of the inset is $2\frac{1}{2}$ times that of the chart. It will be noticed that while Bouvet charted the W. and NW. shores of his discovery with fair accuracy as regards outline and orientation, the foggy weather then prevailing led him to exaggerate their extent considerably.

In 1808 a London firm, Enderby Bros., directed two of their sealing vessels to make a search for Bouvet's land along the parallel of 54° S. from 10° W. to 14° E., thus duplicating and completing the work already performed by Cook and Furneaux. The two ships (snow *Swan*, Captain James Lindsay, and brig *Otter*, Captain Thomas Hopper) left San Sebastian, Brazil, for this purpose on August 22, 1808.

They were completely successful. On October 6th, Lindsay sighted an island about twenty-five miles ahead, and closed it the next day. It proved to be a small island some five miles in diameter, surrounded to a great distance by closely-packed ice. He was unable to land, and left again on the 13th, having in the interval been joined by his consort.

By his observations, the island was in lat. 54° 15′ S., long. 4° 15′ E. (dead-reckoning). By chronometer, this longitude came out at 6° 15′ E., but (with good reason, as afterwards appeared) he preferred to trust to his dead-reckoning. He had but the one chronometer, and had no doubt already found it untrustworthy. In those days chronometers were neither so well made nor so well understood as they are now, and the lot of a merchant skipper's chronometer in a small ship with no proper stowage for it must have been far from a happy one.

It might be thought, then, that the question was settled. But actually, as will be seen, it had barely been opened.

Lindsay's account seems to have been very sceptically received among the cognoscenti. They probably preferred to trust Cook and Furneaux, whom no one could suspect of having an axe to grind; and Lindsay's island, by his statements, lay so close to the tracks of those two explorers that it seemed hardly credible that they should have failed to see it—if it really existed. *Ergo* . . .

I have never seen any contemporary chart which gave credence to Lindsay's perfectly truthful story. A short account of the voyage was printed by Burney in 1817 as an appendix to the account of Bouvet's voyage given in Vol. V of his *Voyages*; and so far as I am aware, this forms the sole authority for Lindsay's doings. His original log does not appear to have been preserved.

In the course of the next twenty years, two men claimed to have seen —and not only seen, but landed upon—Bouvet's island. One, unfortunately, was the American sealer Morrell, already mentioned in connection with Saxemberg Island. There is no doubt that he actually made several voyages in which he combined sealing with a certain amount of exploration—for example, he was the first man to discover the rich guano deposits on Ichabo Island—but the only authority for his work is his own book *A Narrative of Four Voyages* . . ., published at New York in 1832. And what a book it is! Written in the style of the *Watertoast Gazette*, it reveals Morrell as a boastful romancer, suffering from a constitutional inability to refrain from "orating" on all occasions (particularly emergencies calling for instant action) and quite unashamed to acknowledge that it is his constant practice to fill his pages with accounts of the doings of other men, related as his personal experiences. His style alone has a strange power of casting a most convincing air of unreality over his accounts of even quite credible events. As an Antarctic explorer once expressed it to me, "Reading Morrell, you have a feeling that if he came down and told you it was raining in buckets, you would be quite safe in leaving your oilskin below."

By his own account, Morrell anchored off the island, which he seems to have had no difficulty in finding, for two days in 1822. He gives its position as lat. 54° 15′ S., long. 6° 11′ E.—in which case Cook could not have failed to sight it.

Much better authenticated is the visit paid to the island in 1825 by two more of the Enderby vessels—the sealers *Sprightly*, Captain George Norris, and *Lively*. Norris fell in with the island on December 10, 1825, and on the 16th he landed there and took formal possession in the name of King George IV—thus antedating, by a little over a century, Captain Horntvedt of the Norwegian whaler *Norvegia*, who hoisted the Norwegian flag there on December 1, 1927, under the impression that the island had hitherto been a "no man's land".

Thompson Island.

Norris's annexation of Bouvet Island, however, is chiefly interesting as providing grist for the diplomatic mills. He has a better claim to remembrance in that he has provided a puzzle, in connection with his explorations, which was long unsolved. In the interval between December 13th and 16th, he stood away to the north-eastward, and discovered a second island, which no one had ever seen before and only one man has reported again. It was a small, low-lying island, on which the sea was breaking with great violence. Three miles south-eastward of it was a little cluster of three rocky islets, with a solitary rock three miles farther southward still. He called the island "Thompson Island", and the three islets the "Chimneys".

There seems to be no real doubt that he honestly believed he had made these discoveries. The question is, did he really see land—and, if so, where is it situated?

Norris has done what he could to help us; but, unfortunately, when examining the data one finds oneself wishing that he had either done a little more or a little less. He drew a chart of all his discoveries, and entered their positions into his log. Chart and log, apparently, have long been lost, but in the Admiralty archives is a contemporary copy of both, communicated by Messrs. Enderby in November 1826, soon after the *Sprightly's* return. And it is when one examines this document that the difficulties begin.

Norris called the larger island, of which he took possession, "Liverpool Island", and determined its position, by his observations, as lat. 54° 15′ S., long. 5° E. Incidentally, he took the trouble to circumnavigate it, and so made certain that it was an island. From the sketches which he gives of it, and in the light of modern investigation, it is obvious that his "Liverpool Island" was Bouvet Island, whose position is now known within a mile or two, and which lies about 1½° westward of the position he gives—a discrepancy of little moment.

It would seem fairly safe to assume, then, that Thompson Island and its satellites lie somewhere to the north-eastward of Bouvet Island. But as regards their exact position the information which Norris gives is both redundant and contradictory. Summarizing the statements contained in his log (and converting his bearings from points to degrees for convenience), he tells us that Thompson Island bears 22½°, forty-five miles from Bouvet Island; and, intending to make the matter still plainer, gives us the position of each island in latitude and longitude. Unfortunately, as his chart shows and calculation supports, these positions are only twenty-six miles apart, and make Thompson Island bear 42° from Bouvet Island. Furthermore, on this showing the variation of the compass (the divergence of the N. point of the compass-needle from the true north) at Bouvet Island in 1825 would be 19½° E., whereas Lindsay, in 1808, found it to be 17° W. in the same vicinity, and Ross, in 1845, 20° W. It is true that the variation alters, in course of time, at practically every point on our globe—but the process is slow, and such a change as a double swing of 38° in 37 years is a thing unheard of. As I say, one wishes that Norris had told us either more or less; but there is absolutely no reason to doubt his good faith. He was no scientist, it is true; he seems to have been a plain blunt seaman, doing his limited best to set down explicitly, for the benefit of his employers, what he had himself seen and done.

The re-discovery of Bouvet Island.

Norris's work seems to have met with no more general credence than Lindsay's; and the Government appears to have received the news of a new addition to our far-flung Empire with the most awful calmness, unbroken by either announcement or acknowledgment. In view of the fact that particulars of Norris's exploits had been in the hands of the Admiralty since 1826, it seems incredible that Captain James Ross, R.N., when he searched for Bouvet Island in 1843, should never have heard of either Norris or Lindsay. Such, however, is the fact.

Like his great predecessor Cook, whom he resembled in many ways, Ross was coming back from circumnavigating the Antarctic; having, in the course of three years, performed the greatest feat of Antarctic exploration which, so far, it has been given to one man to accomplish. As a useful piece of secondary work, he intended to determine the position of Bouvet Island, "which had so often been sought in vain, . . . with some degree of precision". But Fate, ably assisted by inefficient staff-work in the Hydrographic Department, ordained otherwise.

It must be premised, and it will explain a good deal that would otherwise remain obscure, that the account which Ross gives (in his book) of his search for Bouvet Island is extraordinarily unreliable. To criticize the work of one of the greatest of all Polar explorers, who was also a countryman and a brother officer, is an invidious task; but I think that in this matter there has already been enough paltering with geographical truth, particularly since a Norwegian writer, Mr. Bjarne Aagaard, has endeavoured to bolster up the Norwegian claim to Bouvet Island by vehement appeals to Ross's work as the final authority.

I do not propose to go into the matter here in much detail. Broadly speaking, Ross, writing some years after the event, seems to have compiled the account of his search from his journal, and to have jotted down the courses and distances which he believed himself to have steered from day to day without verifying them from the only reliable source—the ship's log. The positions of his ships (they were, by the way, the famous *Erebus* and *Terror* in which Franklin and his men afterwards perished) at each noon, as given in his account, are correct; much of the remainder is a tissue of inaccuracies. I verified this for myself, many years ago, by consulting the original logs and Masters' journals of the two ships, from which their actual track can be computed with considerable accuracy. In what follows, it must be understood that I speak of what Ross actually did, and not of what he says he did.

Running eastward across the South Atlantic, he crossed the meridian of Greenwich in lat. 54° 07′ S., intending to run Bouvet Island down, if it existed, on the parallel of 54° 15′ S. To avoid the chance of being shipwrecked on it in the night (for the Antarctic summer was over, and the nights rapidly darkening and lengthening), he hove-to every evening until daybreak.

Had he managed to keep to his parallel for a couple of days, he must have accomplished his intention of finding the island. But by a strange chance a shift of wind took him north-eastward just before he could have sighted it, and when he regained his original latitude the island, as we now know, was just out of sight astern. He actually passed in sight of it, but eighteen miles off, a distance at which the best look-out might well be excused (unlike the seaman who received three dozen lashes because the earth was a globe*) for failing to distinguish it from one of the many icebergs then visible.

As if to add point to Ross's failure, a similar fate befell Lieut. T. E. L. Moore, R.N., H.M. hired barque *Pagoda*, who made an unsuccessful search for the island in 1845. Moore had been dispatched by the Admiralty to complete, by running from the Cape to Australia in a high southern latitude, that portion of the magnetic survey of the Antarctic which Ross had been compelled to leave unfinished. He had been a mate in the *Terror* during the whole of Ross's voyage, and had, consequently, taken part in his chief's search for the island two years earlier. Further search for it formed no part of his programme: nor was this, as sometimes stated,† enjoined by his Instructions. None the less he went out of his way, although short of time, to approach the island's charted position (then 54° 16′ S., 6° 14′ E.) from the NE, and to quit it on a southerly course, thus connecting the tracks of two previous searchers—Cook and Ross—and reducing the unexplored area in which, if it existed, the island must lie.

The Admiralty, not unnaturally, seem to have decided, in view of the non-success of Cook, Furneaux, Ross, and Moore, that some peculiar spell cast upon Bouvet Island rendered it invisible to naval officers.‡ They sought for it no more—not even when an opportunity offered itself in the course of the *Challenger's* great oceanographic voyage of 1874–7. As a tardy measure of justice, however, "Lindsay Island", "Bouvet *or Liverpool* Island", "Thompson Island", and "The Chimneys" at last appeared (in 1853) upon the Admiralty charts; although, with singular fatuity, the three last-named were charted in the exact positions reported by Norris—and in which, as had been shown by the work of the unfortunate

* The story was told in print long ago by Capt. Basil Hall, R.N. The seaman in question was the masthead-man of a frigate stationed on the landward beam of the flagship, and instructed to report by signal as soon as she made the land. Owing to the curvature of the earth's surface, the land was seen from the flagship's masthead (which was much more elevated) before it could possibly have been seen from that of the frigate. This not being realized at the time, the latter ship's look-out received three dozen lashes for having, it was considered, neglected his duty.

† By more than one Antarctic historian. I was under the same impression when this book first appeared (1928) and made some scathing and quite unjustified remarks about Moore in consequence. But in 1933 I managed to find his Instructions (P.R.O. Ad.2/1538. 1844) which had previously eluded me. See *Geographical Journal*, April 1934.

‡ This spell, happily, is now broken. Bouvet Island was seen by Lieut.-Commander J. M. Chaplin, R.N., serving in the R.R.S. *Discovery*, Capt. J. R. Stenhouse, on November 17, 1926—also by the C. in C., Africa Station, Vice-Admiral (now Admiral Sir) E. R. G. R. Evans, R.N., flying his flag in H.M.S. *Milford* (Capt. H. C. Phillips, R.N.) on February 23, 1934.

naval officers who had searched the vicinity, it was morally certain that they could not possibly be situated. That two members of this archipelago were identical, and three of them incorrectly charted, was learnt by the Hydrographic Department in 1899 and rectified, with almost Spanish promptitude, in 1917.

The action taken in 1853 is significant as indicating a reversal of the general opinion, held since Cook's time, that Bouvet Island was non-existent. It must be admitted that for such a view there was considerable justification. Barring Bouvet, its discoverer, the only people who claimed to have seen it were three sealers, undoubtedly rule-of-thumb navigators, and not above suspicion of pitching cock-and-bull stories to enhance their own importance. On the other hand four naval officers, all men of disinterested character and two bearing European reputations, had been over the same ground and seen—nothing. Yet, although two of these searches had been made since the last report of sighting the island (Norris's in 1825), opinion had at last swung definitely from scepticism to credence. So true it is that Truth will out, even in an affidavit.

Fortified by this moral support, and possibly assisted by the reduced inaccuracy of the island's charted position, several American seamen (a class always notorious for their rigid adherence to literal truth) were emboldened to report having sighted Bouvet Island. Such were Captain Williams, of the *Golden West* (1878), Captain Church, of the *Delia Church* (1882), and Captain Fuller, of the *Francis Allen* (1893). Fuller also stated that he saw Thompson Island, to the north-eastward of Bouvet Island; a remarkable feat, in that he is the only man, except Norris, who has ever claimed to have done so.

Doubt as to the existence of Bouvet Island having been removed, the question of its position was finally set at rest by C. Chun, in the German oceanographic vessel *Valdivia*, Captain Krech, in 1898. With truly Teutonic thoroughness her navigator, Sachse, took her straight over the reported positions of Norris's "Liverpool Island", Morrell's "Bouvette's Island", and "Lindsay Island" (as reported by Lindsay). No land was seen in any of these positions. Continuing to steer westward, however, a small island came in sight about 3 p.m. in the afternoon of November 25, 1898—a date worth recording, since it marks the definite solution of the problem which Bouvet set geographers on January 1, 1739.

The island proved to be small and valueless—a volcanic cone rising some 3,000 feet, partially covered by an enormous glacier, and reaching the sea as a ring-fence of precipitous cliffs. It was pentagonal in plan, and about five miles in diameter.* Its position, definitely ascertained

---

* As Fig. 17 shows, Bouvet's partial survey of his discovery agrees very fairly well with those made by the *Valdivia* and the *Norvegia*, which differ very little.

for the first time by modern methods, was found to be 54° 26′ S., 3° 24′ E. Le Monnier, of the French Academy, although discredited in his day, had been perfectly right when he maintained that Cook had thrown away his chance of finding the island by starting his search too far to the eastward; and that in all probability it was situated in about 3° 30′ E.*

The searches for Thompson Island.

One piece of verification remained for the *Valdivia*. It was obvious that Bouvet Island was "Liverpool Island"; in consequence it followed that Thompson Island should be situated to the north-eastward of it. Sachse made his way, in foggy weather, to the position given by Norris—45 miles north-north-east from Liverpool Island—but saw nothing, and obtained a sounding of 1,270 fathoms close to this position, rendering it highly unlikely that there could be an island within ten miles. Owing to the poor visibility he did not extend his search, but this was continued in 1926 by another German research-vessel, the *Meteor*. In clear weather, she steamed over the then charted position of Thompson Island (53° 56′ S., 4° 13′ E.). No land at all could be seen, although the visibility was estimated at eight miles. A sounding of 778 fathoms testified, in conjunction with the *Valdivia's* previous sounding, that the island, if it existed, probably lay further eastward.

Its existence, however, still remained an open question. The position searched by the *Meteor* had been accepted for the Admiralty charts (1917) in consequence of an investigation which I had then recently completed. By carefully plotting the tracks of all recorded searches and the varying "areas of good visibility from mast-head height", it became clear that there was an area, some 300 square miles in extent and including this position, which had never been examined at all: and the *Meteor's* search, while reducing this area considerably, did not obliterate it altogether. There was still room for Thompson Island and its dependent islets, the "Chimneys", in about 54° S., 4° 35′ E.

I published this conjecture in August, 1928†—and four months later Consul Lars Christensen of Sandeford, Norway, despatched the *Norvegia* to test it. She made Bouvet Island on Dec..20, and thereafter zig-zagged for eight days between 52° and 55° S., and from 4° 35′ W. to 6° 17′ E. No trace of Thompson Island could be seen, although she reported

---

* He maintained this view in three memoirs read to the Académie des Sciences in 1776 and 1779. His conclusions were attacked by Wales (Cook's astronomer in his Antarctic voyage) in a paper read before the Royal Society and printed, with additions, in the Introduction to *Cook's Third Voyage* (London, 1784).

† In the first edition of this book.

steaming over the positions indicated by Norris, Fuller and myself.* Furthermore, the R.R.S. *Discovery II* obtained, in 1930, a number of consistently-deep soundings on all sides of my position, more or less disposing of the suggestion that, since 1825, Thompson Island might have disappeared as the result of volcanic action. It was removed from the Admiralty charts soon afterwards.†

In all probability, Norris mistook an earth-encrusted iceberg for land —an error which, in the absence of deep-sea sounding equipment, the most experienced navigator might commit. He was aware of this, but could not always avoid it—when charting a detached rock (shown by the *Discovery II* to be non-existent) about 5½ miles 328° from Cape Circumcision, he remarks of it ". . . it is cased with ice and at first we imagined it to be an iceberg. . .". A similar appearance was probably at the bottom of Fuller's report, also.‡

"Vigias".

Still, the curious history of the search for Bouvet Island may well make us cautious as to removing from the charts any island, however doubtful. For example, such action would, from a common-sense point of view, have been perfectly justifiable in the case of Bouvet Island in, say, 1775 (after Cook's search) or in 1846 (after the searches made by Ross and Moore). Yet it would, as we now know, have replaced truth by error—and it might have led to a shipwreck. There is, indeed, a good deal to be said for the point of view indicated, not entirely seriously, in that rare and cynical classic, *The Bogus Surveyor*.

"The most tedious process in boat sounding is that of searching for reported rocks or those known to exist in the old charts. In nearly all cases these are extremely difficult to discover, because—if they *do* exist— it seldom happens that the positions are exactly correct on the old charts, and also because very frequently these dangers only have their being in the brain of some foolish old merchant skipper who has reported their supposed existence. If, after an hour or two's search in the supposed neighbourhood, no traces of the rock or shoal can be discovered, it will be advisable to accept its rather doubtful existence as a fact.§. . . Place the rock on your field board and obtain the necessary angle to fix its position with the station-pointers.

"Some few surveying captains have objected to this plan, but it is

' * I have no details of her track. I should welcome them, since her week's search embraced an area of some 40,000 square miles.

† See Admiralty Notice to Mariners no. 406 of 1931.

‡ See Ad. N. to M. no. 407 of 1931.

§ "You will, of course, be guided by the preconceived opinion of your captain on this subject." (Footnote in original.)

evidently the best under the circumstances, and Marine surveying is, after all, one continual struggle with difficulties, which must be overcome, or the work would not go on.

"There can be no danger to shipping in adopting this course. On the contrary, navigators, seeing the rock marked in your chart, will naturally avoid the risk of approaching it too nearly; or, should they recklessly neglect precautions (as they will do at times), you have the satisfaction of knowing that there is really no rock there to strike upon."*

This plan was followed, in the charts of a century ago, and even later, to such an extent that the chart of so frequented a highway as the North Atlantic became positively peppered with "vigias"—imaginary shoals originating in a misapprehension of such phenomena as discoloured water, floating kelp, a school of porpoises, a water-logged tree-trunk, or a dead whale. Nowadays we are more sceptical, and the list of the classical "doubtful islands" has been severely curtailed in consequence. The last of note to go, "unwept, unhonoured, and unsung", were the Nimrod group, long believed, on the strength of a single vague report, to exist in about 56° 20′ S., 158° 30′ W.; but at least two others of equally dubious pedigree are overdue for removal from the charts.

One is Pagoda Rock (60° 11′ S., 4° 43′ E.), reported by Lt. Moore, of the *Pagoda*, in 1845. This rock only made its début on the Admiralty charts in 1918 (at my suggestion). The idea was to direct attention to its vicinity, and so get the question of its existence settled. Three consequent searches, all fruitless (*Quest* 1922, *Meteor* 1926, *Norvegia* 1928) have left no reasonable doubt that what Moore saw was, as in the case of "Thompson Island", an earth-encrusted iceberg. It is true that Moore got, or thought that he got, a 250-fathom sounding close to his "discovery" —but the *Pagoda* was drifting rapidly before a strong breeze, and without the help of steam, deep-sounding, in the calmest weather, was a wearisome and unreliable business.

The other is that hoary nuisance, Emerald Island. This was reported in 1821 by the ship *Atlantic*, C. J. Nockells master, which only saw it *on the horizon*, 25 miles away! It has never been seen again, and its charted position (57° 15′ S., 162° 50′ E.) coruscates with notes recording the dates of numerous unsuccessful searches. No doubt there is some excellent reason for keeping it on the Admiralty charts, but I cannot imagine what this is—in my opinion, it should never have been placed on them at all. Yet, apparently, *sedet aeternumque sedebit*.

* This extract is perfectly genuine, and from a published book. The latter's full title is: "*The | Bogus Surveyor*" | *or* | *A Short History of a Peculiar People.* | By Whitewash, | The Surveyor's Friend. | Price one shilling. Devonport, A. H. Swiss, "Bremner" Printing Works, 111 and 112 Fore Street (n.d.).

Dougherty Island

There remains, however, one long-accepted island whose existence is still not absolutely disproved, and whose story is curiously similar to that of Bouvet Island. That is Dougherty Island, which, if it exists, is the farthest of all from any inhabited land.

In 1800 an American whaler, Captain Swain, of Nantucket, sighted what he took to be an island south-westward of Cape Horn, "covered with snow, and abounding with sea-dogs and fowl". He named it "Swain's Island", and gave its position, roughly, as lat. 59° S., long. (dead or even corrupt reckoning) 90°–100° W.

A few years later Captain Richard Macy, also of Nantucket, sighted an island "four or five miles in extent in south latitude 59° and west longitude 91°, his ship passing near enough to see the breakers. The island abounded with sea-dogs or seals, and the water was much coloured, and thick with rock-weed". There is also a vague report of a similar island having been seen about this time by a Captain Gardiner, of Sag Harbour, on his way home from New Zealand.

A search, dictated by commercial motives, was made for "Swain's Island" by the American vessels *Anawan*, Captain N. B. Palmer, and *Penguin*, Captain A. S. Palmer, in February–March 1830—but such accounts of their cruise as have survived are vague and confused. It was certainly unsuccessful—they appear to have explored (but with what thoroughness does not appear) the region 54°–61° S., 63°–104° W. It is quite impossible that in so short a time they could have made a thorough search all over this area. Its widely extended limits are an eloquent tribute to the respect in which they held their compatriots' ability as navigators.

The reports of Swain and Macy attracted little attention, and seem to have been entirely forgotten; for when, ten years after the Palmers (they were brothers) had abandoned their search, an island closely resembling Macy's was reported in a position considerably further westward, it was generally regarded as a completely new discovery. There can be little doubt, however, that if the island really exists, the honour of discovering and naming it should rightly belong to Swain.

In this connection, it is interesting to recall the account given by Morrell, in the work already mentioned, of the fate of Captain Robert Johnson, of the schooner *Henry*. Apart from his possible connection with Dougherty Island, it may be noted that Johnson, in 1822, made an exhaustive but futile search for the Auroras—to which group, after a digression extending over two oceans, I am now slowly returning.

Morrell remarks:

". . . In the year 1823, Captain Robert Johnson . . . left New Zealand on a cruise to the south and east, in search of new lands, between the sixtieth and sixty-fifth degrees of south latitude; and as he has never been heard of since leaving New Zealand, it is very probable that he made discovery of some new island near the parallel of 60°, on which the *Henry* was shipwrecked. . . ."

Morrell's standard of probability does not seem to be very exacting; but the suggestion is interesting—if not for its likelihood, at least for the confidence which shines through it that a capable American skipper, as Johnson undoubtedly was, could not possibly lose even a small schooner through her foundering at sea.

In 1841 the eponym of Dougherty Island attracted the world's attention for the first and, so far as I can gather, the only time. Here is a verbatim extract from the log of Captain Dougherty, of the British whaler *James Stewart*:

"May 29, 1841, at 2 a.m., saw land ahead, luffed and cleared it. It appeared an island 5 or 6 miles in length, running N.E. and S.W., with a high round bluff on the N.E. end, with low land to S.W.: between N.E. and S.W. ends there appeared a valley covered with ice and snow; we passed it within a quarter of a mile, going ten knots: lat. 59° 20' S., long. 120° 20' W.: the position for lat. and long. may differ a few miles by reason of not having had proper observations for several preceding and following days."

As in the case of Saxemberg Island, this report was followed, before many years had elapsed, by a second. In 1860 Captain Keates, of the *Louise* of Bristol, reported having sighted an island on September 4, 1859, which he placed, by good observations, in lat. 59° 21' S., long. 119° 7' W. He described it as round and dark-coloured, about 80 feet high, with an iceberg aground on the north-west side of it: and he based this latter assertion on the fact that although the berg was tilted so that one end rode much higher out of the water than the other, yet it remained broadside-on to the wind, in opposition to several other neighbouring bergs, which all lay with their lower ends to windward.

This report, in spite of the island's sadly-altered appearance, was generally accepted as confirming Dougherty's, and "Dougherty Island" became a familiar landmark (in Keates' position) upon the Admiralty and other charts. The fact that Furneaux, in 1774, had passed very close to both Dougherty's and Keates' positions without sighting any land escaped notice—and as the reports of "Swain's Island" had been forgotten, attention was not directed to them, or to the fact that Ross, in 1842, had sailed over two out of the three positions which they assigned to it.

Yet again, in the course of a warm newspaper correspondence in the *Otago Daily News* of 1891 as to the island's existence, Captain William Stannard, of the *Cingalese* (its principal defender), stated that he had sighted the island in 1886, and that Captain Whitson of the *Dunedin* had done so a year earlier and had observed a large number of seal frequenting it. Stannard gave for its position 59° 20′ S., 120° 18′ W., which agreed most singularly with Dougherty's, and in which, with the addition of a subsequent note, "Probably lies further eastward", it was shown on the Admiralty charts until 1935.*

In support of his statements, Stannard produced a sketch of the island executed by himself. If it did not exactly form irrefutable proof that Dougherty Island existed, it at least demonstrated a minor point of some importance—namely, that he was no artist. It looks like a cross between a disreputable iceberg and a "dissipated saw".

Two years later (Feb. 26, 1893) a New Zealand sealer, Capt. White, recorded sighting a considerable number of seal in the vicinity of Dougherty Island. Writing in 1909, he remarked:†

"Any doubt as to its existence is all nonsense. We sighted the island about 6.30 a.m. . . . having passed round three sides, there cannot be much doubt about our having seen it. It is much like Macdonald Island‡ . . . only a little longer. We spent 2–3 hours trying to lasso and club seals, which were plentiful and rubbing against our ship's side. Distance 5–6 miles off the island. . . . We had a very fine sight at noon . . ., so the latitude can be relied on. Longitude fairly good, but may be a few miles farther east. I have given you the position in which we placed it. As for some people saying it does not exist, *I would bet all the tea in China it did exist* on February 26, 1893."

His position was 59° 48′ S., 118° 40′ W.—slightly southward, and rather eastward, of Stannard's. Still, whatever slight uncertainty might attach to its situation, the case for the island's existence certainly looked, at this epoch, overwhelmingly strong.

But, unfortunately, there is another side to the picture. Dougherty Island has been searched for, during the last sixty years, more often than Bouvet Island has ever been; and with a uniformly depressing lack of success. Take the following examples:

S.S. *Ruapehu*, 1889. Passed five miles north of charted position.

S.S. *Aorangi*, 1890. Passed very close to charted position.

S.S. *Mamari*, 1893. Passed over charted position.

S.S. *Niwaru*, 1907. Passed forty miles south of charted position.

---

* In that year, it was removed from them "by square date" (*i.e.* without publication of a Notice to Mariners), as presumably non-existent.

† In a letter to Mr. H. J. Bull, quoted in Mr. Lars Christensen's *Such is the Antarctic* (London, 1935). I am indebted to Messrs. Hodder & Stoughton, his publishers, for permission to make this extract.

‡ 53° 02′ S., 72° 32′ E. It is about 1½ miles long.

None of these vessels saw any signs of land.

More complete searches have also been made by other navigators, who adopted the sound old plan of running along the parallel of 59°–59½° S. between wide limits of longitude. For example, the late Capt. H. E. Greenstreet, of the S.S. *Rimutaka*, in a most praiseworthy attempt to dispose of the problem, executed a whole series of such unsuccessful searches, as follows:

In 1894, from approximately 125° W. to 115° W.

,, 1900,	,,	,,	125°	,,	109° ,,
,, 1902,	,,	,,	124°	,,	105° ,,
,, 1907,	,,	,,	120°	,,	110° ,,
,, 1910,	,,	,,	123°	,,	113° ,,

Again, Scott with the *Discovery*, in 1904, ran along this parallel from 125° W. to 104° W. without sighting the island, and obtained a sounding of 2,588 fathoms in the Dougherty-Stannard position: while the magnetic vessel *Carnegie*, in December 1915, passed within three miles of the same position, and stated that from the masthead the island could have been seen, had it existed, anywhere within a radius of thirty-five miles.

Earlier than the *Carnegie*, too, the *Nimrod*, of Shackleton's first Antarctic expedition, had passed over the charted position of the island in June 1909; but as this search was made in mid-winter it does not carry the same weight as some of the others.

Lastly, on Dec. 25–27, 1930 the *Norvegia* ran along 59° 48′ S. from 121° 30′ W. to 115° 30′ W. without seeing anything of the island, although the average visibility was estimated at nineteen miles. She obtained soundings of 2,335 fathoms, and upwards, in and near Capt. White's position.

It may be added that Ross, while not specifically in search of any island, contributed in 1842 a most useful piece of work to the data supporting the theory of its non-existence. He ran along the parallel of approximately 59° 10′ S. from 117° W. to 109° W., and from 102° W. to 89° W. and onwards. Similar aid can also be obtained from the tracks of Cook and Furneaux in the vicinity, which zigzag extensively among the more regular paths of the later explorers.

The whole question is an extraordinary puzzle, far more perplexing than that of Bouvet Island's existence was in, say, 1850; and it is still disputable. The positive evidence is strong—the negative, if anything, stronger still. Assuredly the island cannot exist in, or anywhere near, 118°–120° W. If it exists (and we can scarcely assert definitely that it does not) it must lie closer to the position originally reported by Swain in 1800—59½° S., 100° W.—although the discrepancy in longitude

between this position and those of Dougherty and Stannard is an appalling
one, even to those who know the haphazard navigation of the early
sealers and whalers. As a class, these have never possessed, or been likely
to possess, either the instruments or the skill necessary for accurate
navigation; and the whalers, in particular, have always been credited,
justly or unjustly, with holding the view that they didn't care two hoots
for their position so long as they had plenty of whales in sight.

As regards the positive evidence in favour of Dougherty Island's existence the remarkable discrepancy between the account of it given by
Captain Keates and by everyone else who has reported sighting it prevents
our giving the former much weight—so that one of (at first sight) the
best pieces of corroborative evidence must be altogether discounted. The
strongest real feature of the case for the island's existence is the agreement
in its length and appearance, as described by Macy, Dougherty, and
Stannard. Macy, it will be remembered, said that it was "four or five
miles in extent": Dougherty stated that it was "five or six miles in length,
with a high round bluff on the north-east end, with low land to south-
west", and Stannard, in the course of some notes accompanying his
sketch, remarks, "north-east end high bluff 300 feet. South-east end very
rugged, and about six miles long".*

It is of course possible that Dougherty knew of Macy's account, but
this certainly was not generally accessible at the time in any work of
reference. The independence of Stannard's account is, unfortunately,
more open to doubt. Broadly speaking, it is a question of his word v.
several circumstances pointing against him. In a letter to the *Otago Daily
News*, he stated that he had originally been doubtful about the island's
existence, as he could find no published account of it. On the other hand,
for that statement to be correct he must have been singularly destitute of
sailing directions, since all available information relating to the island was
given, at that date, both in the Admiralty Pilots and in Findlay's *Pacific
Directory*, and similar works. And the remarkable agreement between his
position for the island and Dougherty's own suggests, in a manner difficult
to gainsay, that he may have obtained it from a chart (or a volume of
sailing directions) and not from his own observations. The same cavil
attaches to his description of the island.

There is, however, one more or less plausible theory to be put forward
—a theory which unfortunately cuts both ways. If accepted, it certainly
clears up many difficulties, but at the same time it relegates Dougherty
Island to the limbo of discarded and erroneous ideas.

The parallel of lat. 59° S. forms, in the region within which all reports

---

* White (1893) described it as being a little longer than McDonald Is.—or some *two*
miles only, at most.

of Dougherty Island lie, a rough limit for the pack-ice and icebergs constantly emanating from the Antarctic Continent. This is not, of course,
an inviolable limit; but in general terms one may say that a navigator who
keeps two or three degrees to the north of it is unlikely to fall in with
many bergs, while one who should persist in keeping a similar distance
southward of it could scarcely avoid doing so.

Now the Antarctic icebergs frequently attain a size which, at first
sight, is apt to disconcert even experienced Arctic navigators. Flat-topped
bergs five or six miles in length and rising several hundreds of feet out
of the water are by no means uncommon. On the other hand, they are
not as plentiful as blackberries, even inside the Antarctic Circle; and
the occurrence of such bergs, allowing for the wastage which goes on
perpetually from the time when a berg is "calved" from its parent
glacier until it disintegrates altogether, is a comparative rarity in such
a latitude as 59° S.: while by the inexperienced eye of a mariner not
accustomed to Antarctic ice conditions, such a berg would be taken for
an island far more often than not. And that a large berg should, in the
absence of near-by land, be resorted to by numbers of seal is not in the least
improbable.

It seems not unlikely, then, that what Swain, Macy, Dougherty, and
the rest saw was a tabular iceberg; not of course the same berg in each
case, but (so to speak) a standard pattern of berg, which they all met in
much about the same latitude because that was a likely parallel in which to
encounter such a berg, and because it was about as far south as they cared
to go. Running along 59° S. they were bound, sooner or later, to fall in
with a berg of the kind: they were equally bound to differ in the longitude
where they met with their particular specimen: and, as explained, they
were not unlikely to mistake such a berg for an island. If this reasoning be
acceptable, *cadit quæstio.*

The Aurora Islands.

And now, at long last, to return, after this well-nigh interminable
digression *"de omnibus et quibusdam aliis"*, to the question (now, perhaps,
more comprehensible) of the Aurora Islands.

It may be as well, in the first place, to give the original authority for
their appearance on the charts—an authority long regarded, with justice,
as unquestionable. Here is an extract from the *Transactions* of the Royal
Hydrographical Society of Madrid, 1809.*

* My version is based on that given by Weddell in his *Voyage towards the South Pole,*
pp. 61–9. I have made one or two slight amendments, and added an explanatory word
or two in brackets.

"THE AURORA ISLANDS

"We do not learn that they were ever seen before the year 1762, in which they were discovered by the ship *Aurora*, which gave them her name. In 1790 they were likewise seen again by the ship *Princess*, belonging to the Royal Philippine Company, Captain Manuel de Oyarvido, who showed us his journal in Lima, and gave us some information with regard to their situation. In 1794, the corvette *Atrevida*, having gone purposely to situate them, practised in their immediate vicinity from the 21st to 27th of January all the necessary observations, and measured by chronometers the difference of longitude between these islands and the port of Soledad in the Maluinas. The islands are three; they are very nearly in the same meridian; the centre one is rather low, and the other two may be seen at nine leagues distance."

Then follows a very impressive set of calculations (which I will spare the reader) as to the position of the islands. The results are as follows:

Southernmost Island	53° 15' 22" S.	47° 57' 15" W.
Centre, or Low Island	53° 2' 40" S.	47° 55' 15" W.
Northernmost, or New Island	52° 37' 24" S.	47° 43' 15" W.

The northernmost island was apparently called New Island by the *Atrevida* because it had not been sighted previously—for a most simple reason.

In justice to Don Manuel Oyarvido, as will appear later, one further extract must be made:

"The captain of the *Princess* says, that to E.S.E. of the southernmost island there is a bank or shoal, at the distance of eleven miles, but the corvette *Atrevida*, which made various efforts to find it, could not discover it. . . ."

In an appendix to this account, there is a detailed account of the *Atrevida's* exploits, presumably from the pen of her commander, Captain J. de Bustamente. One or two passages in it explain a good deal.

Apparently he was not enamoured, as every true surveyor ought to be, of exploration for its own sake. We read:

"We took advantage of the winds, sometimes favourable, sometimes contrary to our course, keeping in the parallel of 53½° (S.) and with prudent moderation determined to lie-to at nights. . . . In these lyings-to, we suffered the double martyrdom of losing precious time, and encountering rollings and a cold that were insufferable even to those who had just experienced the intemperance of Cape Horn."

Then, on the 20th of January, comes the sighting of the southernmost of the Auroras.

"At 5½ p.m. we perceived to the northward, at a great distance a dark lump, which appeared to all of us like an iceberg. Notwithstanding, we bore away for it under a press of sail; and when we were near it, we saw distinctly a great mountain in the form of a tent, divided vertically into two parts; the eastern extremity *white*, and the western very *dark*; on which latter side was a belt of snow: and we noticed some breaks in the dark streak.

"We all agreed that this was *the* island: but we saw no other, and none of the circumstances agreed with those reported of the Auroras.

"We passed within one mile of the island, coasting it on the western side; and from that point, it presented us the view of a sharp rock, trending from north to south. The southern part, constantly exposed to the freezing winds from that quarter, was covered with snow; and, falling perpendicularly on the north-west side, with winds much more temperate and moist, the land was there perfectly discoverable."

They lay-to during the night, hoping for finer weather next day.

"At daylight, we saw another island at a great distance, also covered with snow, but not so high as the former one. At 6h. it might be distant ten miles, to the N. by E., and the first island was seen to the S.E., distant about eight miles. At 9h. we lost sight of it (the second island); and although the wind freshened from the N.W. we went round it without result, because, the clouds not having dissipated, we could not observe the latitude at noon. We nevertheless waited, and at one o'clock had an altitude, and another at three o'clock. . . .

"The wind was now at S.W., and we hauled to the southward, seeking in higher latitudes more favourable winds to get to the westward and make the coast of Patagonia.

"On the 24th, at midday, we were in 55° 28′ latitude S.; and as we did not meet better winds, but rougher seas and more intense colds, it was resolved to lessen the latitude, in search of more favourable weather. We stood to the northward, on the port tack, with all sail; and on the 26th, at evening, discovered to the E. ¼ N.E. a white lump, which at first appeared to us an iceberg; but its immobility soon convinced us that it was an island. It is a large rock, making in sharp pinnacles, but formed like a saddle-hill. The N.E. was covered with snow, but the southern part, being perpendicular, would not retain it. At a mile from this last point, there extended several breaking reefs, terminating in small islands. We coasted along this great rock at a regular distance, and sounded frequently, without finding bottom. On the 27th, in the morning, we had good observations of latitude and longitude. . . ."

Such, in epitome, in Bustamente's account; and, at first sight, it reads most convincingly. But there is a caveat to be entered, which may as well be done here.

I am convinced that Bustamente, at the start of his cruise, had, like the Bogus Surveyor's captain, a preconceived idea as to what he would find; and I think I can indicate what that idea was.

In the reported latitude of the Aurora Islands (53° 33' S.) and some six degrees further eastward (42° 02' W.) there is an undoubted group of small rocky islets, called the Shag Rocks. It is uncertain who discovered them; but they are known to have been shown on a chart which Bellings-hausen, the Russian circumnavigator of the Antarctic, bought in London in August 1819. They are quite close together—not more than a mile or two apart—and form a line of three pinnacles some 150–200 feet high, running about north and south. A shoal awash lies ten miles S.E. by E. of the southernmost of the islets.

Now there is very little doubt that some tidings of these Shag Rocks had reached Bustamente, probably from his informant Oyarvido. The coincidence between the actual shoal 10' S.E. by E. of the Shag Rocks and the shoal stated by the latter to lie east-south-east of his Aurora Islands "at the distance of eleven miles", is proof positive, to my mind, that Oyarvido was, so far as we know, the discoverer of the Shag Rocks, and that he took them for the islands previously reported by the *Aurora* because he was unable to detect the considerable difference in the two longitudes. If so, the information he gave Bustamente actually referred, though neither knew this, to the Shag Rocks; and there are several indications to that effect in Bustamente's journal.

For example, in a passage already quoted he remarks: ". . . We all agreed that this was *the* island; but we saw no other . . .," clearly indicating that he expected to find more than one island in sight at a time. Again, in an earlier passage (not previously quoted) he remarks:

"At daybreak on the 16th, we saw two large icebergs distant 5 miles to the N.E. Their pyramidal shape would not have failed to flatter our hopes if their proximity had not destroyed the illusion. . . ."

Assuredly the man who wrote that was expecting to fall in with "pyramidal shaped" islands.

Cheered, no doubt, by the thought that he had performed a useful piece of exploration, and not suspecting that he had added to the woes of seamen fighting their way round the Horn as well as to the subsequent gaiety of nations, he went his way to the comparative comfort of Pata-gonia, where, in company with his chief, Captain Malaspina, of the *Descubierta*, he executed a number of excellent surveys which have better stood the test of time. His Aurora Islands remained, encumbering the charts—but not, happily, the ocean.

The first seaman to relieve his professional brethren of this incubus was Captain James Weddell, a man of very remarkable character, who lacked nothing but opportunity to have won fame second to none as a Polar explorer. He will never be quite forgotten, for in 1823 he accomplished the remarkable feat of beating, by nearly two hundred miles, the "furthest south" record previously established by Cook, and reaching, with two tiny and feeble ships, the unprecedented latitude of 74° 15' S. The sea which he traversed, and to which he gave the cumbrous name of "Sea of George the Fourth", is now known, most justly, as the Weddell Sea.

Weddell spent many years sealing and exploring in the South, but he never had a chance to repeat his famous exploit. He died at forty-six, esteemed and remembered as a fine seaman, a daring explorer, and—more important than either—a truly noble character; a man who achieved magnificent results with scanty means, and who never grudged either time or trouble in promoting the safety and the prosperity of his brother sailors.

Of this trait, his search for the Auroras in 1820 provides an excellent example. He sailed from Staten Island, off Cape Horn, on January 27th, in the brig *Jane*, and ran eastward along the parallel of 53° 15' S. On Feb. 1st, at noon, he observed his position to be 52° 47' S., 48° 47' W.; only 28 miles 254°, therefore, from the *Atrevida's* "New Island". I continue the story in his own words.*

"At seven in the evening we had passed over the (laid down) latitude and longitude of these islands, without observing the least appearance of land. We *obtained* and continued in the parallel of latitude, running through the place assigned to them till we arrived in the longitude of 46°. I consider this allowance for error in longitude to be pretty ample; particularly since the *Atrevida* sailed from port Soledad in the Falkland Islands; from which, to the place for our investigation, was but about three days' sail: hence her common reckoning could not have erred much, and she had chronometers which should have been nearly exact. *These considerations produced in my mind a degree of surprise; and I could not, at that moment, reconcile my experience with the facts which had been asserted.*† I was resolved, however, not to abandon the object of my pursuit, without being fully satisfied of the truth or falsity of this geographical problem.

"It was now remarkably clear; and, from the masthead, land of common height might have been seen at the distance of eight leagues; but still, nothing of the kind was observed. We next steered S.S.E. into the latitude of 53° 17', and then W. by S., in order to get sight of the southern island; but in vain—not the smallest indication of land appeared. . . .

* *A Voyage towards the South Pole* . . . (London, 1825) pp. 60–74. The book is based, of course, on Weddell's journal: but I believe this to have been revised for publication by his friend William Jerdan, editor of *The Literary Gazette* from 1817 to 1850.

† This passage is not italicized in the original.

"The situation for the middle island bore now S. 33° E., distant eight miles. We had a clear view of 6 or 7 leagues, but nothing like land was to be seen. The only chance now left us for finding these Auroras, I conceived, was by making various courses between the latitudes of 53° 15′ and 52° 37′; and this we did.*...

"We had thus again passed over the site of these islands to no purpose. ... Having thus diligently searched through the supposed situation of the Auroras, I concluded that the discoverers must have been misled by appearances; I therefore considered any further cruise to be an improvident waste of time; and to the gratification of my officers and crew, directed our course to the Falkland Islands."

Perhaps the most striking feature of Weddell's narrative, apart from its evidence of his ability and thoroughness as an explorer, is its urbanity. Surely, if hard Fate should decree that one must publicly be called a liar, one could only wish that such a man as Weddell should have the doing of it. And how staunchly he and his editor must have resisted the temptation to put the word "discoverers" into inverted commas.

After Weddell, several other explorers engaged in the excellent but rather purposeless pursuit of "flogging the dead horse". Johnson, and also Morrell, in 1822, and Biscoe in 1830 made similar protracted and careful searches for the Auroras without success.

But tradition dies hard. As a class, cartographers, like lexicographers, are conservative and seamen credulous. The Auroras survived, on many charts, well into the second half of the nineteenth century—although in this particular the Admiralty charts, on which they never appeared, form an honourable exception. Even Ross, who knew of Weddell's work, accepted their existence, for they appear on the South Polar chart published in his book in 1847; although this may be merely a blunder, since in the same chart he omits the Shag Rocks. And many seamen made the existence of the Auroras an article of their simple faith, fathering upon them a wonderful legend that somewhere on their shores reposed the wreck of a Spanish galleon, offering untold wealth to its fortunate discoverer.

For this "foc'sle yarn" there is a discoverable, if flimsy, foundation. In October 1819 a Spanish three-decker, the *San Telmo*, was lost with all hands on the South Shetland islands. Remains of her timbers, but no records or traces of survivors, were found on some of the islands by the sealers. William Smith, who had discovered the South Shetlands only a few months before her loss, possessed, and perhaps now inhabits, a coffin made from such timbers.

* See Fig. 18. It may be noted that the track there shown is not in exact agreement with this description.

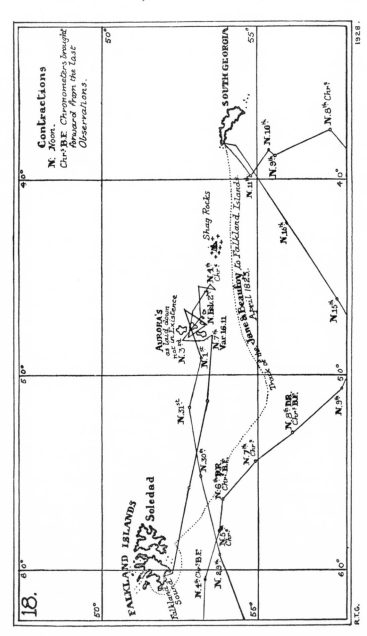

FIG. 18.—Copy of part of a chart by James Weddell, showing his track when in search of the Aurora Islands. The chart originally appeared in his book *A Voyage towards the South Pole* (London, 1825).

The silent tragedy of the *San Telmo*, garbled and distorted by rumour, became, by an easy association of ideas, located at the Aurora Islands. And the treasure, of course, was an inevitable addition. For many people, such as those who persistently subscribe money for diving operations in Tobermory Bay, the ideas "Spanish galleon" and "treasure" are indissolubly associated. With reference to the "treasure-ship *Florentia*", sunk some fifty feet in the Tobermory sands, and devoutly believed in by the late Duke of Argyll and many humbler mortals, it may be pertinent to point out that she is quite certainly not the *Florentia*, which got safely back to Spain, but the *San Juan Bautista*; and that, in all human probability, there never was an ounce of treasure on board of her.

In 1838 the mystery surrounding the Auroras attracted the attention of one of the greatest and most unfortunate of all writers, Edgar Allan Poe (*pace* Mr. H. L. Mencken* and other wielders of the critical broad-axe, who take a perverse pleasure in bespattering the only world-figure of American literature). He embodied it, not without some artistic shaping of the actual facts, in his extraordinary story *Arthur Gordon Pym*, the only long story—except the similarly-unfinished *Journal of Julius Rodman*—which he ever wrote. He seems to have mainly relied for his facts upon Morrell's book; but probably he also obtained a good deal of information from one J. N. Reynolds, a pertinacious advocate of American Antarctic exploration who became, as much as any man could become, Poe's intimate friend—one for whom he called vainly in his last hours.

Another "sighting" of the Auroras took place in 1856. Here is an extract from the log of the *Helen Baird*.

"1856, Dec. 6th.—Moderate breeze and foggy; at 4h. a.m. the chief mate reported icebergs to leeward (eastward); going on deck, pronounced them to be the Auroras covered with snow; two in sight (a large and small one) bearing east (true) distant eighteen miles; at 6h. a.m. more clear, saw two others to the northward—altogether five† islands; at 8h. a.m. the northern island was east 12 miles, with the N.W. and north parts clear of snow—the south covered, the top being flat, with snow; the south end higher than the north. By meridian altitude and chronometric observation the north island is in lat. 52° 40′ S., long. 48° 22′ W.—and the whole may be about twenty to twenty-five miles in extent from north to south."

But by this date the tide had turned, and the fictitious existence of the

---

* Still, I can forgive Mr. Mencken much of his petulant mud-sligning for the sake of that slim book of essays which he has cheerfully entitled *Damn: A Book of Calumny* (New York, 1918).

† It is a curious coincidence that Purdy's *Oriental Navigator*, published in 1816—when the existence of the Auroras was unquestioned—remarks (p. 21):

"16. AURORA ISLES. Five small isles, distinguished by this name, are exhibited in the late Spanish charts. . . ."

Auroras was nearing its close. The captain of the *Helen Baird* (who seems to have possessed his full share of dogmatism and self-importance) might say what he pleased—he was preaching, in general, to deaf ears. Rosser and Imray, however, in their *South Atlantic Directory*, published in 1870, paid him the compliment of examining his report, in conjunction with all the former data, most seriously; and went out of their way to obtain particulars of the tracks of many vessels which had recently traversed the site of the islands. These routes they embodied in a chart in which the unfortunate Auroras are pierced and transfixed, by tracks of damning accuracy, in a manner which brings to mind the pictures showing the martyrdom of Saint Sebastian.

Still, the tradition of the Aurora Islands long survived their removal from the charts: they were once more reported—finally, let us hope—in 1892. Here is an extract from the log of the barque *Gladys*, Capt. B. H. Hatfield, from Iquique to Hamburg, June 26, 1892.

"Lat. 52° 55' S., long. 49° 10' W., land was reported on the lee quarter about 12 or 15 miles distant; it appeared like a long island extending from N. 11° E. to S. 11° W., true, about 10 or 12 miles long, with two hummocks rising up from the top, dividing the island into thirds, which would appear like three islands. . . . It was free from any snow. . . . At 8 a.m. discovered another island . . . distance about ten miles. The part which I saw presented a bold bluff appearance of moderate height, and flat on top, slightly rising towards the south, with greyish appearance, free from snow. . . . It looked as if there might be a passage between this island and the long island. . . . Mu h reliance cannot be put on my reckoning, as I had no observations for several days."

In a subsequent letter to the *Journal of Commerce** (Oct. 10, 1892), Capt. Hatfield remarked:

"I think those islands which I discovered would about tally with the position of the Auroras, which have been so many years unsuccessfully searched for. Captain James Weddell searched for them in 1820, and declared they did not exist. That man went in the middle of the long summer days, when they were covered with snow and ice, and declared them icebergs;† but in the dead of winter, when I saw them, such places are apt to be free from ice and snow."

Unfortunately, contemporary investigation showed conclusively that what the *Gladys* had actually seen, and mistaken for land, was a couple of very large tabular icebergs.

What the *Atrevida* actually saw still remains, and will probably always

* *Liverpool Journal of Commerce*, Oct. 3, 1892.
† See "Icebergs in the Southern Ocean", by Wm. Allingham (*Nautical Magazine*, vol. for 1893).

remain, a puzzle. From his journal, her captain seems to have been perfectly capable of distinguishing between an iceberg and an island; he states emphatically that he saw naked land; and apparently he was by no means without opportunities of making accurate observations. Weddell suggests that what he actually saw was, in the case of the first and third islands, the Shag Rocks—their appearance altered by pack-ice adhering to them, over which their summits would show black—and that the second island was an iceberg encrusted with earth, similar to one which he had himself encountered farther to the south. But while Weddell's views are entitled to considerable weight, his solution is not altogether satisfactory.

Unless we conclude that Bustamente and all his officers were incompetent to navigate a barge from Portsmouth to Spithead—in which case they were scarcely like to find employment as marine surveyors—we must assume that they were at least capable of determining their position (given such chances of observation as they had) within, say, five minutes of latitude and half a degree of longitude. In such a case, it is very difficult to believe that, if he saw the Shag Rocks, he could have been so grossly in error as *six degrees* of longitude; and it is simply inconceivable that his first and third islands, differing in *latitude* some 38', could *both* have been the Shag Rocks. Nor does his account suggest that the land which he saw resembled the Shag Rocks much in appearance; while in view of his emphatic assertions as to the nature of what was seen, which was certainly unlike any iceberg, Weddell's theory as to the origin of the second island seems also untenable.

As suggested, it is possible that Bustamente had at the back of his mind a preconceived idea, inspired by what Oyarvido had told him of the Shag Rocks; and a psychologist might perhaps regard his Aurora Islands as a distorted Brocken-spectre of the Shag Rocks themselves, preserving their number and relative situation, but transferred bodily to the westward, and hugely enlarged both as to their size and as to their distance apart. That he could subconsciously put together, piecemeal, this dream of his and select, in the course of a voyage of considerable range and very varied direction, such appearances—icebergs or whatever else they may have been—as would bring it on to the chart, is, as the American papers used to say, "remarkable—if true": yet I put it forward, with diffidence, as the only attempt at an explanation which I can offer.

"And now," in the manner of Herodotus, "let it suffice to have said this much about the Auroras and all other doubtful islands."

VIII

MERSENNE'S NUMBERS

Many, I have no doubt, have heard of the enthusiastic Don who once proposed a toast to "Pure Scholarship", coupling with it the pious aspiration, "And may it never be of any damned use to anybody". Like most other exemplary and edifying fables, it has been fathered upon many people and located in many places.

There is one department of human knowledge concerning which we may safely assume that this aspiration will always be fulfilled. The utility of the various branches of mathematics is, generally speaking, in inverse ratio to their purity; and even though the abstruse results of non-Euclidean geometry and similar studies are now finding comparatively practical applications in the Theory of Relativity and quantum mechanics, most of us are willing to take such matters on trust, confident that, even if there is an omitted symbol or other loose screw in the reasoning, no shipwreck, structural collapse, or other practical inconvenience can possibly result.

And of no branch of mathematics is this more true than of the Theory of Numbers. It is so utterly devoid of practical value, and so remote from the normal interests of even the majority of mathematicians, that most of the latter have discreetly left it alone. It is a fascinating subject, but one of very limited appeal.

During the seventeenth and eighteenth centuries, the foundations of modern mathematics were well and truly laid by hundreds of willing hands. Yet in the same period there were but four first-class mathematicians—Fermat, Euler, Legendre, and Lagrange—who can be said to have advanced the Theory of Numbers beyond the point at which it had been left by Diophantus some twelve centuries before.

Their work is curiously related. Several of Fermat's results were left in the form of theorems—statements professing to be true, but not accompanied by a proof. About a century later, these proofs were, in most cases, supplied by Euler; who, in turn, left some similar theorems to await proof at the very capable hands of Lagrange. Lagrange also supplied the missing proofs for most of Fermat's remaining theorems. But not for all. The Theory of Numbers is one of those branches of mathematics which are peculiarly prolific of unsolved puzzles. From the eighteenth century down to quite recent times we are constantly finding cases in which some mathematician has enunciated a theorem relating to the Theory of Numbers and has omitted to supply its proof. We believe that the theorem is true—in one or two cases it is practically certain that such is the case—but in the present state of mathematical knowledge such proof is not forthcoming; if it ever existed, it has perished with its discoverer.

It may seem almost incredible that Fermat,* for example, who died on January 12 1665, should have been able to discover valid theorems which none of his successors, equipped with mathematical weapons of which he could never have had any conception, has ever succeeded even in proving; but there is practically no doubt that such is the case. The famous and apparently simple "Fermat's Last Theorem" provides an excellent demonstration of the fact.

Equations such as $x^2 + y^2 = z^2$, $x^3 + y^3 = z^3$, ... $x^n + y^n = z^n$ are algebraical commonplaces. In arithmetic, it is perfectly simple to find integers (whole numbers) which, if substituted for x, y, and z in the first of these equations, will satisfy it. Thus,

$$3^2 + 4^2 = 5^2.$$

But, according to Fermat, it is impossible to find *any* integral values whatever for x, y, and z which will satisfy the equation $x^n + y^n = z^n$ if n is *any* integer greater than two. In other words, the sum of the squares of two whole numbers can be a square; but the sum of two cubes can never be a cube, the sum of two fourth powers can never be a fourth power, and so on for ever. The same holds good, *mutatis mutandis*, for the differences of such powers.

Nothing, apparently, could be simpler than such a theorem—nothing, certainly, has been found harder to prove. The best result up to date has been a demonstration, based on an investigation published by Kummer in 1849, that the theorem is certainly true for all values of n up to 100, and for many higher values complying with certain conditions.† But that is not in the least the same thing as a general proof. None such has yet been given: although a money prize offered in 1907 produced, within three years, a crop of over a thousand false proofs.

It has been seriously questioned whether Fermat himself possessed such a proof. It is a question of assertion *v.* improbability. He definitely stated that he had a general demonstration of it—*demonstratio mirabilis sane‡*— and the balance of evidence seems to be in his favour. It awaits rediscovery.

---

* Pierre de Fermat, Counsellor to the parliament of Toulouse.

† Professor L. E. Dickson, of Chicago, has shown, for example, that if x, y, and z are prime to n, the equation is definitely impossible for all values of n up to 7,000. There is some ground for suspecting that, for cases in which this relation does not obtain, Fermat's theorem does not invariably hold good.

‡ He enunciated the theorem in a Latin note on the margin of his Diophantus, adding (I translate) ". . . of which matter I have found a wonderful and valid proof. This narrow margin cannot contain it".

A famous feat of factorizing which he performed in 1643 affords another example of his extraordinary powers. Having received a letter inquiring whether the number 100,895,598,169 possessed any factors, he replied by return that it was the product of 898,423 and 112,303.* Both of these numbers, as he pointed out, are primes; *i.e.* they have no factors except themselves and 1. The enquiry was certainly addressed to the right man, and its result suggests that Fermat possessed some test for rapidly determining whether any given number is prime or not. No general test of the kind is known at the present day.

The existence of some such test is also suggested by the case of "Mersenne's Numbers"—in all probability a third puzzle provided by Fermat for the bewilderment of later mathematicians. Before going into it, one or two general remarks may be useful.

Prime numbers (I apologize for the repetition) have no factors except 1 (and themselves). When they are small, their recognition is easy. Most people, for example, know that such numbers as 17 and 37 are primes. But it is not so generally realized that there is no limit to the size of prime numbers; and this fact tends to go unrecognized because when an odd number runs into four—or even three—figures it is almost impossible for the ordinary man to say, off-hand, whether it is prime or not.

There is, in fact, only one case on record of a person possessing the ability to factorize mentally, and at sight, any number less than 1,000,000. He was Zerah Colburn (*ob.* 1840), the American "calculating boy". When in London in 1812, being then aged eight, he was asked for the factors of 247,483, which he at once gave as 941 and 263 (both primes) —while on being asked for the factors of 36,083 he replied that it had none. The ordinary man would see no immediate difference in kind between 36,083 and 36,087—yet the first is a prime, while the second is divisible by 3.

But when dealing with primes running into billions, the "calculating boy" and the ordinary man are equally helpless, and even the professional mathematician is far from happy. As a curiosity, I subjoin the largest number which is definitely known to prime. It happens to be one of Mersenne's $(2^{127} - 1)$ as will be seen later.

$$170,141,183,460,469,231,731,687,303,715,884,105,727$$

The fact that it is to be prime was established by E. Lucas in 1876–7, and verified by E. Fauquembergue in 1914.

---

* It seems probable that Fermat was accustomed to factorize large numbers by expressing them as the difference of two squares—a method to which reference is made in the collected edition of his works (*Œuvres de Fermat*, 3 vols., Paris, 1891, 1894, 1896).

Composite numbers are those which can be resolved into factors. All composite numbers belong to one of three classes—abundant, deficient, and perfect numbers—depending upon the relation which they bear to the sum of their factors. For example, of the three numbers 24, 28, and 32, 24 is abundant: the sum of its factors—12, 8, 6, 4, 3, 2, and 1—is 36. 28 is perfect—the sum of its factors is also 28. And 32 is deficient, for its factors only total 31.

The great majority of composite numbers are deficient or abundant. There are, by the way, certain pairs of numbers, one abundant and one deficient, which are called "amicable numbers", and stand in a curious relation. Such are, for example, 220 and 284. 220 is abundant; the sum of its factors is 284. 284 is deficient; and the sum of its factors is 220. 1,184 and 1,210 are another pair of the kind.*

Perfect numbers are very rare indeed. There are two (6 and 28) in the first hundred whole numbers; but there are only four in the first million and seven in the first billion. The eighth is no less than

$$2,305,843,008,139,952,128.$$

The largest *known* perfect number is produced by multiplying $2^{127} - 1$ (previously quoted) by 2^{126}. I have never seen the result in print, but it has been computed at least three times in recent years—by Mr. R. W. Hitchcock (1934), myself (1935), and Mr. E. T. Hall (1942). As all three calculations are exactly accordant, it is safe to accept

14,474,011,154,664,524,427,946,373,126,085,988,481,573,677,491, 474,835,889,066,354,349,131,199,152,128

as the largest number at present known to be perfect. Anyone, with a good deal of time on his hands, who doubts the fact has my full leave to test it by factorising, and summing the factors: but while so far I have shirked this—and shall continue to do so—I am none the less confident that the statement is correct.

The reason for this confidence is that we know, and have long known, the formula governing the form of a perfect number—in other words, the recipe for making them. A great part of the work done on the theory of numbers has dealt with the forms of numbers—for it is quite a mistake to imagine that all numbers are much of a muchness. They can be classified into a very large number of quite well-marked divisions, possessing the most unexpected properties.

* The discovery of this pair, remarkable for their very small difference in value, is due to Nicolo Paganini, who announced it in 1866, being then aged sixteen. It may be noted that he is not identical with the famous violinist—who died in 1840.

For example, all prime numbers greater than 3 are of the form $6n \pm 1$.* That is to say, any such number is within 1 of being divisible by 6. But this is only the beginning of their analysis. They can be further classified into four principal forms and twenty-six sub-forms. The leader in this department of analysis, the "partition of numbers", was Fermat, and after him Lagrange; but in modern times its branches have flowered into such a profusion of "congruences", "residues", "ideal primes", "indeterminates", "ternaries", "sets of points" and other blossoms of mathematical terminology as would make them stare to see.

The form of all even perfect numbers has long been known; and it may be noted that there is some ground for supposing that no odd number can be perfect. No number of the kind is known to exist†—on the other hand, no general proof has yet been given that such a number is an impossibility. As the result of the combined though scarcely simultaneous labours of Euclid and Euler, it is known that all even perfect numbers are of the form

$$2^{p-1} \left(2^p - 1\right),$$

when $\left(2^p - 1\right)$ is a prime: and, also, that all numbers of this form are perfect.

The computation of large perfect numbers, therefore (if anyone should wish to spend his time in such a manner), depends upon our being able to determine whether a given value of p makes $\left(2^p - 1\right)$ a prime or not. And at this point we necessarily come across the very remarkable statement published by Mersenne in 1644.

Marin Mersenne (1588–1648) was a Frenchman who joined the Franciscan brotherhood and was, for some years, the head of a convent at Nevers. Most of his time, however, was spent in mathematical correspondence. Like his successor Collins (1625–83) in England, he acted as intermediary between all the leading mathematicians of his time, and became, in effect, a one-man "Bureau of Mathematical Information". In the preface to his book, *Cogitata Physico-Mathematica*, published in Paris in 1644, there appeared his celebrated statement respecting certain numbers of the form $2^p - 1$.

These numbers are now generally known as "Mersenne's numbers", a name introduced by the late W. W. Rouse Ball, of Trinity College, Cambridge. It is worth noting, however, that Rouse Ball, who had made a special study of the subject, was firmly of opinion that the statement in

* It is not, of course, true that all numbers of this form are prime. Such an assumption would constitute a good specimen of the "converse fallacy of accident". 35, for example (5×7) is of the form $6n - 1$, and 55 (5×11) of the form $6n + 1$.

† If any does, it must exceed 2,000,000—and, as shown by J. J. Sylvester, it must contain at least six prime factors.

question was actually due to Fermat, one of Mersenne's most constant correspondents.* This has not been definitely established, but it appears most probable. Mersenne's own language suggests that the statement did not originate with himself, but had been communicated. In addition, he was quite an ordinary mathematician, not at all likely to propound a problem which has baffled, in part, all succeeding attempts to verify it. On the other hand, such a feat was, from what we know of Fermat, well within his capacity—while there is no other mathematician of the time, except Newton, of whom the same can be said.

Following Rouse Ball (of whose work on the subject, embodied in the various edition of his *Mathematical Recreations and Essays*, I have made free but, I hope, not unfair use) Mersenne's statement—or, rather, Fermat's —can be distilled out of its original Latin and boiled down to this.

"For values of p from 1 to 257, the expression $2^p - 1$ is a prime when p is 1, 2, 3, 5, 7, 13, 17, 19, 31, 67, 127, or 257; in all other cases it is a composite number."

Actually, as it stands, this statement is not quite correct. Of the numbers given, 67 should be 61; Mr. R. E. Powers, an American computer, showed in 1911–14 that $2^p - 1$ is prime, not composite, when p is 89 and 107; and in 1926 Kraitchik† showed that $2^{257} - 1$ was composite. As will be seen, these errors have caused the statement to be regarded, by a very competent judge, as a mere guess.

Apart from these corrections it appears, so far as it has been verified, to be true. Its interest resides in the fact that our present mathematical knowledge does not enable us to discover, in some cases, whether it is true or not; and, while it can hardly have been either due to sheer guess-work or laboriously verified in every case, the principle on which (presumably) it is based remains to be rediscovered.

The difficulty of verifying it is largely due to the huge size of some of the numbers which have, if possible, to be factorized. For example, when p is 257 the resulting $2^p - 1$ contains 78 figures.

The number of cases which have to be examined is fifty-six; the prime values of p between 1 and 257 inclusive—for 'if p is composite, so is $2^p - 1$. Of these, it is stated (with the corrections previously indicated) that 43 values of p make $2^p - 1$ a composite number, and that 13 make it a prime. So far, all of the former cases have been verified, and 7 of the latter. There remain six values of p – 157, 167, 193, 199, 227, and 229

---

* It is, however, possible that the statement was communicated to Mersenne by Frénicle, another contemporary French mathematician. He did a good deal of work in connection with the theory of numbers, but is best known by his researches upon the subject of magic squares.

† His result was verified by Lehmer in 1930.

—for which at present the statement has still to be verified. They yield, in all cases, values of $2^p - 1$ running into a large number of figures, and it is known that none of these values possesses any factor less than a million. According to Fermat, $2^p - 1$ is composite in all six cases.

The history of the problem, which has attracted many eminent mathematicians from Euler onwards, shows, as might be expected, that it has been found relatively easier to factorize the numbers than to show that they are prime. For example, Euler discovered the factors of $2^{251} - 1$, but the highest number which has been definitely shown to be prime is $2^{127} - 1$. In certain cases, factors of $2^p - 1$ are known even for much higher values of p than any of Mersenne's numbers: for example, R. Niewiadomski showed in 1913* that 4,567 is a factor of $2^{761} - 1$; and one factor of $2^{967} - 1$ is known.

In view of that fact that at present we are unable even to test Fermat's statement exhaustively, it is difficult to question the view expressed by Rouse Ball, who speaks of "Mersenne's numbers" as "one of the unsolved riddles of higher arithmetic", and remarks:

". . . It is impossible to believe that the statement made by Mersenne rested on an empirical conjecture, but the puzzle as to how it was discovered is still, after more than 250 years, an unsolved problem."

On the other hand, it is only fair to point out that a very definite opinion of a contrary kind has been expressed by a distinguished mathematician of our own day, Professor G. H. Hardy, of Cambridge. In a paper read before the mathematical section of the British Association in 1922, he remarks:

. . . "The bubble has at last been pricked. It seems now that Mersenne's assertion, so far from hiding unplumbed depths of mathematical profundity, was a conjecture based on inadequate empirical evidence, and a rather unhappy one at that. It is now known that there are at least four numbers about which Mersenne is definitely wrong; he should have included at any rate 61, 89, and 107, and he should have left out 67. The mistake as regards 61 and 67 was discovered as long ago as 1886,† but could be explained with some plausibility, so long as it stood alone, as a merely clerical error. But when Mr. R. E. Powers, in 1911 and 1914, proved that Mersenne was also wrong about 89 and 107, this line of defence collapsed, and it ceased to be possible to take Mersenne's assertion seriously.

"The facts may be summed up as follows. Mersenne makes fifty-five assertions, for the fifty-five primes from 2 to 257. Of these assertions,

---

* *L'Intermédiare des Mathématiciens*, vol. 20 (1913), pp. 78, 167.

† By Seelhoff (but, earlier, by Pervušin—in 1883). Seelhoff's proof is not flawless. Lucas had already found, in 1876-7, that $2^{67} - 1$ was not a prime. (R.T.G.)

forty are true, four false, and eleven still doubtful. Not a bad result, you may think; but there is more to be said. Of the forty correct assertions many, half at least, are trivial, either because the numbers in question are comparatively small, or because they possess quite small and easily detected divisors. The test cases are those in which Mersenne asserts the numbers in question to be prime; there are only four of these cases which are difficult and in which the truth is known; and in these Mersenne is wrong in every case but one.

"It seems to me, then, that we must regard Mersenne's assertion as exploded; and for my part it interests me no longer. If he is wrong about 89 and 107, I do not care greatly whether he is wrong about 137* as well or not, and I should regard the computations necessary to decide as very largely wasted. There are so many much more profitable calculations which a computer could make."

With the last sentence of Professor Hardy's remarks I entirely agree; but with regard to the remainder I must say that while he has performed the functions of *Advocatus Diaboli* with candour and efficiency, and while I am far from imagining that I am competent to argue a mathematical question of this kind with him, it seems to me that there is a good deal to be said, on general lines, for the view taken by Rouse Ball (with whom I used to have very pleasant and, on my part, profitable correspondence on one or two mathematical subjects).

In the first place, I agree with Rouse Ball in regarding Fermat's inclusion of 67 and his omission of 61 as due to a misprint. Mersenne's book was a large one; the statement (in which one or two simple misprints are extremely obvious) occupies an incidental and quite unimportant position in the preface, not in the body of the book; and while mathematical works of the seventeenth century were, as a class, more carefully printed and corrected than most other books, they are, as a rule, very far from flawless. If this view be accepted, it at once reduces Fermat's errors from five to three.

The omission of $p = 89$ and $p = 107$, and the incorrect statement respecting $p = 257$, are more serious; but I cannot see that they should be regarded as outweighing the great preponderance of cases in which Fermat's statement has been shown to be correct—a preponderance which would still be sufficiently striking if we threw into the other scale all the cases yet waiting to be verified. Nor do I consider that it is quite fair to pass over in silence the remaining half of the "forty correct assertions" merely

---

* In an earlier portion of his paper, Professor Hardy had alluded to $2^{137} - 1$ as the smallest Mersenne number whose prime or composite character was still (1922) an open question. Actually it had been shown by Fauquembergne, in 1916, to be prime—as Fermat said. The smallest Mersenne number still (1944) unverified is $2^{157} - 1$.

because they relate to composite numbers. Several of these assertions were so far from being "trivial" that their verification required a great deal of most laborious numerical work; and their correctness is surely no less convincing testimony than that of the numbers asserted to be prime.

If Professor Hardy had written his paper twenty years later he could, of course, have strengthened his case materially by adducing Fermat's erroneous statement that $2^{257} - 1$ was prime; but on the other hand he would have had to weaken it in respect of his totals of "true", "false", and "doubtful" assertions. At present, out of Fermat's fifty-six* assertions forty-seven are now (1944) known to be true, and three† false, while six are still doubtful.

The real objection to the "conjecture", I suggest, is one which Professor Hardy has only implied. The theory that Fermat's statement was not empirical but proceeded from real knowledge presupposes, or at least suggests, that he possessed (as already remarked) some means of rapidly ascertaining whether a given number, of any size, was prime or composite. If he possessed such a test, it is difficult to understand how he failed to detect the true character of $2^p - 1$ when p is 89, 107, or 257. It may have been a simple oversight—the history of science is full of such blunders, committed by the keenest-witted men. Or it may have come about through a mere numerical error, for it can scarcely be assumed that even a test of the kind indicated could be applied without a good deal of calculation. That Fermat had, or thought he had, such a general test is strongly suggested by a later passage in Mersenne's preface, which contains the startling assertion—impossible to test by any known method —that there are *no* values of p between 17,000 and 32,000, or between 1,050,000 and 2,090,000, which make $2^p - 1$ a prime.

For completeness, I may point out that Rouse Ball had not overlooked the error respecting 89 and 107‡ when he published his considered opinion, already quoted, as to the problem still presented by "Mersenne's Numbers".

It may be of interest to add one or two details of other theorems of the kind which still await proof. Apart from Fermat's Last Theorem there are, for example, these:—

Euler's Biquadrate Theorem.—The arithmetical§ sum of the fourth powers of three numbers cannot itself be a fourth power; in other words, $a^4 + b^4 + c^4 = d^4$ cannot be solved numerically.

---

* Fifty-five if, for technical reasons, we do not regard 1 as a prime.

† Assuming that his "67" is a misprint.

‡ That respecting 257 was not discovered until after his death in 1925.

§ This is not true of their *algebraical* sum: Euler himself pointed out that $a^4 + b^4 = c^4 + d^4$ is satisfied by $a = 542$, $b = 103$, $c = 359$, $d = 514$.

Goldbach's Theorem.—All even numbers can be expressed as the sum of two primes. At present the proof of this depends upon that of another theorem, enunciated by Riemann, which is also believed to be true, but at present defies proof. In view of its somewhat formidable appearance, and the high cost of mathematical type, I refrain from giving it here.

Lagrange's Theorem.—Every prime of the form $4n - 1$ is the sum of a prime of the form $4n + 1$ and of twice another prime of the same form. Lagrange reached this result by induction, but could not prove it.

Various theorems dealing with the partition of numbers, and for which a rigorous demonstration is lacking, have also been enunciated, in quite recent years, by the late Srinavasa Ramanujan, F.R.S., of Cambridge. In fact, the field for the amateur computer who decides to devote his time to clewing-up some of the loose ends of the Theory of Numbers is a wide one; and, as Professor J. B. S. Haldane has indicated in his *Possible Worlds,** it offers useful employment even for circle-squarers.

* *Possible Worlds*, J. B. S. Haldane (London, 1927), p. 173—in the essay "Scientific Research for Amateurs".

IX

THE WIZARD OF MAURITIUS

M any years ago, in

> . . . times when I remember to have been
> Joyful and free from blame,

I came across a copy of Sir David Brewster's *Letters on Natural Magic*. It seemed to me then, and it seems to me now, one of the most wonderful books ever written. With advancing and sorrowful years, I have come to know more about Brewster. I am better able to appraise at its true value, for example, that laboured feat of idolatry which he called *The Life of Sir Isaac Newton,* and which, if touched with Ithuriel's spear, must have displayed on the covers of both its portly volumes the legend, "An Opinionated Defence of the Absolute Uprightness, Mental Chastity, and Fair-Mindedness of Sir Isaac Newton against the Clearest Evidence". But although I speedily became aware that Brewster was far more to be respected as the inventor of the kaleidoscope than as a narrator of facts, and although I regretfully decided that in the case of D. D. Home the honours rested with the American "spiritualist" and not at all with the "scientist" who explicitly asserted, in a private and long-unpublished communication, statements which he took the earliest opportunity of disavowing in a letter to the Press, I have never swerved in my allegiance to his amazing collection of scientific marvels.

It is a wonderful book—wonderful both for its matter and its manner. Brewster does not smack you on the back and invite you to laugh at the exploded chimeras which delighted and puzzled our ancestors; nor does he come up to you, with a twitch at your sleeve and a sneer on his lips, and tell you what a fine fellow you are, to be sure, to scoff at anything which Modern Science (always in capitals) cannot explain to your complete satisfaction. He goes to work soberly, honestly, and painstakingly to show you the *raison d'être* of the wonders he recounts; and, if he has a fault, it is one which, in all probability, arises simply from the time which has elapsed since his book was first published. Every now and again he slips in some reference to a matter which, in the first half of the nineteenth century, was probably a thing of common knowledge, but which perplexes us of the twentieth not a little.

I can scarcely give a better illustration of my meaning than the following extract, premising that Brewster is speaking of mirages, and other natural optical illusions:

". . . The representation of ships in the air by unequal refraction has no doubt given rise in early times to those superstitions which have prevailed in different countries respecting 'phantom ships', as Mr. Washington Irving calls them, which always sail in the eye of the wind, and plough their way through the smooth sea, when there is not a breath of wind upon its surface. In his beautiful story of the storm ship, which makes its way up the Hudson against wind and tide, this elegant writer has finely embodied one of the most interesting superstitions of the early American colonists. The Flying Dutchman had in all probability a similar origin, *and the wizard beacon-keeper of the Isle of France, who saw in the air the vessels bound to the island long before they appeared in the offing, must have derived his power from a diligent observation of the phenomena of nature.*"

As I have since learned, there can be no doubt that, when Brewster wrote the singular concluding words which I have italicised, he was referring to a subject which was, for the intelligentsia of his day, a matter of common notoriety. But, at the time when I first read them, I do not think that there were many people alive who could have made head or tail of them. If I am bold enough to think that I have co-opted myself *in nostro docto corpore*, it is because I have since, in the course of a desultory and haphazard process of reading, conducted (to my shame be it written) not entirely apart from Government time, come across some long forgotten papers which throw a flood of light on a very dark subject.

Broadly speaking, the evidence which I have found shows quite clearly that Brewster was well within the truth when he spoke of a man at Mauritius who could foretell the arrival of ships at the island long before they appeared over the horizon. He might have gone further, and told how this man could determine, by his mysterious gift, whether one ship, or more, was approaching, and how long it would be before it, or they, came in sight—and even state in the same manner, when on board a ship, the distance and bearing of the land when it lay a long way below the visible horizon. He might have said all of this, and yet never have departed by one iota from the exact and certified truth.

Of all the remarkable events in connection with the wizard of Mauritius, none, I think, is more remarkable than the extraordinary manner in which some account of his doings has been preserved to our own time. The facts are as follows:

The hero of our story is an obscure Frenchman named Bottineau, who returned from the Isle de France (Mauritius) to his native country in 1784—only to find that France, in travail with an upheaval which was shortly to change the whole face of Europe, had little inclination, and less leisure, to consider or reward his newly discovered art of "Nauscopie"—the discovering of ships, when below the horizon, by means of the effect which their motion produced upon the atmosphere. Bottineau, a shadowy figure who fades out of sight almost before one has time to appraise him, seems to have made but one convert, or semi-convert, of note—the famous or infamous Jean Paul Marat, M.D. of St. Andrew's University, N.B., and some time a troglodytic inhabitant of the Paris sewers; but latterly, until very properly stabbed in his bath* by Charlotte Corday after his forensic defeat of the Girondins, one of the three most powerful men of the Terror. Time enough has gone by to forgive Marat for his crimes—the Cleon of his age, he is no more to be blamed for seizing power when his chance came than a clot of scum is for riding bravely down the stream when once it had been dislodged from its native fastness—and we must at least be thankful that a happy chance has embalmed Bottineau in his correspondence like a fly in amber.

In the year 1806 an English gentleman, whose name, unfortunately, has not been preserved, was residing, on parole,† at Brussels. He seems to have made the acquaintance of Madame Guilleminot, sister-in-law to the General of that name. This lady, being (in common with most French women of the time) smitten with the prevailing craze for collecting autographs, applied to one of Napoleon's numerous and virtuous sisters for a few signatures of celebrated men. The Princess in question forwarded the request to Cambacérès, then Chancellor of the Empire, at whose direction "une énorme tas de papières" was forwarded to Mme. Guilleminot. It is worth while noting that many of these papers had never passed through the post office: they were original drafts, often disfigured by erasures and interlineations. This, in itself, is no marvel. During the First Empire, and still more during the Revolution itself, your private papers and, *a fortiori*, your correspondence, were never regarded as anything more than the raw material of a prosecution; and the "Cabinet Noir" must have accumulated, between 1793 and 1814, sufficient *pièces*

---

* As Mr. A. Neil Lyons has sung:

> . . . there 'e sat
> A spitting up
> The purple blood like wine:
> When Joe Golightly
> Very rightly
> Knifed 'im in the spine,
> 'E sadly sat
> A-spitting up
> The purple blood like wine . . . (*da capo*).

† He was a *detenu*: one of the several thousand English people who visited France in 1802 (during the Peace of Amiens), and of whom the survivors returned to England in 1814.

incriminatoires to carpet the entire surface of the habitable globe.* What is remarkable is that, among the papers which Mme. Guilleminot received, and which she gave to the *détenu* for perusal, were some documents relating to Bottineau and the marvels which he had accomplished at Mauritius.

At this point, unfortunately, there is *hiatus valde deflendus* in our history. All that can safely be asserted is that, in some way or another, the papers in question came, in 1834, into the hands of Captain A. B. Becher, R.N., founder and first editor of that estimable monthly *The Nautical Magazine*. Anyone who doubts my veracity may refer, in the Admiralty Library or elsewhere, to the issue of that periodical which, adorned on its cover by a magnificent steel-engraving of His respected (if sub-normal) Majesty King William IV of happy memory, appeared in March 1834. There, under the suggestive heading "Original Papers" (and what paper, surely, could be more original than the one in question?), they will find, distinguished by the sub-title "The Art of Discovering the Representation of Ships, etc, in the Atmosphere", the raw material of the present essay.

One conceives the meticulous and be-whiskered Becher, type and pattern of all succeeding Assistant Hydrographers, undergoing some conflict of mind before deciding to open his columns to the amazing narrative which had fallen into his hands. His venture, *The Nautical Magazine* (still flourishing, but not conducted quite on its original lines), was only two years old. A breath could make it—or unmake it. To his eternal credit, he took the risk: and his foresight was, if anything, justified only too abundantly. Not one of his readers, so far as I can discover, troubled to enquire either as to the source of his materials or as to the authenticity of the facts there embodied.

One wonders, if Becher had possessed that bent for mystification which produced Locke's *Moon Hoax*, and Poe's *Hans Pfaal, Von Kempelen,* and *Balloon Hoax*—all published, in reputable journals, as matters of sober fact—how far, given his obviously trustful clientèle, he could safely have gone. Surely, there never was a stranger tale than Bottineau had to tell; and, although I believe it to be strictly true, I am still perplexed to understand how his memory (he had long been dead when his narrative saw the light) managed to escape the Jeddart justice which an incredulous public meted out to Marco Polo, Mendez Pinto, du Chaillu, and a hundred others who, foolishly handicapped by veracity, have told it truths which it was not prepared to hear.

The first letter printed by Becher is one from Marat to a Mr. Daly.† It is not dated, but was probably written about 1785.

---

* I once gathered from a correspondence in *The Times* that this property is equally characteristic, in peace-time, of disused safety-razor blades.

† I have not been able to identify Daly with any certainty.

"You know, my dear friend, that much of my time has lately been taken up in preparing my work upon Light, Fire, etc., for the Press: it is, however, nearly completed; you may, therefore, expect to hear from me very regularly in future. M. Bottineau, whom I mentioned to you in my last letter, has experienced every kind of disappointment. If he is able to raise sufficient money, he purposes visiting London very shortly, where he is likely to meet with more success; for you gentlemen of the British Isles will, I am convinced, patronize the discovery which my friend has made. I who have made a study of optics, meteors, etc., am, I must confess, somewhat sceptical respecting the science which he terms *Nauscopie*, or the art of discovering vessels and lands at a considerable distance: but the concurring testimony of hundreds of persons, the certificates which he has obtained from officers of high rank, all tend to show that there must be truth in his statement; and although he may have been neglected in France, I hope, for the honour of science, that a fair trial will be given him in your country, and that he will not be treated as visionary.

"Certain it is, that if his art should prove to be true, incalculable advantages will be derived from it. I have seen an officer who resided six years in the Isle of France, and he assures me that the whole population will corroborate the averments made by M. Bottineau. . . .

"Such, my dear friend, is the account which M. Bottineau has given me; he has also explained the phenomenon, which, he assures me, in order to understand perfectly, only requires being on the seashore for a few hours, and that in less than a week I should understand his art as well as himself. As my poor friend looks very ill, I am afraid he will not be able to visit England, the only resource, he says, that is left to him. Mr. Moore, who has been studying medicine here for some time, leaves Paris this evening for London, and will take charge of this letter.

"I have not time to explain to you the phenomenon perceived in the atmosphere when a vessel approaches land, etc., but I will give you all the explanation in my power in my next letter, and very possibly it may enable you, who have so many opportunities of visiting the coast, to ascertain whether the art of *Nauscopie* be one of those sublime discoveries that do honour to the genius of man. For myself, if I could conveniently visit the seashore, I would certainly make more than one trial. When I have sent you the explanation, you will judge for yourself; and do not act as the Abbé Fontenay, for one of your poets has said wisely, that 'There are more things in heaven and earth than are dreamt in our philosophy'. Adieu.

"MARAT."*

* He follows the accepted French practice of signing with the surname only.

Incorporated in Marat's letter is an account, by Bottineau himself, of the genesis of *Nauscopie*. For the sake of clearness, I print it separately.

"As early as the year 1762, holding then an inferior situation in the King's navy, it appeared to me that a vessel approaching land must produce a certain effect upon the atmosphere, and cause the approach to be discovered by a practised eye even before the vessel itself was visible. After making many observations, I thought I could discover a particular appearance before the vessel came in sight: sometimes I was right, but more frequently wrong; so that at the time I gave up all thoughts of success.

"In 1764, I was appointed to a situation in the Isle de France: while there, having much leisure time, I again betook myself to my favourite observations.

"Here the advantages I possessed were much greater than before. First, the clear sky and pure atmosphere, at certain periods of the day, were favourable to my studies, and as fewer vessels came to the island, I was less liable to error than was the case off the coast of France, where vessels are continually passing, some of which may never arrive in sight, although the indications I allude to may have been witnessed by me. I had not been more than six months upon the island when I became confident that my discovery was certain, and that all that was requisite was to acquire more experience, and then *Nauscopie* would become a real science.

"As the officers in the island led an idle life, they were frequently on the shore looking through their glasses to discover when a vessel was arriving from Europe. I frequently laid wagers that a vessel was arriving, one, two, and even three days before she was actually in sight, and as I was very seldom wrong, I gained a considerable sum of money.

"The officers attributed my success to a particular power of vision I possessed; but then again, they were quite puzzled on reflecting, that although they used glasses, I never employed any.

"In 1780, I wrote to the Minister of Marine, Maréchal de Castries, announcing my discovery. In his answer, he instructed the Governor of the island to enter my *announcements* of arrivals in a private register for two years at least.

"On the 15th May, 1782, my observations commenced.

"On the 16th May I announced to the Governor that three vessels were near the island. Orders were immediately given to the *vigies*;* their glasses were turned to the direction which I had pointed out. Their declaration was—'No vessel in sight.' On the 17th, the *vigies* informed the Governor that a ship had just appeared above the horizon. On the

* The official watchmen, or "look-outs".

18th, a second came in sight, and on the 26th, a third was visible to the naked eye.

"Viscount de Souillac sent for me on the last-named day, and made me an offer of 10,000 livres, and a pension of 1,200 livres a year, on the part of Government, if I would disclose my secret; but not conceiving the remuneration sufficient, I declined accepting the offer.

"Viscount de Souillac, some months after, wrote to M. de Castries: he stated, that I had made the surprising discovery of a new art—that of being able to observe the arrival of vessels 100, 150, and even 200 leagues distant; that for more than fifteen years I had regularly predicted the arrival of vessels, sometimes three or four days before they could be seen with a glass: that the register kept by order of the Minister showed that I had almost always been right in my predictions; and that even when I had announced the approach of a vessel which did not actually arrive, it was proved beyond a doubt that the vessel or vessels in question were foreign ones that had come within two or three days' sail of the island, and had proceeded to their destination without touching at the Isle de France. 'Upon one occasion he asserted that a fleet of eleven vessels were approaching the island; the announcement caused great alarm, as we anticipated an attack from the English. A sloop of war was instantly dispatched to look out; but before she returned, M. Bottineau came to the Governor, and informed him that the signs in the atmosphere had disappeared, and that the fleet had taken a different direction. Some time after this a vessel arrived here from the East Indies, and reported that she had seen a fleet of eleven vessels sailing towards Fort St. William.' *In fine, that from the year 1778 till 1782, he had announced the arrival of 575 vessels, many of them four days before they became visible.*

"The letter terminated thus—'However incredible this discovery may appear, myself and a great many officers, naval and military, must bear testimony to the announcements made by M. Bottineau. We cannot treat him as an impostor, or as a visionary. We have had ocular demonstration for so many years, and *in no instance has any vessel reached the island, the approach of which he has not predicted;* those which did approach, but did not touch the island, were in most cases proved to be foreign vessels.'

"A short time after this letter had been dispatched—(this letter, I am certain, reached the office of M. de Castries, but, I am also certain, was never perused by him)—I determined to return to my native country, and accordingly took my passage on board one of His Majesty's vessels, commanded by Captain Dufour. I felt somewhat anxious to ascertain whether the effect produced on the atmosphere when a vessel approaches, would be somewhat similar, as regards the approach of one vessel towards another, and to my great delight I perceived it to be the same, although less powerful; but my eyes now became so practised, that not once, during the voyage, did I make a mistake.

"I announced to Captain Dufour the approach of twenty-seven vessels, while proceeding to our destination; but (also) what afforded me more heartfelt satisfaction than my previous observations, namely, certain appearances in the skies when a vessel approaches land, the observer being on board; or similar appearances when one vessel approaches another; and, in my opinion, to be able to discover land from a vessel, long before it is in sight, is, if possible, of infinitely greater advantage to navigation.

"Upon one occasion, I told Captain Dufour that we were not more than thirty leagues from some land. This he denied to be possible: however, upon looking attentively to his reckoning, he was compelled to acknowledge that he was in error, and immediately altered his course. I discovered land three times during the voyage; once at the distance of 150 leagues.

"On the 13th June, 1784, I landed at L'Orient, and instantly proceeded to Paris. My applications to the Minister to obtain an audience were not attended to; and the only answer I obtained from the Officer of Marine was, that my memorial was under consideration. Abbé Fontenay, editor of the *Mercure de France*, having heard of my 'pretended' discovery, without even asking to see my certificates, signed by the Governor of the Isle de France, and all the officers of the garrison there, thought proper to turn my discovery into ridicule, and affirmed that it was not 'ships at sea, but castles in the air' I had found out. In this state the affair remains; and all I can add is, that should vexation and disappointment terminate my existence before I can explain my discovery, the world will probably be deprived, for some time, of an art that would have done honour to the eighteenth century."

Poor Bottineau! Assuredly his discovery, could he have shown it to be explicable by the natural science of his time, would have made his reputation, and "done honour to the eighteenth century"; but in view of his proceedings at Mauritius the authorities to whose attention he brought it can scarcely be blamed for thinking that it smacked more of the Middle Ages. If he had wished to build up for himself a reputation as a practitioner of the Black Art, he could scarcely have set about it differently. His unceasing vigils, his definite predictions based (apparently) upon supernatural knowledge, their almost unvarying success, his assertion that he possessed a secret known to no other man, and his refusal to part with that secret even for what, to a man in his circumstances, represented affluence, might not impossibly cause mutterings and shaking of heads among his neighbours even in our own day; eighteenth-century Mauritius and eighteenth-century France probably numbered, even among their professed "free-thinkers", many whom not all the fulminations of

Voltaire and the "appeals to reason" of the Encyclopædists could persuade out of a deep-rooted belief in sorcery.

As Bottineau predicted, the world was deprived of his discovery; as, no doubt, it has also been of many other discoveries made by poor and friendless men who have happened, or managed, to get on the blind side of officialdom. Bottineau was not the first man who has waited, covertly eyed by sneering messengers, in the ante-rooms of Government Departments: and who, as a rare alternative to the customary flat refusal of an interview, has trudged his way along the corridors, hoping against hope that his luck has turned at last—only to be received by some semi-detached private secretary, devoting such time as he can spare from his personal adornment to the neglect of his duties and the sometimes polite but invariably definite discouragement of "outsiders".

Yet there can be little doubt that Bottineau was no charlatan—that he had made a discovery which would be of some interest even in these days of W/T, and must, in his own day, have been of much greater importance. Looking at the matter from the standpoint of the Vicomte de Souillac, it is a little difficult to understand how, in those days of "wars and rumours of wars", Bottineau ever managed to obtain from him permission to leave the island.

The French Governors of Mauritius, from Labourdonnais downwards, seem to have possessed, and exercised, a remarkable measure of absolute power. It is a matter of history that, some thirty years later, the unfortunate Captain Matthew Flinders, R.N., who, duly provided with a French safe-conduct, had done more for the survey of Australia than any one man before or since, was arrested at Mauritius in 1804 when on his way home to England, and was detained there till 1810 by the arbitrary fiat of the Governor, Decaen—and this in spite of the fact that the latter had received instructions for his liberation from Napoleon's Government as soon as the news of the arrest reached Europe. If De Souillac had compelled Bottineau to remain, or had demanded his secret as the price of letting him go, it is quite probable that the French Government, if they ever heard of this high-handed proceeding, would have endorsed it. And it might, in the long run, have been better had De Souillac acted thus. But whatever his motives may have been—and distrust in Bottineau's powers can scarcely have been one of them—he let him go his way to disappointment, neglect, and an unregarded death.

I turn to the certificates which the Abbé Fontenay so derided.

No. 1

A letter from the Governor of the Isle of France to the Marshal de Castries.

"Port Louis, Isle de France,
"18.4.1784.

"Monseigneur,—A letter which you wrote on the 6th of April, 1782, to M. Bottineau, a ci-devant officer of the second class in this colony, in the king's service, as well as in that of the company, renders it imperative on our part to give him one for you, of which he is the bearer.

"It is in order to be useful to his country that he is about to visit France; and he would experience much regret were his discovery lost to the world; a discovery with which he alone is acquainted, and which others have, in vain, attempted to unfathom: it consists of announcing the presence of one or several vessels at a distance of 100, 150, and even 200 leagues. Is this the result of study, or the application of the principles of some science? By no means: all his science is in his eyes. He sees in nature signs that indicate the presence of vessels, as we assert that fire exists in places where we see the smoke; this is the comparison he makes, when speaking to others concerning his art; in keeping his discovery a secret, this is the clearest explanation he has afforded, in order to show that he did not make the discovery by the knowledge of any art, or of any science, or by the application of any previous study.

"He asserts, that it is the effect of chance that led him to the discovery; he has watched Nature, and found out her secret; this science, therefore, has not, it may be said, cost him any trouble: but that which has required much study, and really belongs to him, is the *art of judging of distances.*

"The signs, he says, indicate clearly enough the presence of vessels, but *they only who can read the signs* are able to judge of the distances, and this art, he asserts, is an extremely laborious study. On this very account, he had for a long time been the dupe of his science; *for the last fifteen years he has foretold the appearance of vessels in this island.*

"At first it was merely a gamble: he was in the habit of making bets, and often lost them because the vessels did not arrive at the appointed time: on this account, he studiously applied himself to find out the cause of his errors, and the perfection of his art is owing to his exertions.

"Since the war has broken out, his *announcements* have been very numerous, and sufficiently correct to create a sensation in the island. We have conversed with him upon the reality of his science; and to have dismissed him as a quack would have been an injustice. Moreover, we required proofs, and he regularly supplied us with 'announcements'; and the result was, that several vessels that had been announced several days beforehand, arrived at the precise time; several others were delayed, and several did not arrive.

"It has since been proved, that the delay in the arrival of some of the vessels was occasioned by contrary winds, or currents in the ocean. Those which did not arrive, M. Bottineau is fully persuaded, were foreign vessels which passed by; and, indeed, we have since ascertained that a fleet of English vessels arrived in India which might have been in sight of the island at the time fixed upon by M. Bottineau. *What we can certify is, that M. Bottineau was almost always right.*

"Whether this be the effect of chance, or otherwise, it would perhaps be imprudent in us to determine: this, however, is certain, that the circumstance is so extraordinary, in whichever way we consider it, that we endeavoured to prevail upon M. Bottineau to make us come to a positive conclusion, either by confiding his secret to us, or to any well-informed person who could be depended upon: but he declined to accede to our request; fearing, no doubt, that he should not obtain a sufficient remuneration for his discovery.

"We have the honour, etc.,
"LE VICOMTE DE SOUILLAC.
"CHEVRAU."

No. 2.

"The undersigned, chief officer of engineers of the King in the Isle de France, certifies, that M. Bottineau has, at different periods, announced to him the arrival of more than a hundred vessels, scarcely without ever being mistaken (*sic*); that he announced these vessels, two, three, and even four days before the coast signals; and, moreover, that he stated when there was only one, or when there were several vessels.

"*(Signed)*   GENU.
"TREBOND, *Colonel of Infantry.*
" *November* 16, 1780."

No. 3.

"I cannot refuse my testimony to truth, and I give this certificate in acknowledgment of the pleasure and agreeable surprise I have experienced from your continued and certain announcements. I advise you to cultivate this science, which will prove of immense benefit. The remarks of a few idle persons must not deter you. When Christopher Columbus proposed his discovery, he was treated as a madman by John the Second, King of Portugal, and Henry the Eighth, King of England; and had it not been for Isabella of Castille, who encouraged this celebrated Genoese, America would perhaps not yet have been discovered.

"This example, and a thousand others, show how prudent it is to withhold one's judgment on points of fact, in systems founded on astronomy or philosophy. I am persuaded that nature possesses a thousand secrets which are still hidden from us.

"*(Signed)* LE BRAS DE VILLEVIDERNE,
"*H.M. Attorney-General for the Isle de France.*
"5.11.1781."

No. 4.

"We, Commissary-General of the Navy in this port, certify, that having wished to try whether M. Bottineau really possessed the talent of announcing (before the usual observers placed upon the mountains) the vessels that arrive here, and having desired him to inform us in writing of his predictions, he has announced to us within six months, one hundred and nine vessels, one, two, three, or four days before the signals were made from the mountains, and in this number he only was twice mistaken; moreover, he explained these errors by contrary winds or the currents. We have also to acknowledge, and not without great astonishment, that his art extends so far as to inform him whether there was one, or there were several in the vicinity of the Isle, and if they were together or separated.

"*(Signed)* MELIS.

" PORT LOUIS, ISLE DE FRANCE.
"16.5.1782."

Reading these certificates, it will be conceded that there is at least a *prima facie* case for conceding to Bottineau the power which he claimed of being able, by the recognition of some atmospheric phenomenon (which was, apparently, visible to anyone whose eye had been trained to recognize it), to predict the approach of vessels of which every portion was still a long way below the horizon. No other explanation, I submit, is possible. Those who deny the authenticity of the documents which I have reprinted here are necessarily confronted by the fact that not only Brewster, but also many other people of his time have noted and expressed some garbled version of the story of "the wizard of Mauritius". It came, for example, to the front in the days when the mind of every intelligent person in our country was exercised over the problem of finding traces of Sir John Franklin's ill-fated expedition.* In Brewster's day, there seems to be no doubt that the story of the ill-fated *Nauscopist* was a matter of "common fame", although, as often happens, the actual facts of the case were overlaid by a thick superstratum of rumour.

* See, for instance, a letter (not otherwise remarkable) by one John Christophers, published in the Parliamentary Papers relating to the Franklin search expedition under Capt. Austin, R.N. (1852).

I come now to the last of the documents which I shall reprint: Bottineau's own explanation of the feats which, I submit, there is no doubt that he accomplished. And there is an objection *in limine* of which I should like to dispose.

It has not infrequently been the case that the opinions of the intelligentsia and of οἱ πολλοί (which, as a matter of course, have differed) have ultimately been weighed in the balance of informed general judgment, and the popular opinion confirmed. On the literary side, I need only instance *The Pilgrim's Progress*, whose author Cowper dared not name. To-day, little as we may like Christian's haste to leave behind his wife and family in his eagerness to come first to the Golden Shore, we acknowledge (even without necessarily perusing all, or any, of the pages of that wonderful book) Bunyan's pre-eminence as an allegorist, and as the never-failing guide and solacer of those who are "fast bound in misery and in iron". Similarly we know, as the result of the labours of E. F. F. Chladni (better known as the eponym of "Chladni's figures" and the founder of modern acoustics) that the ages-old theory of the origin of meteorites is, strangely enough, correct, and that the fine-spun theories of those scientists who stoutly denied, *a priori*, that they could possibly have an extra-terrestrial origin were, if possible, less related to fact than the dogmas of any, or all, of the various churches which, being "no connection with the firm over the way", alone promise salvation.

If we seek for a modern case of an undisputable fact being discovered and remaining unexplained, we have not far to look. In 1922, Mr. E. A. Reeves, Map Curator of the Royal Geographical Society, published his discovery of the fact that a freely-suspended piece of paper, exposed to strong sunlight, will always tend to turn so as to set itself north and south. This fact has been repeatedly verified; but, so far, it has not been explained, either by its discoverer or by anyone else. With this passing reference, I wish (greatly daring) to point out that it is entirely unfair to expect the discoverer of such facts to put forward their explanation; just as the local wit of Sir James Barrie's *Window in Thrums* was careful to explain that it was unfair to expect the maker of a joke necessarily to see the humour of it.

This, unfortunately, is a matter upon which, as upon all other subjects, public opinion is incorrectly informed. The discovery of some fact is one thing; the explanation of it quite another. Bacon saw this clearly, when he laid down the rules to be followed by his "Interpreters of Nature". Some men provide the facts: others interpret them. Occasionally, the two rôles are filled by the same man; but this is a rare event, not a natural consequence. The point is put very clearly by Wells (I have too high an opinion of his works to write "Mr. H. G. Wells", any more than I should

write "Pierre Simon de Laplace", or "Charles John Huffham Dickens"*)
in his story *Filmer*, which deals with a man who discovered an entirely safe
method of flying, and killed himself rather than take part in an actual
demonstration of his invention.

I remember coming across, many years ago, a book chiefly written by
John Mullins, who acquired a competence and a considerable reputation
as a successful "dowser", or diviner of subterranean water-springs. In his
later years, he had been induced to put his experiences on paper: and, not
content with recounting simply the facts of his own experience—the
many cases in which he had indicated successfully the place of springs in
situations far remote from any spots where ordinary geologists considered
that there was a probability of finding water—he seems to have felt
impelled to give his conclusions, and theory, as to the *modus operandi*
which he employed. Though he did not know it, he was adding to an
already considerable literature upon his own subject, and his contribution
bore a strange and painful resemblance to a work which was published in
1546.

The book was reviewed, shortly after its appearance, in the scientific
equivalent of *The Times*, that excellent paper *Nature* (of whose founder
and first editor Henry Smith, the Cambridge mathematician and wit,
once said that "he exhibited an arrogance which would still have been
offensive even had he been the Author of Nature"). The review was
entrusted to a deservedly-famous physicist who had done work of first-
class importance. With almost boyish glee, he fell upon his *corpus vile*
much as, one imagines, Macaulay went to work upon the utterly inept
productions of "Satan" Montgomery.

His review was scathing, clear, concise, damning—and absolutely
unfair. In these days, "this ghastly, thin-faced time of ours", we hear,
amid much waving of entirely bathetic red flags, frenzied and Klaxonic
(or should one say Maxtonic?) appeals of "fair play for the underman".
Well, if ever there was an entirely justified appeal of this kind, it was that
of Mullins and Son *v.* Authority. The subject-matter of the case—the
question whether it is possible for certain specially gifted people to detect,
by indications which are impalpable to most of us, the presence of underground water—may reasonably be regarded as still *sub judice*. I will only
say that those who have not read the late Sir William Barrett's book on the
subject—and I have never yet met an opponent of the "dowser" who had
—have still a little to learn; for my own part, I consider that the power of
detecting underground water through one's personal sensations (of which
the hazel twig, like the "planchette", is merely a convenient but by no
means indispensable index) is one scarcely rarer than the ability to move

* Or, for that matter, "John Henry Brodribb Irving".

one's ears independently—a faculty which I happen to possess myself. But whether this be so or not there can, I think, be little question that for a trained physicist to join issue with a well-meaning but imperfectly-educated man on the subject of phenomena which the latter honestly professed to have observed, *and not to take his stand on the facts but upon the explanation of them*, was to gain a Pyrrhic victory by the sacrifice of all traditions of fairness, sportsmanship, and scientific candour. The motto of a celebrated society to which the reviewer belonged is *Nullius in Verba*, and its leading principle has always been that of the man from Missouri—"It's up to you to show me". I could give many instances from its history in which one man has brought the facts of a certain phenomenon into notice, and another has explained them. To gird at a discoverer because he has not hit upon the true explanation of his observations is not far removed from the sin of Ham.

With these petulant but not entirely irrelevant remarks, I return to Bottineau. Here are some notes which have survived upon the subject of his discovery, as explained by himself. It is exasperating to reflect that his secretive "complex", to use a word beloved to those who minister to the ailments of half-witted old women of both sexes, has prevented him, even here, from giving a clear description of the "signs" upon which his "art" was based.

"NAUSCOPIE is the art of ascertaining the approach of vessels, or, being in a vessel, the approach to land, at a very great distance. The knowledge neither results from the undulation of the waves, nor from quick sight, nor from a particular sensation, but simply from observing the horizon, which bears upon it certain signs indicative of the approach of vessels, or land.

"When a vessel approaches land, or another vessel, a *meteor** appears in the atmosphere, of a particular nature, *visible to every eye*, without any difficult effort: it is not by the effect of a fortuitous occurrence that this meteor makes its appearance in such circumstances; it is, on the contrary, the necessary result of the approach of one vessel towards another, or towards land. The existence of this meteor, and the knowledge of its different modifications, constitute the certainty and precision of my announcements.

"If I am asked how it is possible that the approach of a vessel towards land can cause any meteor to be engendered in the atmosphere, and what affinity exists between two effects so removed; I reply, that I must be

* I.e. an atmospheric effect (Fr. "météore"—c.f. our "meteorological"). Compare Gray's *Bard*:

.... his hair
Streamed like a meteor on the troubled air."

excused giving an account of the *why* and the *wherefore*; that it is sufficient I have discovered the *fact*, without being obliged to explain the principle.

"Do not even the learned acknowledge that the explanation of meteors is often beyond their comprehension? Valmont de Bomarre says, 'Almost all meteors present in the mechanism of their formation considerable difficulties, profound mysteries, which all the knowledge of philosophers has not yet been able to penetrate.'

"After this avowal, it certainly is not my province to explain what the most learned men declare to be inexplicable.

"The meteor of which I am speaking, although manifesting its effects, may conceal its principle; and, notwithstanding my discovery, does not the less exist.

"However, the study of twenty years seems to have given me a right to reason upon a subject that has become so familiar to me; and the following is my opinion on this head.

"The vast expanse of water forms an immense abyss, into which substances of all kinds are continually entering. The enormous number of animals, fishes, birds, vegetable and mineral productions, which are decomposed in the vast body of water, produce a continual fermentation of matter, which abounds in spirit of salt, sulphur, bitumen, etc. The presence of these gases is sufficiently apparent, from the smell and disagreeable taste of sea-water. These gases, closely united with the sea-water, remain stationary so long as the waters are quiet, and not disturbed; or they may only experience a slight internal agitation, which is manifested externally in a small degree.

"But when the water is put in motion by stormy weather, or by an active mass which passes over its surface with violence and rapidity (a vessel for instance), then the volatile vapours that are enclosed within the bosom of the deep escape, and rise in smoke (*fumée*), composing a vast envelope around the vessel. As she advances, the envelope advances with her, increased every moment by fresh emanations. These emanations are so many particular clouds, which, by degrees joining each other, form a kind of cloud (*nappe*) that projects forward, one extremity of which touches the vessel, while the other extremity advances to a considerable distance. This train of vapours is not on that account visible; it escapes observation by the transparency of its parts. And it is lost among the other fluids that compose the atmosphere: but as soon as the vessel reaches a situation in which it meets with other homogeneous vapours, such as those which escape from the earth, one perceives, on a sudden, that cloud (*nappe*) until then so limpid and subtle, acquire consistence and colour, by the mixing of the two opposed columns. The change commences at the prolonged extremities, which unite by contact, and are thus strengthened and coloured; and then, every minute, as the vessel advances, the change is graduated, gains the centre, and at length, the *engrainement* being complete, the phenomenon becomes more manifest, and the vessel appears.*

"Such, in a few words, is the revelation of the cause and the effects of a phenomenon which, however wonderful it may be, accords, notwithstanding, with physical notions.

"Whatever cause may be assigned for this phenomenon, it is quite certain that it is the infallible satellite of a vessel; and that, in consequence of its prolonged form, it manifests itself to the eyes one, two, three, four, five, and even six days before the vessel itself, according to the state of the weather and the nature of the obstacles it meets with. When the vessel sails with a fair wind (*en poupe*) and meets with no obstacle, the phenomenon possesses its greatest celerity; and, arriving several days before the vessel, it affords the observer the means of announcing the presence of a vessel at a considerable distance; but when the vessel meets with contrary winds, it will be understood that this circumstance must have a great influence on the progress of the phenomenon. On this account, I state that the phenomenon sometimes appears four or five days before the vessel, and sometimes only one day. This defect of uniformity in the apparition results from the greater or less impediment it meets with.

"It will naturally be supposed that there may be weather when the phenomenon cannot show itself before the vessel: for instance, in a violent gale, which appears, at first sight, capable of carrying away the phenomenon—even dissipating and entirely destroying it. This, however, is not the case. The most impetuous wind only retards the apparition of the phenomenon, without destroying it. But when the vessel has reached a certain distance from land, then the phenomenon has acquired so much consistence, that it overcomes the efforts of the strongest winds, which, though they agitate it, still leave some part which they cannot wholly disperse.

"The whole of my science consists in being able to follow the apparition of this meteor, and distinguish its character, in order not to confound it with the other clouds in the atmosphere, and which are not to be attended to. In order to make these observations, neither telescopes nor mathematical instruments are required; the eyes alone are sufficient.

"It is not even necessary to be upon the coast; where the horizon of the sea can be discovered, the observer can announce the approach of vessels.

"The cloudy mass does not present itself suddenly, and with all its character. The first appearance is equivocal, and only puts the observer

---

* One could wish that the translator, when dealing with this portion, had consulted someone who could read French without a dictionary.

upon his guard, who can then commence his study, without being in haste to certify that the vessel is arriving; but, by degrees, the forms are developed, the colours assume a certain tone, the volume acquires consistence, so that the *Nauscopist* can no longer doubt that a vessel is behind; because these forms and these developments are such, that they can only belong to these kind of vapours.

"As the vessel advances, the meteor extends, and becomes consistent. From the moment I became familiar with this singular analogy, I never failed seeing my announcements followed by complete success; and this punctuality caused the great astonishment, mentioned in my certificates, etc., from the Governor, officers, and inhabitants. Convinced of the effect, but not understanding the cause, they could not conceive that a science existed which could give to Man a foreknowledge of events so distant, with respect to time and place. The people attributed these events to the power of magic; the better informed ascribed them to chance. Nothing, however, is more natural than this principle, which has astonished everyone, and concerning which so much incredulity will be manifested throughout Europe.

"BOTTINEAU".

That is the last of the "original documents"—if one can apply that term to rough translations, by an unknown hand, from originals which have long since disappeared, and whose provenance is entirely uncertain. Yet, as if to provide one little glimmer of light, the translator has kindly added a note, which is given below.

"The *Gazette de France* mentions this discovery; and the Abbé des Fontains wrote several articles upon the subject; but the public mind was at that period so absorbed in matters of political importance, that the unfortunate M. Bottineau was neglected; and a letter from Marat, at the dawn of the French Revolution, merely states that Bottineau had died.* The different biographical dictionaries we have consulted make no mention of him."

The editorial "we" in the last sentence suggests that Becher himself was the translator—which is not at all unlikely. His searching of "the various biographical dictionaries" is evidence of his thoroughness, if not of his common sense. It was scarcely likely that Bottineau would secure the smallest niche in such tomes; he was more likely to have found his way into such a work as Brewer's *Dictionary of Phrase and Fable*. But unfortunately he did not do so. My search in all likely and unlikely quarters has

---

* Marat was wrong in this. The *Scots Magazine* (vol. for 1802, p. 850) records: "....A Mr. Bottineau, the inventor of a method by which the approach of ships at sea may be discovered . . . died lately in great misery at Pondicherry".

had no better result than Becher's; and we are driven to fall back upon such information as can be extracted from the documents already quoted.

I have already indicated my opinion that the story of the wizard of Mauritius is substantially true. This does not mean that I suggest we should accept every part of it *au pied de la lettre*. Some hardened sceptics may deny the whole story; they may suggest that Bottineau never existed, and that Becher concocted the whole thing out of his own head. This theory is attractive by reason of its simplicity; but it breaks down in face of the incontestable fact that Brewster, who speaks of the matter as a thing of common knowledge, wrote the last of his "Letters" in 1832, while the account of Bottineau in the *Nautical Magazine* did not appear until March 1834.

If, however, we accept the fact that a man named Bottineau once resided at Mauritius and, justly or unjustly, acquired a reputation for being able to predict the advent of vessels which, like the Spanish Armada referred to in the *Critic*, could not be seen because they were not yet in sight (and this starting-point is one which, I suggest, very few will refuse to occupy), it becomes a matter for one's individual judgment how much further one can reasonably go. In what follows, I only give my own views, for what they may be worth.

If we give any credence to the certificates, the theory that Bottineau's successes in predicting the arrival of ships at Mauritius were purely a matter of chance must, I think, be dismissed as untenable. In view of the chances against him, to suppose that his exploits were a matter of guess-work involves greater improbabilities than it removes. Let us assume, then, that he had acquired some peculiar skill in observing, and making deductions from, indications which were not apparent to the average man.

Now what were those indications? His language, even allowing for the inevitable crudities involved in "doing into English" what was, probably, not the most classical French, is very obscure. But it seems possible to extract from it both positive and negative evidence.

Neglecting his own theory, except in so far as it gives some indications of the nature of the appearances which he saw, or thought that he saw, the reasonable deductions seem to be these. He had trained himself to see some very faint appearance, like an extremely attenuated cloud, somewhere near the sea-horizon, and he found, by experience, that this heralded the advent of a ship. He speaks of the "form" and "colour" of such clouds, and of their acquiring "consistency"; but there can be little doubt that even when most fully developed this appearance was far from easy to see. There must have been many people in Mauritius who, stimulated both by his example and by the hope of gaining some such reward as was offered to him by De Souillac, strained their eyes, during the interval between one of his announcements and its fulfilment, to discover the data upon which that announcement had been made. Their non-success proves, if it proves nothing else, that "the phenomenon" was not easily perceptible. Bottineau's own statements support this; he remarks that a person practising his "science" must undergo a short period of education; sure proof that his "meteor" did not leap to the eye.

It will, I suppose, always be a matter of doubt how far he may have been assisted by unusually keen vision. Such he may have possessed—and, indeed, probably did possess; but the importance of such a faculty is very easy to overestimate. In astronomy, for example, it has often been shown that observers using telescopes of quite moderate power have been able to confirm and re-observe discoveries originally made with the great telescopes—*once they knew where to look for them*. The satellites of Mars, originally discovered by Asaph Hall in 1877 with the 26-inch Washington telescope, and often re-observed with a 12-inch aperture, are a good example of this. It seems likely that Bottineau, scanning the horizon, saw what others failed to see simply because he had trained his eye to detect faint indications which were invisible to an ordinary observer who did not know what they looked like.

It will always be a matter for regret that (so far as I am aware) Bottineau's narrative never came into the hands of Charles Meldrum (1821–1901), the great meteorologist to whom we owe the first scientific investigation of the laws governing the cyclones of the Indian Ocean, and who was in charge of a meteorological observatory at Mauritius itself from 1862 until 1896. I do not think, from what I know of his character, that he would have scoffed at it; rather do I imagine that he would have devoted considerable time and trouble to making a full investigation of the subject, keeping an open mind until he had accumulated sufficient data to form a considered opinion.

However, the matter is not past mending. If there is any truth in Bottineau's statements as to the general character of the phenomena which he was able to detect, any observer with a camera and a clear sea-horizon, whether at Mauritius or elsewhere, who takes a series of photographs of the sea-horizon at short intervals spread over a considerable period of time, and checks them against a register (obtained by W/T or otherwise) of the movements of shipping within a 200-mile radius, should soon be able, if Bottineau's "meteor" has any real existence, to announce to the world an important rediscovery; while, if he draws blank, the "wizard of Mauritius" will remain, more than ever, an enigmatic figure—far beyond praise or blame—generally regarded as a charlatan, but actually a member of that unfortunate fraternity to whom the world has never listened, because they have not prophesied acceptable things.

POSTSCRIPT.

In 1817 and 1818 Capt. the Hon. Francis Maude, R.N. (1798–1886), then a midshipman of H.M.S. *Magicienne*, frequently met at Mauritius an old resident who had learned the art of "Nauscopie" from Bottineau himself, and habitually practised it—with unvarying success.

Peter Green, of Tristan da Cunha, was also credited (in 1935) with the ability to predict the arrival of ships a day or two beforehand. (*The Star*, 9.1.35.)

X

THE PLANET VULCAN

Many things, ranging from collar-studs to battleships,* are quite easy to lose. Heavenly bodies, however, are not usually regarded as included in that category. Yet for such to be lost is not an absolutely unknown occurrence. Biela's comet, for example, after circling round the sun in a regular and decorous orbit for a considerable time, was seen as two comets in 1852,† failed to return in 1859, and has not since been heard of. Some of the minor planets, too—tiny bodies a few miles in diameter—have proved so troublesome to rediscover that an American astronomer, the late Professor J. C. Watson, endowed a Home for Lost Planets‡—that is to say, he created a special fund for the purpose of having the orbits of the twenty-two minor planets discovered by himself regularly computed and kept up to date, thus ensuring that such planets would always be "present and correct" when required.

The story of the planet Vulcan, however, is not so much that of a lost planet as of one which, although once accepted as a member of the Solar System, never existed.

On January 2, 1860, Urbain J. J. Leverrier, at the time Director of the Observatory of Paris, and world-famous as one of the discoverers§ of Neptune, read a paper to the Académie des Sciences in which he pointed out that the observed motion of Mercury did not agree with theory. This anomaly, it may be noted, has since become one of the pillars of Einstein's theory of relativity. At the time, Leverrier proposed to explain it by assuming that matter, as yet undiscovered, existed in the sun's neighbour-

---

* Some years ago, on draining a disused dock at one of the French naval yards, an old and forgotten submarine was found in it. See *Punch*, 3-11-09.

† One, at least, of its observers was a total abstainer.

‡ In humble imitation of this kindly act, the present writer maintains a Home of Rest for Aged Typewriters—now (1944) sheltering some seventy inmates.

§ The discovery of Neptune in 1846 was made by calculation: not, as in the case of Uranus, by direct observation. Leverrier computed its probable position and aspect from data afforded by the known perturbations of Uranus. His prediction was verified by Galle, of Berlin, the first man to see Neptune. J. C. Adams, of Cambridge, was afterwards proved to have computed its position (slightly more correctly than Leverrier) about a year earlier; but, owing to the inexplicable negligence and apathy shown by Airy (Astronomer Royal), Challis (Director of the Cambridge Observatory), and (in a lesser degree) by Adams himself, his prediction was not verified by actual observation until after the planet had been seen by Galle.

hood—in other words, that one or more small planets probably revolved somewhere in the space between Mercury and the sun.

There are, of course, two planets known to revolve round the sun at a less distance than we ourselves do—Venus, the beautiful twin-sister of our own world, which we know as a morning or evening star, and Mercury, which is smaller and far more difficult to see. Outside us are Mars, the belt of minor planets, and the giants Jupiter, Saturn, Uranus, and Neptune, while there is some evidence that outside those again there may be one, or possibly two, not yet detected.*

It was natural that Leverrier, who had himself added an extra-Uranian planet to the Solar System, should have felt that there was no *a priori* reason against the existence of an intra-Mercurial one. On the other hand, it naturally seemed rather curious that, if a planet large enough to cause the observed disturbances really existed so close to the sun, this should not have been discovered earlier. He announced his conclusion with diffidence, remarking:

"This result naturally filled·me with inquietude. Had I not allowed some error in the theory to escape me? New researches, in which every circumstance was taken into account by different methods, ended only in the conclusion that the theory was correct, but that it did not agree with observations. . . . Does it [the undiscovered matter near the sun] consist of one or more planets, or other more minute asteroids, or only of cosmical dust? The theory tells us nothing on this point."

It is a singular fact that when Leverrier read this paper he had (or might have had) in his pocket a letter which he had received on December 22, 1859, from one M. Lescarbault, a doctor of Orgères, near Orleans, who was also an amateur—a very amateur—astronomer. This letter announced the discovery of an intra-Mercurial planet.

Lescarbault stated that on March 26, 1859, he had seen a round black spot, apparently a planet in transit, moving across the upper part of the sun's face on a path which slanted upwards. It had remained in view for an hour and a quarter, during which time it had progressed for a distance rather less than a quarter of the sun's diameter.

Very shortly after reading his paper, Leverrier went to Orgères—apparently with the intention of exposing an impostor. It must be remem-

---

* Some investigations made by Professor George Forbes, F.R.S., of Edinburgh, and based on the curious "grouping" of cometary orbits, strongly suggest the existence of at least one unknown exterior planet. A search made in 1890–92 by Dr. Isaac Roberts at Crowborough has shown that, if it exists, it must appear as of less than the 15th magnitude. It will probably be discovered, if at all, by calculation, as Neptune was—and, not improbably, it is outside the range of even the largest modern telescopes. It is certainly not identical with Pluto, the outermost known planet of our system (discovered by Tombaugh, of Flagstaff Observatory, in 1930).

bered that he was a man of very peculiar temperament. Sir J. J. Thomson has told how, as a young man, he paid a scientific visit to Paris and, wishing to call on Leverrier, enquired about him from a common friend. "I do not know", was the rather startling reply, "whether M. Leverrier is actually the most detestable man in France—but I am quite certain that he is the most detested." However, he showed himself most unexpectedly amiable to his English visitor.

He was an extreme example of a man possessing an absolutely first-class brain and almost completely devoid of ordinary human sympathy and tolerance. His manner was not only frigid but repulsive, he made no allowances for human error and frailty, and in the earlier part of his career as Director of the Paris Observatory he conducted himself towards his subordinates so tyrannically that he was removed from his position.* With all this, there can be no question of his genius as an analyst—and much can be forgiven to a man who accomplished such an amount of magnificent work, and of whom it can at least be said that he spared himself no more than he spared others.

Leverrier went down to Orgères in a state of considerable irritation. It appeared to him exceedingly unlikely—and, if true, most irregular—that anyone who had made, or believed himself to have made, so important a discovery should have neglected for nine months to communicate it to anyone—not even to the official head of the French astronomical world, Urbain Jean Joseph Leverrier, Director of the Observatory of Paris, Professor of Astronomy in the Faculty of Sciences, Senator, and decorated with the Grand Cross of the Legion of Honour, as well as a multitude of lesser distinctions. Assuming his most Rhadamanthine manner, he called at Lescarbault's house and, while declining to give any name, insisted upon seeing him immediately. I imagine that Lescarbault must have taken him for a detective, or even a "Juge d'instruction".

The meeting has been inimitably described by R. A. Proctor.†

". . . The interview was a strange one. Leverrier was stern and, to say the truth, exceedingly rude in his demeanour, Lescarbault singularly

---

* He left the Observatory in 1870, but became its Director again three years later, his successor, Delaunay, having been drowned while boating—a fate which he had always dreaded. Leverrier's second tenure of office lasted until his death on September 23, 1877.

It may be noted that methods similar to Leverrier's were once employed at Greenwich—by John Pond, the only Astronomer Royal who has been requested (*i.e.* compelled) to resign his appointment.

† The extract here given is taken from Proctor's *Rough Ways Made Smooth* (London, 1880, pp. 40, 41). The story is also told in several of his other books: it was one of various themes—other examples are "Oxford and Cambridge rowing-styles" and "star-distribution"—to which he often recurred.

lamb-like. If our chief official astronomer called uninvited upon some country gentleman who had announced an astronomical discovery, and behaved as Leverrier did to Lescarbault, there would most certainly have been trouble; but Lescarbault seems to have been rather pleased than otherwise.

" 'So you are the man,' said Leverrier, looking fiercely at the doctor, 'who pretends to have seen an intra-Mercurial planet. You have committed a grave offence in hiding your observation, supposing you really have made it, for nine months. Tell me at once and without equivocation what you have seen.'

"Lescarbault described his observation. Leverrier asked for his chronometer, and, hearing that the doctor used only his watch, the companion of his professional journeys, asked how he could pretend to estimate seconds with an old watch.* Lescarbault showed a silk pendulum† 'beating seconds'—though it would have been more correct to say 'swinging seconds'. Leverrier then examined the doctor's telescope, and presently asked for the record of the observations. Lescarbault produced it, written on a piece of laudanum-stained paper which at the moment was doing service as a marker in the *Connaissance de Temps.*‡

"Leverrier asked Lescarbault what distance he had deduced for the new planet. The doctor replied that he had been unable to deduce any, not being a mathematician: he had made many attempts, however. Hearing this, Leverrier asked for the rough draft of these ineffective calculations.

" 'My rough draft?' said the doctor. 'Paper is rather scarce with us here. I am a joiner as well as an astronomer' (we can imagine the expression of Leverrier's face at this moment); 'I calculate in my workshop, and I write upon the boards; and when I wish to use them in new calculations, I remove the old ones by planing.' On adjourning to the carpenter's shop, however, they found the board with its lines and its numbers in chalk still unobliterated.

"This last piece of evidence, though convincing Leverrier that Lescarbault was no mathematician, and therefore probably in his eyes no astronomer, yet satisfied him as to the good faith of the doctor of Orgères. With a grace and dignity full of kindness, which must have afforded a singular contrast to his previous manner, he congratulated Lescarbault on his important discovery. He made some enquiry also at Orgères concerning the private character of Lescarbault, and learning from the village *curé*, the *juge de paix*, and other functionaries, that he was a skilful physician, he determined to secure some reward for his labours. At Leverrier's request

---

* It had no seconds hand. (R. T. G.)

† An ivory ball suspended by a silk thread. (R. T. G.)

‡ The French equivalent of the *Nautical Almanac*. It has been published uninterruptedly since 1696; the *Nautical Almanac*, since 1767. (R. T. G.)

M. Rouland, the Minister of Public Instruction, communicated to Napoleon III the result of Leverrier's visit, and on January 25th the Emperor bestowed on the village doctor the decoration of the Legion of Honour."

Leverrier, once convinced as to the real character of Lescarbault's discovery, lost no time in performing the necessary calculations which that worthy had found so baffling. He obtained, for the new planet's mean distance from the sun, about 13,000,000 miles, and for its period of revolution 19 days 17 hours. Lescarbault, who had seen Mercury in transit over the sun with the same telescope, and the same magnifying power, on May 8, 1845, considered that the new planet (which he decided to name "Vulcan") had a disc rather less than a quarter as large. Accordingly, Leverrier calculated that Vulcan's volume was probably about one seventeenth that of Mercury. It did not escape him that, supposing its mass to be in anything like the same proportion, Vulcan could not be held responsible for more than a small fraction of the disturbances observed to be taking place in Mercury's orbit.

He also calculated that Vulcan ought to be in transit on the sun's face on or about April 3rd and October 6th of every year, at which times it should, of course, be visible in the same manner as it had been to Lescarbault. He did not hold out much hope of its being seen at other times, since he computed that its lustre would be so feeble that it might easily remain unseen, even during a total eclipse of the sun.*

The existence of Vulcan did not remain unchallenged for long. Shortly after Lescarbault had been decorated, news arrived from Brazil that another astronomer, Liais, whose observations exactly coincided, in point of time, with Lescarbault's, had been examining the same part of the sun with a more powerful telescope, and had seen no vestige of any such spot as Lescarbault had described. Animated, apparently, by the scientific equivalent of the old *odium theologicum*, Liais made no bones about imputing bad faith to his French *confrère*; and he took especial glee in pointing out that while Lescarbault had originally stated that he had watched the black spot enter on to the sun's disc, he had afterwards admitted to Leverrier that it was already on the sun when he first noticed it. A slanderous personal attack of this kind was quite unwarranted, and it is scarcely surprising that Lescarbault (who, whatever his defects as an observer†, was an honest man) did not reply to it.

---

* Proctor has questioned this statement. By his calculations, Vulcan and Mercury, seen during eclipse at their greatest angular distance from the sun, would appear about equally bright.

† Long afterwards, early in 1891, he announced the discovery of a new and brilliant star—which proved to be Saturn!

For some years astronomers in general, stimulated by a circular issued from the Paris Observatory, kept a special watch upon the sun during the periods indicated by Leverrier, hoping to see Vulcan in transit. They were uniformly disappointed. On April 4, 1875, however, interest in the missing planet was revived by a telegram from Weber, a German astronomer stationed at Pechili, N.E. China, stating that he had observed a small round spot upon the sun, which had vanished a few hours later. As Leverrier had indicated April 3rd as one of the two possible dates for seeing Vulcan in transit, the coincidence was sufficiently striking.

Unfortunately, this spot had also been carefully examined at Madrid through a much more powerful telescope than Weber's, while it had been photographed at Greenwich. It proved to be an ordinary sun-spot, and not even quite round.

Another German astronomer, Wolfe, patiently collected details of nineteen observations, made during the period 1761–1865, of dark bodies, unlike sun-spots, having been seen on the sun's disc. It is, however, a significant fact that such appearances have almost invariably been reported by men who are almost unknown as observers, and never by any of the astronomers who, like Schwabe, Carrington, and Secchi, have devoted many years of their lives to making a daily scrutiny of the sun.

But although Leverrier's predicted transits of Vulcan had failed to materialize, it appeared in 1878 as if his views as to the impossibility of seeing Vulcan near the eclipsed sun had been over-cautious.

During the total eclipse of July 29, 1878, Professor Watson, already mentioned, who was well known both as a competent observer and a mathematician, made a careful search for intra-Mercurial planets, and believed himself to have discovered no less than two. Unfortunately, neither of these could be identified with Vulcan, and the question was further complicated by a report from Lewis Swift (another American observer) that he, too, had discovered an intra-Mercurial planet during the eclipse—which planet differed, as was apparent by its position, both from Watson's pair and from Vulcan.

The matter is somewhat confused and difficult to follow. Briefly, the facts are these. Watson, at Rawlins, Wyoming, sweeping with his tele-- scope over the space on the western side of the eclipsed sun, picked up a star which he took to be ζ Cancri, and then, on the way back towards the sun, observed another star, θ Cancri, with, close eastward of it, a much brighter body, which showed a perceptible disc.* It did not correspond in position with any known star, and he took it to be an intra-Mercurial planet.

Subsequently, when checking the position of the pointers which he had

* The magnifying power used by Watson was only forty-five.

used for recording the various star-positions (eclipses do not last long, and he had adopted this device to save time as much as possible), he became convinced that the star which he had taken to be ζ Cancri was itself a new body, about a degree eastward of that star, and presumably another intra-Mercurial planet.

Swift, a man of less standing than Watson and without (at that time) much astronomical experience, made his observations at Pike's Peak, Colorado. He observed two stars close together on the western side of the sun, of which one was apparently θ Cancri, and the other an intra-Mercurial planet. So far, his observation might be regarded as corroborating Watson's. Unfortunately, he did not determine which of his pair was θ Cancri, giving as his reason that both appeared equally bright; and it will be remembered that the new body seen by Watson close to θ Cancri was, most definitely, very much the brighter of the two.

It was found quite impossible to reconcile Watson's observations with Swift's, and the conclusion generally arrived at was that both observers had made several mistakes. It was considered that what Watson thought he mistook for ζ Cancri was, actually, that star: that his other intra-Mercurial planet was really θ Cancri: and that what he thought to be θ Cancri was a small 6th-magnitude star near it. By a similar process of substitution, it was inferred that what Swift took for θ Cancri and an adjacent intra-Mercurial planet were really 25 Cancri and a neighbouring 7th-magnitude star. These suppositions at least explain the various contradictions and discrepancies in the evidence. Fig. 19 shows the positions of the various bodies supposed to have been seen by Watson and Swift, and of the other stars referred to.

As already stated, whatever Watson and Swift saw it was not Vulcan. Since their time no one claims to have seen that planet, unless we except an American weather-prophet named Tice, the John Partridge of his day. During the 'eighties he evolved various astronomical theories in connection with his system of weather-prediction, and as these theories postulated, inter alia, the existence of Vulcan, he took the bold step of asserting that he had himself witnessed, on a certain day in September, a transit of that planet across the sun. Incidentally, he mentioned that he had at first mistaken it for Mercury—a statement affording quite conclusive evidence as to the extent of his astronomical knowledge.* He pointed out that this transit was separated by an exact number of "Vulcanian years" (19 days 17 hours) from that seen by Lescarbault in March 1859. Unfortunately, he had not realized (although he was afterwards given every opportunity of doing so) that the interval between a spring and an autumn transit of Vulcan ought (the Earth being then at the

---

* A transit of Mercury can only occur in May or November.

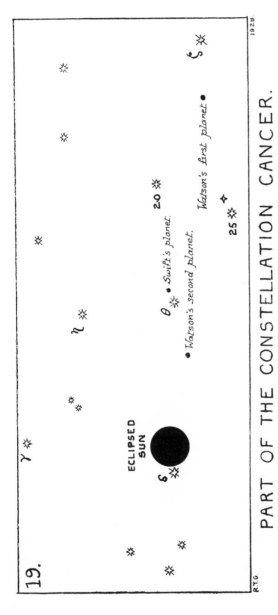

PART OF THE CONSTELLATION CANCER.

Fig. 19.—Diagram showing the supposed intra-Mercurial planets reported by Professors Watson and Swift as having been observed during the total solar eclipse of July 29, 1878.

Note.—The western side of the sun is to the right—the eastern to the left.

opposite side of her orbit) to be a whole number of "Vulcanian years" *plus* 9 *days* 20½ *hours*, and that what he was really claiming was that he had seen Vulcan *through* the sun.

"The planet of romance," as the Abbé Moigno, one of its staunchest champions, once termed Vulcan, is now definitely regarded as "the planet of fiction". It is, perhaps, fitting that it should play a considerable part in a serial story "Planetoid 127" (*penes me*), written by Edgar Wallace, an author whom, although the fact is not definitely stated, I identify (by internal evidence) with the celebrated and prolific author-dramatist who gave us *The Four Just Men*, *The Strange Countess*, *Sanders of the River*, and many other novels whose number and circulation alike, I understand, have attained almost astronomical figures.

Professor Watson and his work figure in the story, which deals with a planet (hitherto undiscovered) of which the bodies supposed to have been seen by Watson are, in reality, the satellites. The planet is a duplicate, in all essential particulars, of our own earth, and revolves in exactly the same orbit at exactly the same speed. But, being situated diametrically opposite to us, it is perpetually obscured by the sun, and in consequence invisible! It is a great pity that Leverrier is no longer alive to discuss the mathematical consequences of this remarkable theory.

Our present telescopic resources do not permit of our making certain that there are no intra-Mercurial planets, but it is safe to say that if any such do exist they must be of the nature of asteroids (minor planets) and small at that. There is practically no doubt that Lescarbault's Vulcan cannot be one of them. It is, however, still doubtful what he actually saw.

In all probability it was a sun-spot. On the other hand, it must have been a very peculiar one, for he had already observed Mercury in transit, and therefore knew, at least, what a planet should look like when on the sun's disc. Another objection is the rapid motion of the body he observed. The sun-spots have an apparent motion due to that of the Earth, and they also are carried round by the sun's rotation at a speed which, curiously enough, is not the same for all parts of the sun's disc, but diminishes towards its poles. But the combined effect of both these motions would not account for more than a fraction of the rapid movement observed by Lescarbault.

On the other hand, if he actually saw an intra-Mercurial planet which has never been seen since, it must have been an exceedingly small one—from which two conclusions necessarily follow. In the first place, he must have been greatly deceived as to the apparent size of the body which he saw; and, secondly, if it was so small that it has not been seen since by the most powerful modern telescopes, it is almost incredible that Lescarbault, with his rather rudimentary telescopic equipment, could ever have seen it at all.

He is by no means the first observer to be misled by appearances. That has occurred to many quite eminent astronomers. The satellite of Venus is a case in point. During the seventeenth and eighteenth centuries it was observed by many astronomers of standing—by the elder Cassini in 1672 and 1686, by James Short in 1740, by Mayer in 1759, by Montbarron in 1764, by Montaigne in 1791, and at various other times by such men as Rodkier and Horrebow. All agreed that it appeared to be about a quarter as large as Venus (i.e. about two thousand miles in diameter). Yet it is quite certain that Venus has no satellite of this size—nor, so far as we know, has she any at all; from which it follows that she never can have had one, since if it had fallen on to her surface in the last century her aspect and orbit would have altered considerably; if it had fallen into the sun the resulting conflagration would be a commonplace of the astronomical text-books; while if (which is quite impossible) it had fallen on to the earth it would have changed the face of every continent and might even, conceivably, have interfered with the publication of this book.

Some of the observations of this satellite may be explained by reflection in the object-glass, after the manner of the celebrated "companion of Procyon".* But Short observed it with two *reflecting* telescopes, employing with one of them three different eyepieces of varying powers.† It is quite impossible that he could have been so deceived—and he was a most careful observer.

There can be little doubt, finally, that most, if not all, of the celebrated "canals" of Mars (first reported by Schiaparelli in 1877 and since observed in large numbers by the late Professor Lowell, of Flagstaff, Arizona, and others) are the product of imagination—not, of course, of deliberate deception. It is claimed that some have been photographed; but, as a well-known amateur astronomer, the late Dr. W. H. Maw, once remarked to me, "I've had a look at those photographs, and you want the eye of faith to see the canals on them". And it is worth noting that Barnard (Director of the Lick Observatory at the time when it possessed the largest telescope in the world), when asked whether he had made many observations of the canals, replied gravely that he regretted his telescope was too powerful to show them.

---

* Otto Struve, of Pulkova, announced in 1873 that he had observed the dark companion of Procyon, whose existence had been suspected, on theoretical grounds, by Bessel (1844) and Auwers (1861). He continued, for some years, to publish his observations of it. It was then discovered to be an optical illusion, due to a flaw in his object-glass, which was found to give similar spurious companions to Arcturus, Capella, and Regulus.

† 60, 140, and 240. A reflecting telescope, of course, has no object-glass.

XI

NOSTRADAMUS

"A Prophet is not without honour, save in his own country." It is a hard saying, but a true one. In this land of ours the prophet, unless he be connected with the Turf, has an unenviable legal status. Witness the following stereotyped reply which it was the custom of a former Astronomer Royal, the late Sir William H. M. Christie, to transmit to the numerous domestic servants and other persons of imperfect education who wrote to consult him upon matters relating to astrology rather than astronomy.

"Sir or Madam,*

"I am directed by the Astronomer Royal to inform you that he is unable to rule your planets. Persons professing to do so are rogues and vagabonds.†

"I am, yours faithfully,

"——(Secretary)."

It was not always so, even at Greenwich. Flamsteed—the first Astronomer Royal, who founded in 1675 a brilliant and long-lived‡ dynasty—performed the first official act of his reign by casting the horoscope of the Observatory. The calculation still exists—although he has written across it the sarcastic comment *Risum teneatis, amici?*§ On another occasion he was made to appear, by an unfortunate coincidence, as one well-skilled in conjuration.

An old woman, no wiser than most of them, once called at the Observatory to enlist his aid in recovering a piece of property (by some accounts, a bundle of washing) which she had lost. Flamsteed, wishing to give her a lesson against believing in soothsayers, listened gravely to the details of the

* It was usually the latter.

† Such is the case. Here is an extract from 5 Geo., IV c. 83 (s. iv), which is still in force:

"... And be it further enacted that ... every Person pretending or professing to tell Fortunes, or using any subtle Craft, Means, or Device, by Palmistry or otherwise, to deceive and impose on any of His Majesty's Subjects ... shall be deemed a Rogue and Vagabond, within the true Intent and Meaning of this Act; and it shall be lawful for any Justice of the Peace to commit such Offender ... to the House of Correction, there to be kept to hard Labour for any Time not exceeding Three Calendar Months. ..."

‡ There have only been ten Astronomers Royal in 269 years.

§ "Can you keep from laughing, my friends?"

case, and having drawn a plan of her house and grounds, which he adorned with various fearsome symbols, directed her to search at a particular point which he had carefully selected at random. He intended, when she should call or write complaining of her fruitless search, to administer the lesson in question. To his confusion, she informed him soon afterwards that she had found the bundle in the exact spot he had indicated. He ascribed the coincidence, in all seriousness, to the craft and malice of the Evil One.

Nowadays, however, Sir William Christie's caustic remark forms a perfectly correct description of the manner in which that majestic if impersonal entity, our British Common Law, regards prophets—or, in its own phraseology, "persons pretending to tell fortunes". In so far as this affects those traders in human credulity who batten in Bond Street, and elsewhere, upon the guineas of the feeble-minded, no great harm is done. But I have often speculated as to the legal position of a person, charged with "pretending to tell fortunes", who really possessed the ability to do so. Suppose that he offered to give the Court a demonstration of his powers, and began by predicting that, like Mr. Justice Talfourd,* the presiding judge should then and there expire upon the Bench in horrid agony. If this lamentable event were actually to occur, would he be acquitted? Or would he, as seems more likely, be indicted for murder?

The word "pretending" begs the whole question. It is reminiscent of the very clever political trick played by the Whigs of 1701, when they translated the French nickname for James II's unquestionably-legitimate son as "The Pretender" instead of "The Claimant" (*Le Prétendant*). Still, its employment is strictly in keeping with the best historical traditions, for the lot of the prophet in all ages has generally been a hard one, and the only well-defined distinction between true and false prophets appears to be that the former, as a class, have fared worse than the others.

Of false prophets, such as those misguided individuals who confidently foretold the destruction of Weymouth by a "tidal wave" on the 29th of May, 1928, at 3.53 p.m., England has, I suppose, been as prolific as most other nations. But she can also point to her fair share of prophets who, to the confusion of common sense, have taken their job seriously, and performed it in a workmanlike manner. For example, William Lilly (the astrologer) predicted in his *Monarchy or No Monarchy* (1651) the

---

* Sir Thomas Noon Talfourd, of the Court of Common Pleas, died on the Bench at Stafford, on March 13, 1854, while in the act of charging the Grand Jury. The late Lord Darling commemorated this calamity in bastard but dignified hexameters. See his *On the Oxford Circuit* (London, 1909).

Talfourd is, I believe, the only English judge who has actually died on the Bench. Others, however, have died on circuit, such as Mr. Justice Watkin Williams, of whom a professional brother remarked, in a threnody remarkable for its masterly distortion of unpleasant facts, that he met his end "while engaged in the work which he loved".

advent of a plague which should leave London with insufficient hands to bury its dead, followed by a devastating fire. He was rewarded by a severe examination before the magistrates, being suspected of knowing more about the Fire of London than he should have done.

The prophecies of Alexander Peden, the Covenanter (1626?–86), are still remembered in the Lowlands, and Walker's collection of them has frequently been reprinted. Many were strikingly successful, although I do not remember to have come across one predicting the most singular event of his strange life. He was originally buried in the parish church of Boswell, Auchinleck (the ancestral home of Johnson's biographer). Some dragoons exhumed the body, with the intention of hanging it in chains on Cumnock gallows. Failing in this, they buried it at the gallows-foot. Such was the veneration which "the Prophet Peden" had inspired among the men of Cumnock, that after the Revolution they deserted their old burying-ground, and formed a new one around the gallows-hill.

And who has not heard of Sam Weller's "red-faced Nixon",* although many, possibly, have wondered whether he was a real person or another example of "what the soldier said".

There is little doubt that Robert Nixon was a real person, but the facts relating to him are "wropt in mystery". He was known as "the Cheshire Prophet" and, by one account, was born in that land of cheeses and cats in 1467, at Over Delamere. Another account, unfortunately, makes him flourish in the reign of James I (1603–25). He seems to have been a sort of Mad Mullah (the *D.N.B.* remarks: "All accounts point to his having been an idiot"), inspired at intervals to emit both local and national prophecies. The tale is told that his fame led to his being summoned to Court, where by a chapter of accidents he was locked up and starved to death, a fate which he had foretold for himself. This recalls the similar

---

* "Vell now," said Sam, "you've been a-prophesyin' away, wery fine, like a red-faced Nixon as the sixpenny books gives picters on."

"Who was he, Sammy?" inquired Mr. Weller.

"Never mind who he was," retorted Sam; "he warn't a coachman; that's enough for you."

"I know'd a ostler o' that name," said Mr. Weller, musing.

"It warn't him," said Sam. "This here gen'l'm'n was a prophet."

"Wot's a prophet?" inquired Mr. Weller, looking sternly on his son.

"Wy, a man as tells what's a-goin' to happen," replied Sam.

"I wish I'd know'd him, Sammy," said Mr. Weller. "P'raps he might ha' throw'd a small light on that 'ere liver complaint as we wos a-speakin' on, just now. Hows'ever, if he's dead, and ain't left the bisness to nobody, there's an end on it."

Pickwick Papers, chap. xliii.

It does not appear that Robert Nixon suffered from *acne rosea*, or tippled; but it was customary for chap-books of the "tuppence coloured" species to depict him as of a ruddy countenance.

story of Cardan, the celebrated mathematician and astrologer, who predicted the date of his own death and considered that he owed it to his reputation to commit suicide when "Der Tag" (September 21, 1576) arrived.

It is certain, at any rate, that Nixon impressed his contemporaries, and that his prophecies had long been orally current in Cheshire before John Oldmixon, the antiquary, published a collection of them in 1714. It went into innumerable subsequent editions.

I am afraid that I cannot admit Mother Shipton into this gallery. She is as much of a myth as Robin Hood. It is true that a work breathing fire, slaughter, and all manner of terrible calamities appeared in 1641 under the title of *The Prophecie of Mother Shipton* . . . and that a life of the good lady was published in 1687 by Richard Head, but the provenance of both books is more than doubtful.

In 1862 a north-country bookseller, Charles Hindley, published a reprint of Head's life together with a text of the *Prophecie* containing some additional verses, said to have been found in a MS. copy dated 1488. These verses, which contained fairly explicit prophecies of such inventions as the steam-engine and the electric telegraph, together with a forecast of the Crystal Palace and a most definite prediction that the end of the world would occur in 1881, attracted considerable attention. Unfortunately, Hindley confessed in 1873* that they were of his own composition.

Of single successful prophecies there are innumerable instances. For example, it seems fairly well authenticated that when Jacques du Bourg-Molay, Grand Master of the Templars, was burned at Paris on March 18, 1314,† he summoned the Pope to appear within forty days, and the King of France within a year and a day, at the bar of judgment. Whether they entered an appearance, I do not know; but they both died within the time specified.

Another case, which has always interested me, occurred during the first circumnavigation of the world. After Magellan had got half-way through the tortuous strait which bears his name, he waited six days for one of his ships, the *San Antonio*, which had lagged behind. No sign of the lame duck appearing, the voyage was resumed. But Magellan, anxious to discover what had become of her, directed his astrologer Andreas de San Martin—who apparently held a position on his staff analogous to that of the Commander (N) or Commander (G) of a modern flagship—to cast

---

* *Notes and Queries,* 4th series, xi. 355.

† A most vivid and haunting picture of this judicial murder, as it might have appeared to one "Master Gysbrecht, Canon-Regular of Saint Jodocus-by-the-Bar, Ypres City", is given in Browning's *Heretic's Tragedy.*

her horoscope, and so ascertain her fate. San Martin, a man obviously skilled in his profession, made the necessary calculations, and reported that her crew had mutinied, made their captain a prisoner, and set sail for Europe. Curiously enough, that was exactly what had happened.

But for the leading case of a famous and successful prophet we must look to France. I do not mean, by a "successful" prophet, one who engages in prophecy as a trade or profession by which he endeavours to earn a livelihood. Such prophets generally end up as successful financiers or convicts. I mean a person who really possesses, and has demonstrated, his ability to foretell the future.

I cannot hope to conceal from the acute reader my belief that such persons have occasionally appeared, and may do so again. But it is coupled with a conviction that the power of prophecy is a rare mental abnormality, which can no more be controlled or exploited by its unfortunate possessor than a heart-attack or a paralytic stroke. As in the case of Nixon, already described, and that of Nostradamus, to be described shortly, the real prophetic afflatus seems usually to be a kind of obsession, seizing its victim at irregular intervals, and unconnected with his normal life and occupation.

For the rationale of the matter, I cannot do better than refer to Mr. J. W. Dunne's remarkable book *An Experiment with Time*. He shows, in a manner which arouses my respectful envy, the possibility of (so to speak) remembering the future as we do the past. It may be found possible to cultivate this ability—in which case I imagine that modern life will become even more complicated, and that the bookmakers (already cowering, like partridges, under the shadow of the "Tote") will go out of business, deeply regretted—by a fortunate few. In the past, however, I suspect that this peculiar faculty was, in most cases, natural, and neither acquired nor cultivated.

And so to the story of Nostradamus.

Michael Nostradamus,* to use the Latinized form of his name Michel Nôtredame, was born at St. Remy, in Provence, on December 14, 1503. He is believed to have been of Jewish descent. He took his medical degree at Montpelier in 1529, and after spending some time in practice at Marseilles, settled at Salon, near Aix, where he soon became reputed one of the first physicians of his time.

At the age of fifty or so he took, for no very apparent reason, to composing prophecies, which he did not immediately publish; apparently fearing, as well he might, that such an act would injure his reputation. He cast them into the form of rhymed quatrains, and arranged them in sets of a hundred, which he termed *Centuries*. Overcoming his diffidence, he published the first three *Centuries* in 1555. Owing, probably, to the

* See Frontispiece.

striking and almost immediate fulfilment of a prophecy in the first *Century* (described later), the work met with very considerable success. A further seven *Centuries* appeared some years later. The exact date is doubtful. That generally given is 1558—but Le Pelletier, an acknowledged authority on the subject, considers it to have been 1566, the year of Nostradamus's death. There have been many succeeding reprints of the *Centuries*, as well as some spurious editions—one of these in particular, published at Lyons in 1568, being remarkable for containing two interpolated and libellous quatrains attacking Cardinal Mazarin.

The *Centuries* are not easy reading. Nostradamus's French, like Milton's English, is full of Latinized constructions. The book abounds also with technical terms, anagrams, and puns. As for its style, Le Pelletier has sufficiently described it in the following passage, which shall not receive, at my hands, the harsh fate of being done into English.*

"Le style enfin est artificieux comme la pensée. Sous les dehors factices d'une rime prime sautière & d'un jargon polyglotte qui n'appartient en propre à aucune langue, l'auteur montre une poésie sauvage, une érudition profonde & la science de tous les idiomes usités par les savants. Le texte est hérissé de mots hébreux, grecs, latins, italiens, espagnols, celtiques, romans. C'est un feu d'artifice perpétuel sous un ciel toujours sombre. Les clartés & les ombres s'y succèdent, s'y entre-choquent & sont autant de surprises ménagées à l'inexpérience du spectateur."

Here, however, I am not concerned with the manner of the *Centuries*, but only with their matter. I do not propose to follow Le Pelletier in his resolute and persevering determination to fit no less than 213 of the quatrains to succeeding events in European history. Such a proceeding is almost bound to give, in many cases, far-fetched and misleading results. I intend only to discuss four cases, in all of which the predicted event can be identified with certainty, while there can be no doubt as to the explicit prediction having antedated it.

The first instance is that already mentioned as having made Nostradamus's prophetic reputation. On July 10, 1559, Henri II, king of France, was killed in a tournament while running a course with one Montgomery, a Scottish nobleman, captain of his guard. Montgomery's lance passed between the bars of the king's gold vizor, and entered his eye. This untoward event was found duly predicted in the 35th quatrain of the first *Century*, which had appeared four years earlier, in 1555. The text runs:

> Le lyon jeune le vieux surmontera
> En champ bellique par singulier duelle:
> Dans cage d'or les yeux crevera,
> Deux classes une, puis mourir, mort cruelle.

* "An apt expression, suggesting the violence of the transaction."

Here, again, are Nostradamus's prophecies of the execution of Charles I and of the Fire of London.

> Gand et Bruccles marcheront contre Anvers,
> Senat de Londres mettront à mort leur Roy. . . .
>
> *(Century* IX, quatrain 49.)
>
> Le sang du iuste à Londres fera faute
> Bruslez par foudres de vingt trois les six. . . .*
>
> *(Century* II, quatrain 51.)

The first of these appeared at some date before 1566, and the second in 1555. Charles I was beheaded on January 30, 1649, the year after the wars in the Low Countries had been terminated by the Treaty of Munster; the Fire of London, of course, occurred in 1666.

But one of Nostradamus's prophecies stands out above all the others by reason of the singularly complete manner of its fulfilment. It is the eighteenth quatrain of the ninth *Century*,† which runs as follows:

> Le lys Dauffois portera dans Nanci
> Jusques en Flandres electeur de l'Empire;
> Neufve obturée au grand Montmorency,
> Hors lieux prouvés delivré à clere peyne.

which may be roughly Englished as follows:

"The lily of the Dauphin shall enter Nancy; and sustain, as far as Flanders, an Elector of the Empire. There shall be a new prison for the great Montmorency; who, not in the customary place, shall be delivered to public punishment."

It will be conceded that this prophecy, as it stands, is not very illuminating. In the light of after events, however, it appears very simple and marvellously accurate.

The two sentences are unconnected, and only appear in the same quatrain because, as will be seen, they relate to events of about the same period (1632–5). On September 24, 1633, Louis XIII of France, who had been the first man since Nostradamus's death to bear the title "Dauphin de France", entered Nancy at the head of his troops. Two years later, the Elector of Treves having been made prisoner by the Spaniards (March 26, 1635), Louis declared war on Spain and marched into Flanders, where he laid siege to Louvain. So much for the first half of the quatrain. What follows is more remarkable.

---

* I do not think this phrase can fairly be taken as a definite indication of the date of the Fire. It might equally well be regarded, by the persons who like to do that sort of thing, as the Number of the Beast.

† See Fig. 20.

CENTVRIE IX.

L'ambaſſadeur non plaiſant fera ſciſme,
Ceux de Ribiere feront en la meſlée:
Et au grand goulphre deſnier ont l'entrée.
XVII.
Le tiers premier pis que ne fit Neron,
Vuidez vaillant que ſang humain reſpandre:
R édifier fera le forneron,
Siecle d'or, mort· nouueau Roy grãd eſclandr¡
XVIII.
Le lys Dauffois portera dans Nanſi,
Iuſques en Flandres Eleéteur de l'Empire:
Neufue obturée au grand Montmorency,
Hors lieux prouez deliure à clere peyne.
XIX.
Dans le milieu de la foreſt Mayenne,
Sol au Lyon la foudre tombera:
Le grand batard yſſu du grand du Maine,
Ce iour Fougeres pointe en ſang entrera.
XX.
De nuiét viendra par la foreſt de Reines,
Deux pars voltorte Herne la pierre blanch¡
Le moine noir en gris dedans Varennes,
Eſleu cap. cauſe tempeſte, feu, ſang tranche.
XXI
Au temple hault de Bloys ſacre Salonne,
Nuiét pont de Loyre, Prelat, Roy pernic
Cuiſeur viétoire aux mareſts de la Lone,
D'où prelature de blancs abormeant.
XXII.

FIG. 20.—Facsimile reproduction of one page of a copy of Nostradamus's *Centuries*, printed in 1605. Quatrain XVIII contains his prediction of the Duc de Montmorency's death.

NOTE.—The title-page of this copy is shown in the frontispiece. (British Museum.)

On October 30, 1632, Henri, second Duc de Montmorency, who had been made prisoner at the battle of Castelnaudary by Marshal Schomberg, being then in open rebellion against Louis, was beheaded at Toulouse. While awaiting trial, he had been confined there in the newly-built prison of the Hotel de Ville; and, as a concession to his rank, the execution took place in the courtyard of that prison, and not on the public gallows.

Note that the prophecy was certainly in print in 1566, and that this most accurate fulfilment of it took place in 1632. And now mark what follows.

In many of the quatrains of the *Centuries*, it is no uncommon thing to find some important statement made in the form of a pun, or other play upon words. So it is in this case. The term "clere peyne" (Lat. *clara poena*) literally signifies a public or celebrated punishment. But as regards Montmorency's execution it has a second and most singular application.

I have said that a concession was made to his rank, in that the execution was private. A second concession was also made, the mode of death being changed from hanging to beheading. The executioner, too, was not the ordinary "M. de Paris", or a provincial "Performer of the High Works of the King", but a common soldier, chosen by lot. *His name was Clerepeyne.*

The fact is attested by two contemporary authorities, Etienne Joubert* and the Chevalier de Jant.† An excellent summary of the evidence bearing upon the point is to be found in a monograph by Motret, published in 1806.‡

I remember to have seen, some years before the War, the results of a calculation, made by (not unnaturally) a German author, as to the probability of this prediction having been fulfilled by pure chance. According to him, it represented a chance of, roughly, one in thirty millions—or, as he put it, about the same risk that any given person would run of being accidentally killed in the course of a single railway journey from Berlin to Munich. I do not know the basis of calculation employed —I should imagine that much of it rested on pure assumption.

Personally, I should have put the "cases of failure" at a considerably higher figure. To my mind, it is a sheer impossibility that the prophecy could have been fulfilled in such minute detail by accident. Chance, or coincidence—call it whichever you please—can explain, or be made to explain, many extraordinary occurrences: but, in my submission, anyone who believes that this prophecy was fulfilled by pure chance is a much

---

* *Eclaircissements des veritables quatrains de maistre Michel Nostradamus,* 1656, p. 18 (no name or place of printing).

† *Prédictions tirées des Centuries,* 1637, p. 12.

‡ *Essai d'explication de deux quatrains de Nostradamus* (Nevers, 1806), pp. 30–9.

more credulous person than the one who, after examining the evidence, forms the conviction that Nostradamus possessed, and exercised, the power of foretelling the future.

However, I suppose that there will always be many who reverse Tertullian's saying,* and regard a statement as incredible because it is well-attested—in the manner of the countryman who, confronted with his first giraffe, remarked, "I don't believe there's no sich creature". It is probably a waste of time to commend to their attention the essential cowardice, as well as the virtue, of "philosophic doubt" in the presence of unexplained facts.

* "*Mortuus est Dei filius . . et sepultus resurrexit: certum est, quia incredibile. . . .*"
—Tertullian, *De Carne Christi*, v.

INDEX

134, 140; searches for Saxemberg Island, 134; encounters cloud effect, 134; claims to have sighted and landed on Bouvet Island, 139-40; conjecture on fate of Robert Johnson, 148-49; searches for Aurora Islands, 158

Motret (author of monograph on Nostradamus), 212

Mullins, John, 186

Musgrave, Rev. G. M., on hoof-marks in Devonshire, 11; see also G. M. M..

Narrative of Four Voyages to the South Seas, A (Morrell), 139-40; quoted, 134, 148-49

Narrative of the Discovery of the Fate of Sir John Franklin, A (McClintock), quoted, 80n

"Nauscopie" (discovery of ships below the horizon through effect of their motion on atmosphere), 174-92

Nautical Magazine, The, 176

Naval Museum, Greenwich, 53n

Neptune (planet), 195; discovery, 194 and n

Nerita, see Graham Island

Newfoundland Banks, 54

Newton, Devonshire: mysterious hoofmarks in, 15

Newton, Sir Isaac, 95

Niewiadomski, R., 169

Nimrod (ship), 151

Nimrod Islands, 147

Niwaru (ship), 150

Nixon, Robert: prophecies of, 206-7

Noad, H. M., 118n

Nockels, C. J.; reports Emerald Island, 147

Norris, George: lands on Bouvet Island, 140; takes possesion of Bouvet Island for England, 134; discovers Thompson Island, 140-41; discovers Chimneys, 140; discovers "Liverpool Island" (Bouvet Island), 141

Northwest Passage, 52, 53

"Nostradamus," 204-13

Norvegia (whaler), 140, 144n, 147, 151

Nostradamus, Michael: birth, 208; education, 208; career as physician, 208; composition and publication of prophecies, 208-9; difficulty of reading and interpreting, 209; prophecy concerning death of Henri II, 209-10; prophecies of execution of Charles I and of Fire of London, 210;

prophecies concerning Louis XIII and the execution of Henri, 2d Duc de Montmorency, 210-12, 211 (facsimile); calculation of odds against chance fulfillment of prophecy concerning execution of Montmorency, 212

Notes on a Cellar-book (Saintsbury), quoted, 44

Oates, Lawrence Edward Grace, 50

Odd I (whaler), 126

Oldmixon, John, 207

Ommaney, Erasmus: makes inquiries of Robert Simpson concerning ships sighted by *Renovation,* 60, 62-64, 66; character and career, 60; questions Thomas Davis, 64; conclusion, quoted, 64

Opinion, informed versus popular, 185-86

Orderson, Rev. Thomas H.: accounts of disturbances in vault of Christ Church churchyard, Barbados, 23 ff.

Orffyreus (Johann Ernest Elias Bessler), 91 ff.; comes under protection of Karl, Landgrave of Hesse-Cassel, 94-95; becomes Town Councillor, 95; exhibits fourth wheel, 95-98; destroys fourth wheel, 98-99; begins to rebuild wheel, 99; dies, 99; pamphlet concerning his wheel, 107-8; see also Wheels, of Orffyreus

"Orffyreus' Wheel," 89-116

Oriental Navigator (Purdy), 133n

Orrery, 97n

Otago Daily News, 149

Otter (ship), 139

Otter, as possible source of mysterious hoof-marks in Devonshire, 16

Oudeman, A. C.: explains Crosse's Acari, 123

"O" version of Orderson MS. concerning disturbances in vault in Christ Church churchyard, Barbados, 27, 29, 47, 48

Owen, Richard: letter on mysterious hoof-marks in Devonshire, 16-17; controversy with Huxley over *hippocampus major,* 17; theory on adult skull, 17; explanation of "sea-serpent," 17

Owen, Robert Dale: on disturbances in vault in Buxhoewden chapel, 35-39 *passim,* 47

Oxenstiern, Axel, 89